CONTENTS

ACCOUNTANCY

Fifth edition January 1989

ISBN 0 86277 107 2

A CIP catalogue record for this book is
available from the British Library

Published by

BPP Publishing Limited
BPP House
Aldine Place
142-144 Uxbridge Road
London W12 8AA

We are grateful to the Chartered Institute of Bankers for permission to
reproduce past examination questions. The suggested solutions have been
prepared by BPP Publishing Limited.

DACOSTA PRINT
111 SALUSBURY ROAD
LONDON NW6 6RG
01-969 1111

PREFACE

The examinations of the Chartered Institute of Bankers are a demanding test of students' ability to master the wide range of financial, commercial and legal knowledge required of the modern banker. The extent and complexity of statutory provisions and professional pronouncements increase each year. The Institute has shown itself to be responsive to the rapid pace of economic and financial developments both in its syllabus and in the style of questions set in the examinations. There is a need for study material which is equally responsive to change.

BPP practice and revision kits are designed to fill the gap. Each kit is tailored precisely to accommodate recent developments in the style and format of the examinations. Annual updating is an essential feature of the process.

This edition of the 'Accountancy' kit contains a bank of 81 questions covering all aspects of the syllabus. Many of the questions are taken from past examination papers and all are provided with full solutions. To assist you in planning your revision, these introductory pages provide detailed guidance on how to approach the main subject areas, together with the syllabus, notes on the format and style of the paper, an analysis of topics examined in recent papers, updating notes on recent developments and extracts from the reports published by the examiners. A quiz on page 16 is designed to test your basic knowledge of the syllabus.

To answer the questions in this kit is equivalent to attempting 20 examination papers. If you are able to accomplish this you will be very well prepared for anything that may arise in the exam.

BPP Publishing Ltd
January 1989

SYLLABUS

Aim

To provide an appreciation of the uses and limitations of accounting information as a basis for understanding the financial affairs of bank customers.

Content

(a) The nature and interrelationships of balance sheets, profit statements and funds flow statements; the concept of the operating cycle; distinctions between working capital flows, cash flows and profit flows.

(b) Costs and 'internal' accounting information from the lending viewpoint; cash budgets and other forecasts, sunk costs, marginal costs and breakeven analysis.

(c) Capital structure: long-term financing; risk implications of gearing; working capital.

(d) Interpretation measures: funds flow, accounting ratios and rates of return.

(e) Valuation: 'going concern' valuation of businesses and shares on the basis of dividend yield, earnings yield, price/earnings ratio and cash flow; historical cost, replacement cost and 'break up' valuation of businesses; re-organisation, reconstruction, and the ranking of claims on liquidation.

(f) Taxation and cash flows: the nature and timing of tax payments by incorporated and unincorporated businesses; treatment of taxation in final accounts. (Questions on tax computations will not be asked, except that students may be required to make adjustments for 'timing' differences between taxable and reported profit.)

(g) The appraisal of simple capital projects including discounted cash flow methods. Cost of capital in 'money' and 'real' terms (allowing for anticipated inflation). Questions on this syllabus area will be confined to Section B of the paper and taxation will be ignored.

(h) The presentation of the accounts of limited companies in accordance with the accounting requirements contained in selected SSAPs (1, 2, 6, 8, 9, 10, 12, 13, 14, 15, 17, 18, 22 and 23) and in the Companies Act 1985 (outline formats provided). The calculation of divisible profits. The redemption and purchase by a company of its own shares.

(i) Group accounts: main principles for consolidating subsidiary and associated companies. Students will be expected to be able to make the main consolidation adjustments under the acquisition and merger methods, namely distributable profits, minority interest, goodwill (acquisition method only) and merger reserve (merger method only). They will be expected to be familiar with, but not to make calculations which take account of, such matters as inter-company loans, transfers of goods, unrealised profit, and dividends paid out of pre-acquisition profits. (Students must also be able to compute the balance of profit for inclusion in the balance sheet but will not be asked to prepare a consolidated profit and loss account or to present the consolidated balance sheet in a form suitable for publication, though they may choose to do so.)

(j) The nature and limitations of standard and conventional accounting procedures, including current cost accounting. Questions on current cost accounting will be confined to Section B and deal with the main principles. Candidates will be expected to be able to make adjustments in the profit and loss account to reflect the increased cost of replacing tangible assets (stock and fixed assets) and carry these adjustments through to the balance sheet. A knowledge of the arguments for and against introducing a system of inflation accounting is also required, as is an appreciation of the limitations of historical cost-based accounting statements as the basis for business decisions during a period of rising prices.

2

THE EXAMINATION PAPER

Paper format

The examination paper is in two sections, each containing three questions. Candidates must attempt two questions from each section. Questions in section A carry thirty marks each; questions in section B carry twenty marks each. The division of the paper into sections does not correspond to any split in the syllabus. Topics from any area of the syllabus may be examined in either section, except that questions on investment appraisal and current cost accounting will be confined to section B.

In the examination, candidates will be allowed 15 minutes reading time before the start of the three-hour period. During the reading time candidates may mark the question paper but may not write in the answer book.

The pass mark for the exam is 51%. In marking, the examiner takes into account handwriting and spelling, as well as the content and general style of the answers.

Analysis of past papers

A brief analysis of the topics covered in recent papers is given below.

Autumn 1988

		Marks
1	Cash budget and forecast accounts	30
2	Preparation of statutory balance sheet; the limitations of published accounts	30
3	Ratios and interpretation of accounts	30
4	Breakeven analysis	20
5	Maintenance of capital; redemption of shares	20
6	Taxation in company accounts	20

Spring 1988

1	Funds statement; the creation of reserves	30
2	Consolidated balance sheet: acquisition method and merger method	30
3	Breakeven analysis	30
4	Treatment of transactions in accordance with SSAPs	20
5	Investment appraisal: payback and DCF	20
6	Liquidation	20

Autumn 1987

1	Accounting for stocks, plant and machinery, and R & D	30
2	Summarised profit and loss account and funds flow statements	30
3	Forecast profit and loss accounts; ratios	30
4	Share valuation under different methods	20
5	Effect of various options on net profit, bank balance, and working capital	20
6	Exceptional and extraordinary items	20

THE EXAMINATION PAPER

All of these questions, and many others from earlier examination papers, are included in this kit.

STUDY GUIDE

Introduction

In your work for the Accountancy paper there are a number of points you should bear in mind.

(a) Study each topic carefully before attempting the related questions. Answering questions is a test of what you have learnt and also a means of practising so that you develop skill in presenting your answers. To attempt them before you are ready is not a fair test of your proficiency and the result may discourage you.

(b) In some areas, such as cash budgets, business valuations, discounted cash flow, group accounts and published accounts, it is useful to consolidate your knowledge by attempting a perfect solution to one question. Take as much time as you need and in the last resort refer to your study text. Then study the suggested solution carefully and be sure to identify any incompleteness or inaccuracy in your own attempt.

(c) Once you are confident of your grasp of a topic, attempt as many further questions as you have time for, this time under examination conditions. Unless time is very short, write full-length answers rather than notes or an outline. Avoid the temptation to skimp on the discussion part of questions. The examiner is testing your ability to take practical banking decisions; he is looking less for mechanical facility in computation than for evidence of sound reasoning based on a thorough grasp of principles.

(d) It is a common failing to rush into writing an answer which you hope displays what you know. This is not sufficient unless it is also what the examiner has asked for. No credit is given for irrelevant material, however correct it may be. You are allowed fifteen minutes before the exam begins to read through the paper. Use the time well to ensure you are quite clear about what the questions require. In particular study the discussion or interpretative part of each question and decide how to lay out the computations so that the figures you will require for comment are clearly derived.

The questions in this kit are designed to provide a wide coverage of the syllabus. By working through the questions, you should therefore be going over all the topics you ought to learn, and assessing your ability to answer examination-style questions well.

To use this kit properly, you should prepare your own answers to questions first, and then compare them with ours. Look to see how many points of similarity and difference there are between them.

Most of our solutions are lengthy, and deliberately so. Given the time pressures in an examination, there is a limit to the amount that candidates can write. However, we take the view that if you are using the kit as a study aid, we would be doing you a disservice by giving you the bare minimum of a solution. You will find, therefore, that our answers go into detail that you might find useful for study or revision: after all, an examination question that you eventually face might tackle the same topic from a slightly different angle, and so you need to learn the topic well.

(a) If you have omitted some points that we include, think about how significant your omissions are, and make a note of the points you ignored for future reference.

(b) If your solution includes points that we omit, think about whether your own answer is fully relevant to the question. (A tutorial note might make a comment on points that would be irrelevant.)

(c) If the question calls for a numerical solution, the workings that we provide should be sufficient to establish where your solution differs. (There may be an error, or a difference in the assumptions used.)

Questions that call for a written answer are difficult to revise with, because it is human nature to be easily bored by writing out lengthy solutions. What we would suggest as a possible remedy for this problem is that:

(a) You should attempt a full written solution to one or two questions, in order to gain experience and familiarity with the task of producing solutions within the timescale allowed in the examination itself.

(b) For other questions you should prepare an *answer plan*. This is a list of the points that you would put into your solution, preferably in the order that you would make them. The Institute encourages answer plans to be prepared in the examination itself, because it helps the examiner to gauge the ability (and intentions) of a candidate.

(c) You should then read our solution; and

  (i) make a note of points that are new to you and that you think you should learn (eg by underlining certain sentences in the solution for future reference);

  (ii) *prepare an answer plan from our own solution*, to make sure that you understand the relevance to the question of the points we raise. This useful discipline will ensure that you absorb the points in our solution more thoroughly. (We deliberately exclude answer plans to give you the chance to do this.)

Your own solutions in the examination

Your own solutions to questions in the examination should take heed of the advice given by the Institute:

(a) prepare an answer plan;

(b) be concise (remember, our own solutions are deliberately lengthy, in order to provide suitable study material);

(c) use tabulation where appropriate - ie present your answer as a series of points. This saves time, and helps to provide a well-structured answer;

(d) show all workings for numerical calculations.

The main causes of examination failure

The Institute also explains the main reasons why candidates fail an examination. These are:

(a) Failure to prepare:

  (i)   inadequate depth of knowledge;
  (ii) failure to keep up-to-date;
  (iii) misconceptions.

(b) Failure to answer the question set:

    (i)   candidates waffle too much - perhaps because they have nothing better to write or cannot see the point of the question;

    (ii)   candidates fail to read the question properly. Make sure you answer every part of the question, and look for key words in a question that might help you to recognise what it is all about.

(c) Failure to complete the paper:

    (i)   inadequate use of time;

    (ii)   'question spotting' - ie revising only a limited number of topics by guessing what might be in the paper. When the guesses turn out wrong, the question spotters find themselves unable to answer enough questions.

A few extracts from recent examiner's reports illustrate similar reasons for examination failure.

Examiner's reports

'On the whole candidates achieved a satisfactory standard when preparing routine accounting statements, such as balance sheets, cash budgets and the statement of funds. In contrast, the standard of analysis and discussion was disappointing. Answers were, in the main, long-winded, irrelevant and covered only a minority of the matters which needed consideration. Candidates must develop a precise analytical style which focuses on the crucial issues and excludes background discussion.'

'Many of the students who fail this examination do so because of what might be broadly described as poor examination technique. In the recent examination a noticeable weakness was the absence of sufficient care taken when reading the questions.'

'A further weakness was the failure to present information, particularly financial statements, in a clear and concise manner.'

'Areas of the syllabus which traditionally cause candidates particular problems (include) discounted cash flow and regulatory requirements. More attention must be devoted to these topics if an acceptable standard of performance is to be achieved.'

'Accountancy is not a subject which lends itself to last minute cramming in the hope that the right questions will come up, and it is therefore important that students work steadily throughout the months available for study prior to the examination.'

The examiners' reports for previous years have also indicated which parts of the syllabus have caused most trouble for candidates. Those which constantly recur are:

(a) ratio analysis;
(b) source and application of funds statements;
(c) regulatory requirements, particularly of SSAPs; and
(d) the basic difference between cash and profit.

A few notes on these specific syllabus areas are given below.

Ratio analysis

In past years, the examiners have been concerned, not so much with the standard of *calculating* ratios, but with the standard of *interpreting* them. A question on ratio analysis will invariably ask for some discussion based on the ratios you have calculated, so it is essential for you to know what each one signifies.

As a first step, think about which ratios are needed in order to answer the question. There is no point in doing more work than necessary, and the examiner will not be impressed by the calculation of irrelevant ratios. When you have picked out which ratios you need, calculate them and set them out in a table, where they can easily be referred to during the discussion part of the question.

The *main* ratios to remember (the list below is not exhaustive) are:

(a) *Profitability ratios*

It should go without saying that a company ought to be profitable, and obvious checks on profitability are:

(i) whether the company has made a profit or loss on its ordinary activities;
(ii) by how much this year's profit or loss is bigger or smaller than last year's profit or loss.

Profit on ordinary activities *before* taxation is generally thought to be a better figure to use than profit after taxation, because there might be unusual variations in the tax charge from year to year which would not affect the underlying profitability of the company's operations.

Another profit figure that should be calculated is PBIT - profit before interest and tax. This is the amount of profit which the company earned before having to pay interest to the providers of loan capital. By providers of loan capital, we usually mean *longer term* loan capital, such as debentures and medium-term bank loans, which will be shown in the balance sheet as 'Creditors: amounts falling due after more than one year.'

Profit before interest and tax is therefore:

(i) the profit on ordinary activities before taxation; *plus*
(ii) interest charges on long term loan capital.

It is impossible to assess profits or profit growth properly without relating them to the amount of funds (capital) that were employed in making the profits. The most important profitability *ratio* is therefore return on capital employed (ROCE), which states the profit as a percentage of the amount of capital employed.

$$\text{ROCE} = \frac{\text{Profit on ordinary activities before interest and taxation (PBIT)}}{\text{Capital employed}}$$

Capital employed = Shareholders' funds plus 'creditors: amounts falling due after more than one year' plus any long term provisions for liabilities and charges

It is often a good idea to sub-analyse ROCE, to find out more about why the ROCE is high or low, or better or worse than last year.

There are two factors that contribute towards a return on capital employed, both related to sales turnover.

(i) *Profit margin.* A company might make a high or low profit margin on its sales. For example, a company that makes a profit of 25p per £1 of sales is making a bigger return on its turnover than another company making a profit of only 10p per £1 of sales.

(ii) *Asset turnover.* Asset turnover is a measure of how well the assets of a business are being used to generate sales. For example, if two companies each have capital employed of £100,000, and Company A makes sales of £400,000 per annum whereas Company B makes sales of only £200,000 per annum, Company A is making a higher turnover from the same amount of assets - ie twice as much asset turnover as Company B - and this will help A to make a higher return on capital employed than B. Asset turnover is expressed as 'x times' so that assets generate x times their value in annual turnover. Here, Company A's asset turnover is 4 times and B's is 2 times.

Profit margin and asset turnover together explain the ROCE, and if the ROCE is the primary profitability ratio, these other two are the secondary ratios. The relationship between the three ratios can be shown mathematically.

Profit margin x Asset turnover = ROCE

$$\text{ie} \quad \frac{\text{PBIT}}{\text{Sales}} \quad \text{x} \quad \frac{\text{Sales}}{\text{Capital employed}} \quad = \quad \frac{\text{PBIT}}{\text{Capital employed}}$$

It might be tempting to think that a high profit margin is good, and a low asset turnover means sluggish trading. In broad terms, this is so. But there is a trade-off between profit margin and asset turnover, and you cannot look at one without allowing for the other.

(i) A high profit margin means a high profit per £1 of sales, but if this also means that sales prices are high, there is a strong possibility that sales turnover will be depressed, and so asset turnover lower.

(ii) A high asset turnover means that the company is generating a lot of sales, but to do this, it might have to keep its prices down and so accept a low profit margin per £1 of sales.

(b) *Debt and gearing ratios*

Debt ratios are concerned with how much the company owes in relation to its size, whether it is getting into heavier debt or improving its situation, and whether its debt burden seems heavy or light.

(i) When a company is heavily in debt, and seeming to be getting even more heavily into debt, the thought that should occur to you is "This can't go on!" If the company carries on wanting to borrow more, banks and other would-be lenders are very soon likely to say "No more!" and the company might well find itself in trouble.

(ii) When a company is earning only a modest profit before interest and tax, and has a heavy debt burden, there will be very little profit left over for shareholders after the interest charges have been paid. And so if interest rates were to go up (on bank overdrafts etc) or the company were to borrow even more, it might soon be incurring interest charges in excess of PBIT. This might eventually lead to the liquidation of the company.

The *debt ratio* is the ratio of a company's total debts to its total assets.

(i)   Assets consist of fixed assets at their balance sheet value, plus current assets.

(ii) Debts consist of all creditors, whether amounts falling due within one year or after more than one year.

You can ignore long term provisions and liabilities, such as deferred taxation.

There is no absolute guide to the maximum safe debt ratio, but as a very general guide, you might regard 50% as a safe limit to debt. In practice, many companies operate successfully with a higher debt ratio than this, but 50% is nonetheless a helpful benchmark. In addition, if the debt ratio is over 50% and getting worse, the company's debt position will be worth looking at more carefully.

The *capital gearing ratio* is a measure of the proportion of a company's capital that is prior charge capital. It is measured as:

$$\frac{\text{prior charge capital}}{\text{total capital}} \text{ ; where}$$

(i)   Prior charge capital = Creditors: amounts falling due after more than one year, (*including loan capital, if itemised separately* in the balance sheet, and *excluding long term corporation tax liabilities*, since these do not have a claim over any profits in the form of interest) plus preference share capital (if any). There is also a view that a bank overdraft, although shown as a current liability in the balance sheet, is often a permanent feature of a company's debt structure and so is as good as long term debt. If this view is taken, the bank overdraft should also be included as prior charge capital, together with any other short term loans which are likely to be replaced when they mature with a new longer term loan.

(ii) Total capital is ordinary share capital and reserves plus prior charge capital plus any long term liabilities or provisions. We would also include minority interests in group accounts.

   It is easier to identify the same figure for total capital as total assets less current liabilities, which you will find given to you in the balance sheet.

   As with the debt ratio, there is no absolute limit to what a gearing ratio ought to be. a company with a gearing ratio of more than 50% is said to be high-geared (whereas low gearing means a gearing ratio of less than 50%). Many companies *are* high geared, but if a high geared company is becoming increasingly higher-geared, it is likely to have difficulty in the future when it wants to borrow even more, unless it can also boost its shareholders' capital, either with retained profits or a new share issue.

A similar ratio to the gearing ratio is the *debt/equity ratio*, which is the ratio of:

$$\frac{\text{prior charge capital}}{\text{ordinary share capital and reserves}}$$

This gives us the same sort of information as the gearing ratio, and a ratio of 100% or more would indicate high gearing.

The significance of the gearing ratios is that:

(i)   the more highly geared the company, the greater the risk that little (if anything) will be available to distribute by way of dividend to the ordinary shareholders; and

(ii) a high geared company has a large amount of interest to pay annually (assuming that the debt is external borrowing rather than preference shares). If those borrowings are 'secured' in any way (and debentures in particular are secured), then the holders of the debt are perfectly entitled to force the company to realise assets to pay their interest if funds are not available from other sources. Clearly, the more highly geared a company the more likely this is to occur when and if profits fall.

(c)   *Working capital liquidity ratios*

The 'standard' test of liquidity is the *current ratio*. It can be obtained from the balance sheet, and is the ratio of:

$$\frac{\text{current assets}}{\text{current liabilities}}$$

The idea behind this is that a company should have enough current assets that give a promise of 'cash to come' to meet its future commitments to pay off its current liabilities. Obviously, a ratio in excess of 1 should be expected. Otherwise, there would be the prospect that the company might be unable to pay its debts on time. In practice, a ratio comfortably in excess of 1 should be expected, but what is 'comfortable' varies between different types of businesses.

Companies are not able to convert all their current assets into cash very quickly. In particular, some manufacturing companies might hold large quantities of raw material stocks, which must be used in production to create finished goods stocks. Finished goods stocks might be warehoused for a long time, or sold on lengthy credit. In such businesses, where stock turnover is slow, most stocks are not very 'liquid' assets, because the cash cycle is so long. For these reasons, we calculate an additional liquidity ratio, known as the quick ratio or acid test ratio.

The *quick ratio*, or *acid test ratio*, is $\dfrac{\text{current assets less stocks}}{\text{current liabilities}}$

This ratio should ideally be at least 1 for companies with a slow stock turnover. For companies with a fast stock turnover, a quick ratio can be comfortably less than 1 without suggesting that the company should be in cash flow trouble.

Both the current ratio and the quick ratio offer an indication of the company's liquidity position, but the absolute figures should not be interpreted too literally. It is often theorised that an 'acceptable' current ratio is 1.5 and an 'acceptable' quick ratio is 0.8, but these should only be used as a guide. Different businesses operate in very different ways.

What is important is the trend of these ratios. From this, one can easily ascertain whether liquidity is improving or deteriorating. If a company has traded for the last 10 years (very successfully) with current ratios of 0.43 and quick ratios of 0.12 then it should be supposed that they can continue in business with those levels of liquidity. If in the following year their current ratio were to fall to 0.38 and their quick ratio to 0.09, then further investigation into their liquidity situation would be appropriate. It is the relative position that is far more important than the absolute figures.

Don't forget the other side of the coin either. A current ratio and a quick ratio can get bigger than they need to be. A company that has large volumes of stocks and debtors might be over-investing in working capital, and so tying up more funds in the business than it needs to. This would suggest poor management of debtors (credit) or stocks by the company.

(d) *Working capital turnover ratios*

A rough measure of the average length of time it takes for a company's debtors to pay what they owe is the *'debtor days' ratio*, or average debtors' payment period.

It is only an estimated average payment period, but it is calculated as:

$$\frac{\text{trade debtors}}{\text{sales}} \quad x \quad 365 \text{ days}$$

Sales are usually made on 'normal credit terms' of payment within 30 days. Debtor days *significantly* in excess of this might be representative of poor management of funds of a business. However, some companies must allow generous credit terms to win customers. Exporting companies in particular may have to carry large amounts of debtors, and so their average collection period might be well in excess of 30 days.

The *trend* of the collection period (debtor days) over time is probably the best guide. If debtor days are increasing year on year, this is indicative of a poorly managed credit control function (and potentially therefore a poorly managed company!)

Another ratio worth calculating is the *stock turnover period*, or stock days. This is another estimated figure, obtainable from published accounts, which indicates the average number of days that items of stock are held for. As with the average debt collection period, however, it is only an approximate estimated figure, but one which should be reliable enough for comparing changes year on year.

The number of stock days is calculated as: $\dfrac{\text{stock}}{\text{cost of sales}} \quad x \quad 365$

The reciprocal of the fraction, ie $\dfrac{\text{cost of sales}}{\text{stock}}$

is termed the stock turnover, and is another measure of how vigorously a business is trading. A lengthening stock turnover period from one year to the next indicates:

(a) a slowdown in trading; or
(b) a build-up in stock levels, perhaps suggesting that the investment in stocks is becoming excessive.

Source and application of funds statements

A statement of source and application of funds (often called a funds flow statement) is a method of showing where a business gets its funds from and how those funds are then applied. Its starting point is always profit before taxation, and it goes on to reconcile the amount of profit earned in a period of time with the increase or decrease in net liquid funds during the same period.

The idea is that items not involving the movement of funds (eg depreciation) are added to the profit before tax figure, to arrive at total funds generated from operations. To this is added any other funds (eg issue of new shares), to arrive at total figure of funds available to the business - from which is taken the application of funds (eg purchase of fixed assets), to arrive at a final balance.

You will notice that none of the working capital figures have appeared so far in the statement. What should happen is that the balance calculated so far should equal the total increase (or decrease) in working capital. The increase (or decrease) of all the items comprising working capital (ie stocks, debtors, creditors, cash etc) are added up, and the total should be the same as that derived from the funds figures in the paragraph above.

The arithmetic in preparing a funds flow statement is not usually very difficult. It is understanding which figure goes where that can cause problems. One way to give yourself a better chance of coming up with the right solution to a funds flow question, is to write out a skeleton statement straight away, and then slot the required figures into the statement afterwards. The skeleton statement could be:

A COMPANY LTD
STATEMENT OF SOURCE AND APPLICATION OF FUNDS
FOR YEAR ENDED _____

	£	£
Profit before taxation		X
Adjustments for items not involving the movement of funds:		
eg Depreciation	X	
Profit (or loss) on sale of fixed asset	(X) or X	
		X
Total funds generated from operations		X
Other sources of funds:		
eg Proceeds from sales of fixed assets	X	
Proceeds from sale of investments	X	
Issue of new shares	X	
New loan	X	
		X
		X
Application of funds:		
eg Purchase of fixed assets	(X)	
Purchase of goodwill	(X)	
Taxation paid	(X)	
Loan repaid	(X)	
		(X)
		X or (X)
Increase/(decrease) in working capital:		
Increase/(decrease) in stocks	X or (X)	
Increase/(decrease) in debtors	X or (X)	
(Increase)/decrease in creditors	X or (X)	
		X or (X)
Movement in net liquid funds:		
Increase/(decrease) in cash	X or (X)	
Increase/(decrease) in short term investments	X or (X)	
		X or (X)
		X or (X)

Regulatory requirements

Time and time again, the examiner reports that candidates give a poor showing in the examination when it comes to preparing a profit and loss account and/or balance sheet under the various rules which apply to these statements. Statements of standard accounting practice represent the main problem. There is no denying that the content of the SSAPs is both dry and voluminous. But unfortunately there is no way around them - they simply have to be learned by heart. Before sitting the examination you should be able to:

(i)   list the SSAPs (by name and number) which are examinable according to the syllabus;

(ii)   make brief notes on the contents of each of these SSAPs; and, most important of all

(iii)   understand the problem which each of the SSAPs addresses. If you do not understand the purpose of an SSAP, how can you possibly apply it to a particular set of figures presented to you in an examination question?

The difference between cashflow and profit

The fact that the examiners have found it necessary to comment on candidates' apparent failure to understand the cashflow/profit difference is remarkable. This difference is fundamental to accounting, and is even enshrined in SSAP 2 *Disclosure of Accounting Policies* and in Companies Act 1985 as a fundamental accounting concept - the accruals concept.

The difference between cashflow and profit can be simply demonstrated. Suppose a business receives £1,000 cash in one year (all relating to sales) and spends £800 in the same year (all relating to purchases). Then the cashflow for the year is simply:

	£
Income	1,000
Less outgoings	800
Net inflow	£200

But the £200 is not necessarily the same as profit, because the sales and purchases may not necessarily relate to the year in question. Profit always relates to a specific period: cash flows do not. For example, suppose £200 of the £1,000 income actually related to payments owed by debtors from the previous year, and that £150 of the £800 expenditure actually related to the purchase of materials to be used in the following year. Then profit for the year would be:

	£
Sales	800
Less purchases	650
Profit	£150

So although the business has gained £200 in cash over the period, its profit was only £150 for that period.

Of course, the above example is only a simplified example of what you may meet in real life or in the examination. But if you bear the principle in mind, you should not go far wrong.

SSAP 9 (revised)

If you have been studying with the latest edition of the BPP Accountancy study text, you will already be up to date for events up to the end of August 1988. Since then, the ASC has published a revised version of SSAP 9 *Stocks and long-term contracts*.

The revised SSAP 9 has emerged from an exposure draft (ED 40 *Stocks and long-term contracts*) published as long ago as November 1986. The main aim of ED 40 was to regularise the accounting treatment of long-term contract work in progress, which in the past had presented two anomalies:

(a)   The attributable profit on long-term contracts was usually established by a separate calculation which was not integrated into the turnover and cost of sales figures shown in the profit and loss account.

(b)   The balance sheet valuation of long-term contract work in progress included an element of profit. This conflicted with the CA 1985 requirement that current assets should be stated at purchase price or production cost (or net realisable value if lower).

To overcome these difficulties, ED 40 proposed a system in which the turnover and cost of sales generated by a long-term contract would be reflected in the profit and loss account year by year. The balance sheet presentation of long-term contract balances would be substantially revised. No changes were proposed to the principles on which profit calculations were based, and companies would therefore be reporting the same net profits as under the old system.

The proposals of ED 40 were eventually adopted almost unchanged in SSAP 9 (revised). The principal features of the new system are set out below.

(a)   As a long-term contract progresses, an amount of turnover is recognised in some appropriate manner and is included in the profit and loss account. Related costs are similarly recognised and disclosed in the profit and loss account under the appropriate headings (mainly cost of sales). The result is that the profit and loss account reflects a net profit earned on the contract.

(b)   Once the work done on a contract has been recognised as turnover, it must be disclosed in the balance sheet under debtors. (The caption recommended by the ASC is 'amounts recoverable on contracts'.) The amount so disclosed must be reduced by any payments received on account.

(c)   Work in progress on long-term contracts (ie the costs of work done but not yet recognised in the turnover and cost of sales figures) will continue to be shown in the balance sheet under stocks. (The caption recommended by the ASC is 'long-term contract balances'.) The amount so disclosed must be reduced by any foreseeable losses and by payments on account, other than those already matched with turnover (see (a) above).

The new system of accounting for long-term contracts will lead to certain practical difficulties, particularly in establishing the amounts to be recognised as turnover and cost of sales. Until it becomes clear how companies will apply the new rules you are unlikely to be examined on the subject in any detail.

TEST YOUR KNOWLEDGE: QUESTIONS

1 List seven categories of users of accounts.

2 What is the basic valuation rule for stocks and work in progress?

3 What is franked investment income?

4 What components of the year's taxation charge would you expect to find disclosed in a note to the profit and loss account?

5 In what circumstances may research costs be shown as an asset in a company's balance sheet?

6 Under what caption in a company's balance sheet would a balance on deferred taxation account be disclosed?

7 Explain the general rule restricting the amount which a private company may distribute by way of dividend (s263 CA 1985).

8 Distinguish between an accounting basis and an accounting policy.

9 What is an extraordinary item?

10 How are exceptional items disclosed in a company's profit and loss account?

11 Describe the accounting treatment of unrealised stock profits in preparing a consolidated balance sheet.

12 What accounting treatment does SSAP22 prescribe in respect of goodwill arising on consolidation?

13 What is an associated company?

14 Define the additional depreciation adjustment in the context of current cost accounts.

15 Give the formulae for:
   (a) debtors' collection period; and
   (b) finished goods turnover period.

16 Give the formula for breakeven volume of sales.

17 Where would the following items appear in a statement of source and application of funds:
   (a) profit on disposal of fixed assets;
   (b) premium received on a new issue of shares;
   (c) profit and loss charge for taxation?

18 Arrange the following liabilities according to their order of priority in a liquidation:

   preferential creditors
   secured creditors with a fixed charge
   secured creditors with a floating charge
   liquidation expenses

19 A company has regular annual equity earnings of £100,000. There are 500,000 50p ordinary shares in issue. Similar companies have price earnings ratios of 5. What value would you place on the company's shares using the price/earnings ratio as your valuation basis?

20 Name three methods of evaluating a capital investment project.

1   Managers; shareholders; trade contacts; providers of finance; Inland Revenue; employees; financial analysts.

2   Stocks and work in progress should be valued at the lower of cost and net realisable value.

3   Franked investment income is dividends received (plus the associated tax credit) by a UK company from its shareholding in another UK company.

4   The following components of the year's taxation charge are commonly disclosed by note:

   (a) the charge for UK corporation tax on profits for the year;
   (b) the transfer to or from the deferred taxation account;
   (c) tax attributable to dividends received;
   (d) any underprovision or overprovision of tax in the previous year.

5   Neither SSAP13 nor statute permits research costs to be shown as an asset in any circumstances. *Development* costs, however, may be shown as an asset in circumstances defined by SSAP13, principally relating to the project's feasibility and commercial viability.

6   Deferred taxation would be disclosed under the caption 'Provisions for liabilities and other charges: taxation, including deferred taxation.' This caption comes after 'Creditors: amounts falling due after more than one year'.

7   A company may only pay a dividend out of its accumulated *realised* profits (less realised losses) so far as these have not already been paid out as dividends.

8   An accounting basis is one of the detailed methods available for applying an accounting concept. An accounting policy is an accounting basis selected and consistently applied by management as being most appropriate to the circumstances of the business. For example, the straight line method and reducing balance method are both possible *bases* on which depreciation may be accounted for. Whichever method management chooses becomes the accounting *policy* of the business.

9   SSAP6 defines extraordinary items as 'material items which derive from events or transactions that fail outside the ordinary activities of the company and which are therefore expected not to recur frequently or regularly'.

10 Exceptional items are charged in arriving at the 'profit or loss on ordinary activities before taxation'. They are usually disclosed by way of note. They are stated gross, and any related taxation is included in the tax charge for the year.

11 Intra-group profits on goods remaining in group stocks at the balance sheet date are:

   (a) deducted from the value of group stocks; and
   (b) deducted from group reserves.
   Any proportion of such profits which is attributable to minority interests may optionally be deducted from minority interests rather than from group reserves.

12 SSAP22 treats goodwill arising on consolidation in the same way as any other purchased goodwill. The normal accounting treatment is to eliminate goodwill immediately against reserves. Alternatively, purchased goodwill may be carried as an asset in the balance sheet; in this case, the balance must be amortised over the useful life of the goodwill.

13 SSAP1 defines an associated company as one over which the investing company can exercise significant influence (eg by board representation or by holding equity shares in the associate. A holding of 20% or more of the ordinary shares will give rise to a presumption of associated company status).

14 The additional depreciation adjustment is the difference between:

(a) depreciation based on the historical cost of a fixed asset; and
(b) depreciation based on the current cost of the asset.

15 (a) Debtors' collection period = $\dfrac{\text{Average debtors}}{\text{Annual sales}}$ x 365 days

(b) Finished goods = $\dfrac{\text{Average finished goods stock}}{\text{Cost of goods sold in year}}$ x 365 days
turnover period

16 Breakeven sales volume = $\dfrac{\text{Total fixed costs}}{\text{Unit contribution}}$

17 (a) As a deduction, under 'adjustments for items not involving the movement of funds'.
(b) As a source of funds.
(c) Nowhere - but the tax actually *paid* during the year would appear as an application of funds.

18 The order is:
secured creditors with a fixed charge
liquidation expenses
preferential creditors
secured creditors with a floating charge

19 Value of the company   = £100,000 x 5
= £500,000

∴ Value of each share   = $\dfrac{£500,000}{500,000}$

= £1

20 The return on investment method; the payback method; discounted cash flow.

INDEX TO QUESTIONS AND SUGGESTED SOLUTIONS

As far as possible, questions have been listed under the appropriate headings from the syllabus. But some questions span more than one area of the syllabus: where this is the case, a question has been placed under the heading which is most relevant to its content.

QUESTIONS

QUESTIONS

1. BASIC (20 marks)

The following information relates to a business with year end 31 December 19X4.

(i) *Office equipment*

	£
At cost, 1 January 19X4	13,500
Accumulated depreciation 1 Jan 19X4	4,700
Additions in year at cost	7,200
Disposals in year at cost (NBV £1,700)	2,400

Depreciation policy: 10% per annum on the reducing balance

(ii) *Telephone expenses*

	£
Accrued expense at 31 December 19X3	112
Quarterly bills:	
1.11.X3 – 31.1.X4 (paid 5.2.X4)	180
1.2.X4 – 30.4.X4 (paid 4.5.X4)	190
1.5.X4 – 31.7.X4 (paid 10.8.X4)	195
1.8.X4 – 31.10.X4 (paid 6.11.X4)	210
1.11.X4 – 31.1.X5 (paid 5.2.X5)	216

(iii) *Rates*

	£
Six months to 31.3.X4 (paid 3.10.X3)	1,200
Six months to 30.9.X4 (paid 4.4.X4)	1,400
Six months to 31.3.X5 (paid 4.10.X4)	1,400

(iv) *Debtors*

	£
Provision for doubtful debts at 1 Jan 19X4	380
Cash received during year from debtor previously written off as bad debt	90
Bad debts written off during year	130
Debtors' balances at 31 Dec 19X4	24,800

Of the debtors' balances of £24,800 outstanding at 31 December 19X4 £300 is regarded as doubtful. A provision of 2% is required at 31.12.X4 in respect of balances not specifically provided for.

(v) *Rental income*

The business owns a property which it rents to a local trader. Rent is payable quarterly in advance on 28 February, 31 May, 31 August and 30 November.
The following sums were received in 19X4:

		£
2 Jan	Quarter to 28 February	240
26 Feb	Quarter to 31 May	240
31 May	Quarter to 31 August	270
30 Aug	Quarter to 30 November	270

A payment of £270 in respect of the quarter to 28 February 19X5 was not received until January 19X5.

QUESTIONS

You are required to compute the amounts which would appear in the 19X4 profit and loss account for:

(a) depreciation of office equipment;
(b) telephone expenses;
(c) rates;
(d) bad and doubtful debts;
(e) rental income.

2. **TREND** (25 marks)

Trend Limited began trading on 1 April 19X0. The following figures are available for cost and depreciation of plant in the three years to 31 March 19X3.

Year ended 31 March	19X1	19X2	19X3
	£	£	£
(A) Plant at cost	80,000	80,000	90,000
(B) Accumulated depreciation	(16,000)	(28,800)	(36,720)
(C) Net (written down value)	£64,000	£51,200	£53,280

The only other information available is that disposals have taken place at the beginning of the financial years concerned.

	Date of Disposal	Original acquisition 12 months ended 31 March	Original cost	Sales proceeds
			£	£
First disposal	19X3	19X0	15,000	8,000
Second disposal	19X4	19X0	30,000	21,000

Plant sold was replaced on the same day by new plant. The cost of the plant which replaced the first disposal is not known but the replacement for the second disposal is known to have cost £50,000.

You are required to:

(a) identify the method of providing for depreciation on plant employed by Trend Limited, stating how you have arrived at your conclusion; (2 marks)

(b) reconstruct a working schedule to support the figures shown at line (B) for each of the years ended 31 March 19X1, 19X2 and 19X3. Extend your workings to cover year ended 31 March 19X4; (16 marks)

(c) calculate the figures for cost, accumulated depreciation and net book value for the year ended 31 March 19X4; and (3 marks)

(d) calculate the profit or loss arising on each of the two disposals. (4 marks)

26

3. LAURA (20 marks)

Laura carries on a business as a clothing manufacturer. The trial balance of the business as on 31 December 19X0 was as follows:

	£	£
Capital account - Laura		30,000
Freehold factory at cost (including land £4,000)	20,000	
Factory plant and machinery at cost	4,800	
Travellers' cars	2,600	
Provision for depreciation 1 January 19X0:		
Freehold factory		1,920
Factory plant and machinery		1,600
Travellers' cars		1,200
Stocks 1 January 19X0	8,900	
Trade debtors and creditors	3,600	4,200
Provision for doubtful debts		280
Purchases	36,600	
Wages and salaries	19,800	
Rates and insurance	1,510	
Sundry expenses	1,500	
Motor expenses	400	
Sales		72,000
Balance at bank	11,490	
	£111,200	£111,200

You are given the following further information:

(a) stocks on hand as on 31 December 19X0 were £10,800;

(b) wages and salaries include the following:

drawings	£2,400
motor expenses	£600

(c) provision is to be made for depreciation on the freehold factory buildings, plant and machinery, and travellers' cars at 2%, 10% and 25% respectively, calculated on cost;

(d) on 31 December 19X0, £120 was owing for sundry expenses, and rates paid in advance amounted to £260;

(e) of the trade debtors, £60 for which provision had previously been made is to be written off. It is thought that the remaining provision will be adequate.

You are required to effect the necessary adjustments at 31 December 19X0 and to prepare the balance sheet and profit and loss account at that date.

4. EXPLAIN (30 marks)

(a) You are required to explain the following terms:

    (i)   bonus issue;
    (ii)   share premium account;
    (iii) capital redemption reserve.   (10 marks)

(b) A company has the following capital structure at 31 March 19X4:

	£'000
Ordinary shares of 50p each	200
10% preference shares of £1 each	30
Share premium account	10
Retained profits	430
Shareholders' funds	670
12% debentures	20
	690

The information below relates to the year ended 31 March 19X5.

(i)   On 1 April 19X4 £10,000 of the preference shares were redeemed at par out of profits.

(ii)   A new issue of 50,000 ordinary shares was made on 1 June 19X4 at a premium of 10p per share.

(iii) On 1 July 19X4 a bonus issue of 1 for 5 was made on the ordinary shares. The issue was funded partly from share premium account and, when that was exhausted, from retained profits.

(iv) The operating profit for the year ended 31 March 19X5 was £200,000 after charging all expenses except the debenture interest.

       The directors propose a dividend of 10% on all the ordinary shares in issue at 31 March 19X5.

You are required to prepare:

(i)   the profit and loss and appropriation accounts and the statement of retained earnings for the year ended 31 March 19X5. (Begin with operating profit and ignore taxation);   (10 marks)

(ii)   the capital structure of the company as it would appear in the balance sheet at 31 March 19X5.   (10 marks)

5. **GRAFTON** (20 marks)

The following extracts are taken from the balance sheet of Grafton plc at 31 August 19X8:

BALANCE SHEET EXTRACTS

	£
Ordinary shares of £1 each, fully paid	500,000
Share premium account	150,000
Profit and loss account balance (all distributable)	370,000
	1,020,000
Net assets (including cash)	1,020,000

The above balance of ordinary shares includes 200,000 redeemable ordinary shares which are to be redeemed on 1 September 19X8 at a price of £1.60 per share.

Required:

(a) The Companies Act 1985 contains provisions enabling limited companies to redeem or purchase their own shares. Outline the provisions contained in the Act designed to ensure 'permanent capital' is maintained intact in these circumstances. (6 marks)

(b) State the figure for Grafton plc's permanent capital at 31 August 19X8.

(2 marks)

(c) Revised balance sheet extracts as at 1 September 19X8, following redemption, taking separate account of each of the following assumptions:

(i) The shares were issued at par.
(ii) The shares were issued at par and, to help finance the redemption, 100,000 £1 9% preference shares are issued at par.
(iii) The shares were issued at £1.20 per share and, to help finance the redemption, 80,000 ordinary shares are issued at £2 per share.

(Set out these extracts under three separate headings - (i), (ii) and (iii).)

(12 marks)

Note: assume there are no other transactions on 1 September 19X8.

6. **TRAFFORD** (20 marks)

The equity section of the balance sheet of Trafford Limited as at 31 December 19X4 is as follows:

BALANCE SHEET EXTRACT

	£
Ordinary shares of £1 each	1,000
Share premium account	400
Distributable profits	600
Shareholders' equity (net assets)	£2,000

The above balance sheet includes redeemable ordinary shares possessing a nominal value of £200. These are to be redeemed on 1 January 19X5.

Required:

Revised balance sheet extracts as at 1 January 19X5, following redemption, taking separate account of each of the following assumptions:

(a) The shares were initially issued at par and are redeemed at par.   (5 marks)

(b) The shares were initially issued at £1.10 per share and are redeemed at £1.50 per share.
                                                                                        (5 marks)

(c) The shares were initially issued at par and are redeemed at £1.20 per share. To help to finance the redemption a new issue of 100 shares is made at £1.05 per share.
                                                                                        (5 marks)

(d) The shares were initially issued at £1.25 per share and are redeemed at £1.40 per share. To help to finance the redemption a new issue of 100 shares is made at £1.10 per share.
                                                                                        (5 marks)

Note: assume that no other transactions occur on 1 January 19X5.

7.   **RIVERSIDE AND ORLANDO (20 marks)**

Riverside plc and Orlando plc are companies engaged in the same kind of business in the United Kingdom. The business is cyclical and from past experience, profits before deducting loan interest are liable to fluctuate up to 50% above or below the 19X2 level.

The following information is provided for 19X2:

	Riverside	*Orlando*
	£'000	£'000
Ordinary share capital (£1 shares)	2,000	1,000
Reserves (average figure for 19X2)	1,500	1,000
15% debentures repayable 19X8/X9	500	4,000
Profit for 19X2 before deducting loan interest	600	900

Required:

(a) Calculations for each company of the rate of return on shareholders' equity.
                                                                                        (8 marks)

(b) A discussion of the capital structure of each company from the viewpoint of the shareholders and management. The discussion should include calculations of the possible variations in the rate of return earned for the shareholders.   (12 marks)

8. ALLERTON (20 marks)

The following is the summarised balance sheet of Allerton Limited at 31 March 19X3.

	£'000	£'000
Fixed assets		
Freehold building at cost less depreciation	40	
Plant and equipment at cost less depreciation	504	
		544
Current assets		
Stocks	420	
Debtors	316	
	736	
Current liabilities		
Bank overdraft	195	
Sundry creditors	205	
	400	
Net current assets		336
Total assets less current liabilities		880
Long-term liability		
12% debentures 19X9		(480)
		400
Capital and reserves		
400,000 shares of £1 each fully paid		400
Profit and loss account		80
		480

The bank overdraft is secured by a fixed charge on the freehold building; the debentures, all held by Shipley plc, are secured by a floating charge over the remaining assets of Allerton.

Allerton has been trading unprofitably for over two years and is now finding it impossible to meet its financial obligations. A meeting of creditors has been called to examine its affairs, and the following proposals are put forward for consideration.

1 *Piecemeal liquidation of the company*
It is estimated that the company's assets, sold individually, would realise the following amounts:

	£'000
Freehold building	70
Plant and equipment	20
Stocks	290
Debtors	250

Liquidation costs are estimated at £10,000 and sundry creditors, in the above balance sheet, include preferential creditors of £30,000.

2 *Sale of company as a going concern*
Shipley would purchase the shares for a token sum and pay immediately the preferential creditors, in full, and the other sundry creditors and the bank 20p in the £ on account of the amounts shown as due to them in the above balance sheet. 75% of the balances then remaining outstanding would be repaid after one year but would not attract interest during the interim period.

Assume that:

(a) the current rate of interest on all forms of borrowing is 12%;

(b) the £195,000 overdraft in the balance sheet included interest to date;

(c) the calculations are being made on 1 April 19X3;

(d) piecemeal liquidation, if selected, would occur immediately, alternatively the company could be sold to Shipley at once.

Required:

(a) Calculations showing the amount which would be received by the bank under each proposal.
(14 marks)

(b) A brief explanation of the relative merits of the two proposals from the bank's point of view. (6 marks)

9. **LION (20 marks)**

The following is the summarised balance sheet of Lion Ltd at 30 April 19X6:

	£'000	£'000
Fixed assets		
Freehold property at book value		70
Plant and machinery at book value		200
		270
Current assets		
Stocks	82	
Debtors	57	
	139	
Creditors: amounts due within one year		
Creditors	95	
Bank overdraft	105	
Taxation and national insurance	20	
	220	
Net current assets		(81)
		189
Creditors: amounts due after one year		
12% debentures repayable 19X8		(50)
		139
Capital and reserves		
Ordinary share capital (£1 shares)		200
Profit and loss account		(61)
		139

The 12% debenture holders have a first charge on the freehold property and the bank has a second charge.

The demand for Lion's products has collapsed over the last five years owing to the availability of cheap imports. Trading losses are mounting steadily and a meeting of creditors has been called to examine Lion Ltd's affairs. The following alternative proposals are put forward by the directors of Lion:

A. *Liquidation of the company*

It is estimated that business assets, if sold individually, would realise the following amounts:

	£'000
Freehold property	120
Plant and machinery	18
Stocks	57
Debtors	50

Liquidation costs are estimated at £5,000. The amount due for tax and National Insurance and £10,000 of the creditors are 'preferential'.

B. *Sale of company to Gulf plc*

Gulf, which is Lion's main supplier and also the debenture holder, is willing to purchase the shares for a token sum and take over the business as a going concern. Under the scheme, the preferential creditors would be paid in full, the debentures would be converted into ordinary shares and the remaining creditors and the bank would receive the full amount owing in twelve months' time. These debts would not attract further interest over the twelve month period.

Assume that:

(i) The bank lends money at 12%.
(ii) The calculations are being made on 1 May 19X6.
(iii) Piecemeal liquidation could occur, in which case cash would be received immediately; alternatively, the company could be sold to Gulf at once.

Required:

(a) Prepare a statement showing the distribution of the proceeds assuming the liquidation option is chosen. Show clearly the amount received by each provider of finance.

(10 marks)

(b) Examine the two proposals from the bank's point of view. (10 marks)

10. SUTHERLAND (30 marks)

Sutherland Ltd is a private company. Three quarters of the issued share capital is held by the directors or members of their families. The company's draft balance sheet as at the end of 19X5 was as follows:

BALANCE SHEET AT 31 DECEMBER 19X5

	£	£
Fixed assets		
Intangible assets		
Development costs		85,000
Goodwill		60,000
Tangible assets		
Land and buildings		270,000
Plant and machinery		326,000
		741,000
Current assets		
Stocks	426,000	
Debtors	531,000	
	957,000	
Creditors: amounts falling due within one year		
Bank loans and overdrafts	687,000	
Creditors	393,000	
	1,080,000	
Net current liabilities		(123,000)
Total assets less current liabilities		£618,000
Capital and reserves		
Called up share capital (800,000 shares of £1 each)		800,000
Share premium account		50,000
Profit and loss account		(232,000)
		£618,000

Bank loans and overdrafts consist of a 10% loan of £400,000 repayable in 19X6 carrying a fixed charge on the company's land and buildings, and an unsecured overdraft of £287,000.

The demand for the company's products has fallen drastically in recent years owing to the import of high quality and cheaper products from south-east Asia. The development costs appearing in the balance sheet above relate to a new product which has been perfected to a marketable stage, and for which there is believed to be a strong demand. The costs have been properly capitalised in accordance with the provisions of SSAP 13. The company is in urgent need of capital to meet existing liabilities and the necessary new investment in plant and working capital.

A scheme for financial reorganisation has been drawn up for the consideration of shareholders and creditors. The terms are as follows:

(i)   The shares of £1 each are to be written down to 20p per share and subsequently every five shares of 20p each are to be consolidated into one fully paid share of £1.

(ii)   The existing shareholders are to subscribe for a rights issue of two new £1 ordinary shares, at par, for every share held after the proposed reduction and consolidation.

(iii)   A major supplier agrees to exchange a debt of £180,000, included in creditors, for 180,000 ordinary shares of £1 each fully paid.

(iv)   In full satisfaction of the £687,000 owing, the bank agrees to accept an immediate payment of £87,000 and to consolidate the balance of £600,000 in five equal annual instalments commencing 21 December 19X7. The loan is too be secured by a fixed charge on the land and buildings and a floating charge on the company's remaining assets.

(v)   The credit balance on share premium account and debit balances on the profit and loss account and goodwill, considered valueless, are to be written off.

(vi)   The assets listed below are to be restated at the following amounts:

	£
Plant and machinery	125,000
Stock	210,000
Debtors	500,000
Land and buildings	320,000

A group of dissatisfied shareholders plan to oppose the scheme on the following grounds: 'We have to bear the whole burden of the reorganisation whereas the bank loses nothing.'

The company has received a cash offer of £1,120,000 for its fixed and current assets.

Required:

(a)   The revised balance sheet of Sutherland Ltd at 1 January 19X6 giving effect to the proposed scheme for reorganising the company.   (14 marks)

(b)   A report for the group of dissatisfied shareholders explaining whether they should accept or oppose the scheme.   (8 marks)

(c)   A report for the bank explaining the matters to be taken into account in deciding whether it would be better to support the scheme or press for immediate liquidation of the company.   (8 marks)

Note: assume you are making the calculations and writing the reports on 1 January 19X6 and that no other changes occur.

11. GRASSINGTON (20 marks)

The following forecasts are provided in respect of Grassington Ltd, a company trading in a single product, for 19X4:

	£
Sales	2,700
Purchases	1,800
Cost of goods sold	1,830
Average trade debtors outstanding	300
Average trade creditors outstanding	160
Average stocks held	305

All purchases and sales are made on credit, and trading transactions are expected to occur at an even rate throughout the year.

Required:

(a) Calculations of the rate of payment of creditors, the rate of collection of debtors and the rate of stock turnover. (9 marks)

(b) A calculation of the expected cash operating cycle (ie the time lag between making payment to suppliers and collecting cash from customers in respect of goods purchased and sold) for 19X4. (5 marks)

(c) Using the information provided, explain any one method by which the directors might achieve a reduction of £20,000 in the company's bank overdraft requirement at 31 December 19X4, and demonstrate the effect on the cash operating cycle. (6 marks)

(*Note:* assume a 360 days year for the purpose of your calculations.)

12. MANUFACTURING COMPANY (20 marks)

The managing director of a manufacturing company has been studying the comparison of working capital at the end of the last two financial years shown in the statement which is reproduced below. He is concerned that the control of working capital seems to be inefficient as both stock and debtors show increases greater than would be expected from the increased level of sales. He is also worried that, although the increase in creditors may give the use of valuable extra funds, it may cause a reduction in the company's credit rating.

As he is anxious to start talks with the stock and credit controllers soon, he needs some preliminary information which can be used as a basis for discussions. As a first step he would like the statement below to be extended with some budget figures at the end of the financial year to 30 June 19X2 added on the following assumptions:

(a) that the average number of days allowed in 19X0 and 19X1 for materials stocks, finished goods stocks, debtors and creditors (as indicated in the statement) will all be reduced by ten per cent in 19X2;

(b) that bank/cash balances at 30 June 19X2 will be £50,000;

(c) that expense creditors at 30 June 19X2 will be £15,000;

(d) that the dividend for 19X2 will be maintained in real terms; and

(e) that the rate of inflation for the year to 30 June 19X2 is expected to be 15 per cent.

Comparison of working capital

	At 30 June 19X0 £	Days	At 30 June 19X1 £	Days
Stock of raw materials at cost	45,077	28	68,613	32
Stock of finished goods at cost including a proportion of variable production costs	36,900	12	31,428	8
	81,977		100,041	
Debtors	847,816	85	897,949	75
Bank/cash	15,874		8,760	
Total current assets	945,667		1,006,750	
Trade creditors	38,697	24	76,971	36
Expense creditors	10,000		17,000	
Provision for dividend	30,000		40,000	
Net working capital	£866,970		£872,779	

Additional information to help in reading the statement:

	Year to 30 June 19X0 £	Year to 30 June to 19X1 £	Budget year to 30 June 19X2 (at current prices) £
Sales	3,645,000	4,370,000	5,244,000
Cost of sales:			
Materials/labour	806,000	1,040,000	1,200,000
Factory overheads: variable	312,000	390,000	520,000
fixed	390,000	560,000	630,000
Purchases of materials	586,000	780,000	1,020,000

Required:

Prepare a suitable comparative statement of working capital to satisfy the points raised by the managing director which shows clearly the steps in calculating the working capital requirements at 30 June 19X2.

13. DEEPDALE (20 marks)

The summarised balance sheet of Deepdale Limited as at 31 March 19X5 is as follows:

SUMMARISED BALANCE SHEET

	£'000		£'000
Ordinary share capital		Fixed assets at cost	
£1 shares	90	less depreciation	182
Retained earnings	70	Temporary investments	
10% debentures	100	(market value £19,000)	13
Creditors	60	Stocks	108
Taxation due 1 January		Debtors	80
19X6	75	Cash at bank	12
	395		395

Additional information:

(1) The company keeps in its bank account the minimum amount of cash needed to meet day-to-day requirements. Any surplus cash is used to purchase temporary investments.

(2) The directors plan to expand the level of activity during the year to 31 March 19X6. Sales will increase from £800,000 to £1,000,000 and this is expected to produce a proportional increase in stocks, day-to-day cash requirements and creditors, while the period of credit allowed to customers will be increased by 50%.

(3) To meet additional production requirements, plant costing £110,000 will be acquired early in the year.

(4) It is estimated that profits before interest charges for the year to 31 March 19X6 will amount to 10% of sales after charging depreciation of £50,000.

(5) Taxable profits for the year are estimated at £80,000 and these will be subject to corporation tax at 35%.

(6) All the shares in Deepdale are owned by the directors who receive salaries at normal market rates.

Required:

(a) Calculate:
   (i)   the additional investment required to achieve the planned increase in sales;
   (ii) the funds expected to be generated from operations during the year to 31 March 19X6. (Ignore interest on any bank borrowings). (10 marks)

(b) Consider the implications of your calculations under (a) and advise management how they might finance the planned expansion. (10 marks)

14. GREENHAYES (30 marks)

Chris Slaughter set up in business a few years ago as a manufacturer of specialised garden implements. His friend, James Hutton, has recently graduated from university where he studied mechanical engineering, design and computing. They decide to form a company to manufacture and sell a sophisticated appliance, designed by James, to regulate the heat in greenhouses. James comes from a wealthy family who provide him with £8,000 to help to start this venture. Chris is able to transfer to the new business plant valued at £8,000 which is surplus to his existing requirements. A new company, Greenhayes Limited, is formed to carry on the business and Chris and James are each issued with shares with a total nominal value of £8,000. The balance sheet of the business at 20 September 19X4 is as follows:

BALANCE SHEET OF GREENHAYES LTD AT 20 SEPTEMBER 19X4

	£		£
Share capital	16,000	Plant	8,000
		Cash at bank	8,000
	£16,000		£16,000

The two directors of Greenhayes Limited approach your bank for an overdraft to finance the planned operations and have provided the following plans and estimates:

(a) Greenhayes will carry on business from rented accommodation. A rental payment of £1,600 for the forthcoming six months will be made on 30 September 19X4, of which three-quarters is for factory accommodation and one quarter for office accommodation.

(b) The plant is expected to have a four year life and a nil scrap value at the end of that period. Depreciation is to be provided on the straight line basis.

(c) Purchases of materials, sufficient to enable the production of 500 units, will be made on 21 September and at the beginning of each subsequent month. Materials will cost £8 per unit payable at the end of the month following the month in which the purchases are made.

(d) Production will commence on 1 October 19X4. It is expected that 500 appliances will be produced in October and in each subsequent month.

(e) Direct wages, payable on a weekly basis, will amount to £6 per unit. In addition, James Hutton, who is to be the production director, will be paid a salary of £800 per month, commencing October.

(f) Factory overhead expenses, other than the rental and James's salary, are estimated at £500 per month payable in October and each subsequent month.

(g) Chris Slaughter will be part-time managing director, receiving a salary of £500 per month from October onwards. Other office and selling expenses will amount to £100 per month payable in October and each subsequent month.

(h) Sales are forecast at the rate of 500 appliances per month commencing 1 November. The selling price is to be £20 per unit payable at the end of the month following the month in which the sale is made.

(i) The stock of finished goods (ie completed appliances) is to be valued on the prime cost basis for internal reporting purposes. There is no work in progress at the end of any month.

Required:

(a) A cash budget for the six months to 31 March 19X5. The cash budget should show the cumulative surplus or deficit at the end of each month. (6 marks)

(b) A forecast manufacturing trading and profit and loss account for the six months to 31 March 19X5, and forecast balance sheet at 31 March 19X5, valuing finished goods on the prime cost basis. (16 marks)

(c) An examination of the forecast profitability of the new venture and of Chris Slaughter's suggestion that the closing stock of finished goods should be valued on the total cost basis for the purpose of preparing the accounts to be presented to the bank. Your examination should include a calculation of the financial effect of valuing finished stock on the total cost basis. (8 marks)

Notes:
1 Ignore taxation
2 Assume that each month consists of four weeks
3 Ignore bank interest, if any.

15. KENDAL (30 marks)

The summarised balance sheet of Kendal Limited, a well established private company which has banked with you for many years, contained the following information.

SUMMARISED BALANCE SHEET
AS AT 31 MARCH 19X4

	£	£
Fixed assets		
Tangible assets:		
cost	920	
depreciation	170	
net book value		750
Current assets		
Stocks	350	
Trade debtors	320	
Investments at cost	70	
Bank balance	35	
	775	
Current liabilities		
Trade creditors	200	
Corporation tax (due 1.1.19X5)	120	
	320	
Net current assets		455
		1,205
Capital and reserves		
Share capital		1,000
Profit and loss account		205
		1,205

The company's managing director, who is also the major shareholder, believes that there is a strong demand for the products Kendal supplies, and he intends to expand the level of activities by renting additional premises and acquiring new plant. He is attempting to assess the financial implications of his plans and he approaches you for advice. He provides you with the following forecasts and information:

(a) Plant will be purchased in May 19X4 at a cost of £270,000 and from 1 June onwards, the level of business activity will be 50% above the previous level. The rate of stock turnover and the period of credit obtained from suppliers are expected to remain unchanged, but the period of credit allowed to customers will increase, on average, by 25%.

(b) The following are extracts from the company's forecast profit and loss account for the year to 31 March 19X5, which takes account of the plans and assumptions made in (a) above.

	£'000	£'000
Operating profit before charging depreciation:		
April–May		60
June–March		450
		510
Less: Depreciation	130	
Corporation tax on profit from operations	180	
		310
		200
Add: Gain arising on sale of the company's temporary investments, in May, net of a tax charge of £16,000		24
		224

Required:

(a) The forecast balance sheet at 31 March 19X5 (a bank balance or bank overdraft may be inserted as the balancing item). (12 marks)

(b) An assessment of the financial implications of the proposals for expansion. The assessment should include calculations of relevant 'solvency' ratios and an indication, so far as the information permits, of the overdraft requirement on 1 June 19X4 assuming that the bank agrees to help to finance the project. For this purpose, you may assume that the increase in the working capital requirement occurs on 1 June 19X4. (18 marks)

Notes:
1 Ignore interest payable on any bank overdraft.
2 A year consists of twelve calendar months of equal duration.
3 There are no seasonal fluctuations in the level of trading activity.

16. BLAIR (30 marks)

Peter Blair has worked for some years as a sales representative, but has recently been made redundant. He intends to start up in business on his own account, using £15,000 which he currently has invested with a building society. He has a number of good business contacts, and is confident that his firm will do well, but thinks that additional finance will be required in the short term. Peter also maintains a bank account showing a small credit balance, and he plans to approach his bank for the necessary finance. Peter, whom you have known for some time, asks you for advice. He provides the following additional information:

(a) Arrangements have been made to purchase fixed assets costing £8,000. These will be paid for at the end of September and are expected to have a five year life, at the end of which they will possess a nil residual value.

(b) Stocks costing £5,000 will be acquired on 28 September, and subsequent monthly purchases will be at a level sufficient to replace forecast sales for the month.

(c) Forecast monthly sales are £3,000 for October, £6,000 for November and December, and £10,500 from January 19X4 onwards.

(d) Selling price is fixed at the cost of stock plus 50%.

(e) Two months' credit will be allowed to customers but only one month's credit will be received from suppliers of stock.

(f) Running expenses, including rent but excluding depreciation of fixed assets, are estimated at £1,600 per month.

(g) Blair intends to make monthly cash drawings of £1,000.

Required:

(a) A cash forecast for the six months to 31 March 19X4, showing the accumulated cash surplus or deficit at the end of each month.   (9 marks)

(b) A forecast trading and profit and loss account for the six months to 31 March 19X4, and a forecast balance sheet at 31 March 19X4, showing the accumulated cash surplus or deficit as a separate item.   (11 marks)

(c) A full assessment of Blair's forecasts and financial requirements from a lender's viewpoint.   (10 marks)

17. **KEHL (30 marks)**

Kehl Limited is engaged in the design and construction of exotic gardens and ornamental pools. The company which was incorporated and commenced business on 1 January 19X5 operates from a small unit on a factory estate. All the shares are owned by the two directors, John Lardner and June Clapham.

The profit and loss account for the first year of operations showed a profit before tax of £6,000, after charging total directors' remuneration of £20,000 and the summarised balance sheet at 31 December 19X5 is as follows:

	£	£
Fixed assets		
Plant and equipment at book value		20,000
Current assets		
Stocks of materials	8,000	
Work in progress	30,000	
Bank balance	2,000	
		40,000
		60,000
Current liabilities		
Trade creditors	4,800	
Taxation due 1 October 19X6	1,800	
Advance payments from customers	20,000	
		(25,800)
		£34,200
Capital and reserves		
Share capital (£1 ordinary)		30,000
Retained profit		4,200
		£34,200

The company carries out work on the basis of contracts with householders and the policy has been to insist on an advance payment of 50% of the total contract price, with the balance payable when work is complete. On this basis the company entered into contracts worth £40,000 during the last quarter of 19X5. As from 1 January 19X6 the directors have decided to reduce the advance payment to 25% of the contract price, with the remaining 75% payable on completion. A substantial increase in sales is expected to result and the forecast profit and loss account for 19X6 is as follows:

FORECAST PROFIT AND LOSS ACCOUNT FOR 19X6

	£	£
Turnover (value of contracts completed		220,000
Less: Opening stock of materials	8,000	
Materials purchased	76,000	
Closing stock of materials	(12,000)	
Materials consumed	72,000	
Other direct costs	108,000	
Total direct costs	180,000	
Opening work in progress	30,000	
Closing work in progress	(45,000)	
	165,000	
Depreciation	2,000	
Directors' remuneration	30,000	
Other indirect costs	12,000	
		209,000
Profit		£11,000

The directors believe that cash requirements will increase and they have private resources totalling £6,000 which they are willing to inject on 1 January 19X6 in exchange for additional shares issued at par. They have approached their bank to finance any shortfall which might arise during 19X6 and the following additional information is made available.

(i) Contracts worth £20,000 will be entered into each month during 19X6.

(ii) All contracts will last three months, so that the balance due on completion is always received in the quarter following commencement of the contract.

(iii) It is the company's policy to take credit for the profit arising on the contract only when the balance payable on completion is received.

(iv) Purchases of raw materials will amount to £10,000 in January and £6,000 in each following month. One month's credit is received from suppliers.

(v) Other direct costs and other indirect costs will be incurred at an even rate during the year and are payable immediately the work is done or services received.

(vi) The director's remuneration is paid in equal amounts at the end of each month.

(vii) Tax at 30% is to be provided on the forecast profit.

(viii) Under an agreement with the local authority, no rent or rates are payable for the first two years of operation but thereafter these will amount to £6,500 per annum.

Required:

(a) A quarterly cash forecast for 19X6 in columnar form, showing the expected cash surplus or requirement at the end of each quarter. (13 marks)

(b) The forecast balance sheet at 31 December 19X6. (19 marks)

(c) A report for the bank on the proposals and prospects of Kehl Ltd. (8 marks)

Note: assume all the calculations are being made on 1 January 19X6. Ignore interest on any additional cash requirements.

18. DODD (20 marks)

The summarised balance sheet of Arthur Dodd at 31 December 19X5 is as follows:

BALANCE SHEET AT 31 DECEMBER 19X5

	£
Fixed assets at book value	40,000
Working capital	25,000
	65,000
Capital at 1 January 19X5	61,000
Profit earned during 19X5	20,000
Drawings	(16,000)
	£65,000

Arthur Dodd plans to expand his business and this will involve acquiring fixed assets for £24,000 and increasing his working capital requirement to £36,000 on 1 January 19X6.

He forecasts that the expansion will cause his profit to increase by 60%. This is after charging depreciation of £8,000 but before interest charges which at present are zero. His bank has agreed to provide a 12% bank loan on 1 January 19X6 to cover the cost of his additional investment. Interest is payable on 31 December each year.

Drawings during 19X6 will amount to £28,000. Cash generated surplus to working capital requirements will accrue at an even rate and be kept in a bank deposit account paying 8% per annum interest credited on 31 December. The interest due on the bank loan will be paid from the deposit account.

Required:

(a)   Prepare a forecast statement of funds for 19X6 to show the amount of cash generated surplus to working capital requirements. You should ignore the interest accruing on the deposit account balance when making this calculation.   (7 marks)

(b)   Calculate the interest credited to the deposit account at 31 December 19X6.
                                                                                                                (2 marks)

(c)   Prepare the forecast balance sheet at 31 December 19X6.   (8 marks)

(d)   Advise Dodd whether, instead of borrowing from the bank, he should finance the planned expansion by selling privately owned securities currently yielding 15% per annum.
                                                                                                                (3 marks)

19. LISTER (30 marks)

Lister Ltd is a manufacturing company; about one third of the issued share capital is owned by the directors. On 1 Ju'y 19X5 plant costing £1,000,000 was purchased and became fully operational. A 50% increase in sales was immediately achieved as the result of a heavy advertising campaign undertaken during June 19X5 at a cost of £150,000. The company's policy is to amortise the advertising expenditure by three equal annual instalments. The figures opposite have been extracted from the company's published account for the two years to 30 June 19X6.

The loan shown in the balance sheet opposite is repayable at the rate of £200,000 per annum, the first payment being due 1 July 19X7.

PROFIT AND LOSS ACCOUNT EXTRACTS YEAR TO 30 JUNE

	19X5 £'000	19X6 £'000
Turnover		
	4,500	6,750
Operating profit	225	472
Less interest payable	-	177
Net profit before tax	225	295
Less corporation tax	77	88
Net profit after tax	148	207
Less dividends proposed	100	150
Retained profit for the year	48	57

SUMMARISED BALANCE SHEETS AT 30 JUNE

	19X5	19X6
Fixed assets		
Cost	2,000	3,000
Less accumulated depreciation	800	1,100
	1,200	1,900
Deferred expenditure		
Advertising campaign	150	100
Current assets		
Stock and work in progress	300	440
Debtors	600	1,163
Cash at bank and in hand	35	-
	935	1,603
Creditors: amounts falling due within one year		
Bank overdraft	-	293
Creditors and accruals	220	293
Taxation due 31 March	77	88
Proposed dividend	100	150
	397	858
Net current assets	538	745
Total assets less current liabilities	1,888	2,745
12% Loan	-	800
	1,888	1,945
Capital and reserves		
Issued share capital (£1 ordinary shares)	1,000	1,000
Reserves and retained profits	888	945
	1,888	1,945

It is expected that turnover and operating profit for the year to 30 June 19X7 will remain at approximately the levels achieved during the year to 30 June 19X6. All fixed assets at present employed have a minimum future useful life of three years, except for a fully depreciated machine which must be replaced in March 19X7 at a cost of £120,000.

Required:

(a) A statement of source and application of funds for the year to 30 June 19X6. (7 marks)

(b) A discussion of the company's financial progress and position, based on the calculations in (a) above together with relevant 'solvency' and 'asset turnover' ratios. (13 marks)

(c) Your views on whether the company will be able to meet a requirement imposed by the bank to eliminate the overdraft shown in the balance sheet opposite by 30 June 19X7. You should produce figures to support your conclusions. (10 marks)

20. ROKER (30 marks)

Roker has recently returned home after spending some time overseas working for a multinational company. Whilst abroad he made regular remittances to his bank. The balance on his account stands at £20,000, and he intends to use this sum to start a business. In the course of his travels he was very impressed by the quality and price of bamboo furniture obtainable in the Far East, and he reached the conclusion that these items would find a ready market in the UK. He has found a reliable supplier and plans to start trading on 1 July 19X5. Roker provides you with the following information:

(a) He has made arrangements to lease lock-up premises where the furniture will be deposited until it is sold. The ten-year lease involves a total outlay of £15,000 which will be paid in full at the end of June 19X5. In the same month Roker expects to acquire a van costing £3,000 in which to transport the furniture. The van will last four years and then be valueless.

(b) He will take delivery of his first consignment of stock on 1 July 19X5 at a cost of £6,000. Further consignments of furniture costing £4,500 each, will be received at two-monthly intervals commencing August 19X5. Payment for purchases of stock will be made in the month following delivery.

(c) Roker will advertise his furniture in trade catalogues and this will cost him £150 per month commencing July 19X5.

(d) Sales will be made at cost plus a mark up of 100%. He estimates that sales will take place as follows:

July 19X5:	zero
August - September 19X5:	£2,000 per month
October 19X5 onwards:	£5,000 per month

Payment will be received in the month following sale.

(e) Rates will amount to £600 per year, payable in half yearly instalments on 1 April and 1 October. However, an initial payment of £150 will be made on 1 July for the three months July-September 19X5.

(f) Other operating expenses of £200 will be paid each month, commencing July. Roker will make monthly drawings of £700, also commencing July.

Required:

(a) A cash budget for the twelve months to 30 June 19X6 showing the
     cash surplus or deficit at the end of each month.   (9 marks)

(b) An estimated profit statement for the year to 30 June 19X6.   (7 marks)

(c) A numerical reconciliation of the forecast change in the cash position, between 1 July 19X5
     and 30 June 19X6, and the estimated profits for that period.   (6 marks)

(d) An assessment of Roker's proposals.   (8 marks)

Notes:
(i)   Ignore interest on any forecast cash deficit
(ii) Ignore taxation.

21. SHEDFORD (30 marks)

Alan Cheep is the managing director of Shedford Sports Ltd which runs a chain of shops selling
sportswear and equipment. The company owns some of the shops and rents the others. Cheep has the
opportunity to purchase two of the shops (currently rented from Newbolt City Council) at a total
cost of £120,000 payable in two equal instalments at 31 January 19X7 and 31 January 19X8. Cheep
has decided to approach the company's bank to finance the acquisition. His accountant has
prepared the following forecasts and estimates:

(i) FORECAST BALANCE SHEET AT 31 DECEMBER 19X6

	£	£
Fixed assets at cost less depreciation		425,000
Current assets		
Stocks of sportswear and equipment	172,000	
Due from credit card companies	22,500	
Balance of cash at bank	1,500	
	196,000	
Current liabilities		
Trade creditors	42,000	
Net current assets		154,000
		579,000
Capital and reserves:		
Share capital		200,000
Reserves		379,000
		579,000

(ii) FORECAST REVENUES AND EXPENSES FOR 19X7

Quarter	1st	2nd	3rd	4th
	£	£	£	£
Sales	200,000	220,000	250,000	240,000
Purchases of stock	135,000	165,000	165,000	150,000
Wages	26,000	27,000	27,000	28,000
Other expenses	43,000	41,000	43,000	40,000

(iii) The balance outstanding from credit card companies at the end of each quarter is consistently in the region of 10% of quarterly sales. All other sales are for cash.

(iv) Suppliers allow one month's credit and you may assume that purchases accrue evenly within each quarter.

(v) Wages include monthly director's remuneration of £2,500 for Alan Cheep.

(vi) Other expenses include a charge for depreciation of £7,000 in the first quarter and £8,000 for each of the remaining quarters.

(vii) Wages and other expenses (excluding depreciation) are paid in the quarter in which they are incurred.

(viii) Interest is charged by the bank at 12% per annum and debited to the customer's bank statement on 30 June and 31 December. The interest charge for each half-year is to be based on the estimated cash deficiency (if any) mid-way through each half-year, ie on 31 March and 30 September respectively.

(ix) Closing stock at 31 December 19X7 is estimated at £180,000.

Required:

(a) A cash budget prepared on the quarterly basis for 19X7. Show the cash surplus or deficit at the end of each quarter. (7 marks)

(b) A forecast of the profit for 19X7. (7 marks)

(c) A forecast balance sheet at 31 December 19X7. (8 marks)

(d) An estimate of the time it will take to repay the bank overdraft, assuming the forecast quarterly trading results for 19X7 are repeated in future years. (8 marks)

Notes:

(i) Assume a corporation tax rate of 30% on reported profit.

(ii) No dividends are to be paid in the foreseeable future.

(iii) Assume each quarter consists of 90 days.

(iv) Ignore credit card charges.

22. SHELTON (30 marks)

The following information is provided for the Shelton Manufacturing Co Limited.

(a) BALANCE SHEET AS AT 30 JUNE

	19X5 £	19X4 £
Capital and liabilities		
Ordinary share capital (£1 ordinary shares)	100,000	100,000
Reserves	52,500	44,000
	152,500	144,000
14% bank loan	60,000	-
Creditors and accruals	24,000	15,000
Taxation payable 31 March	15,100	10,000
Proposed dividend	15,000	15,000
	£266,600	£184,000
Assets		
Plant and machinery at cost	200,000	100,000
Less accumulated depreciation	75,000	40,000
	125,000	60,000
Freehold property at cost	25,000	25,000
Investments at cost	-	11,000
Stock and work in progress	74,000	43,000
Debtors and prepayments	41,000	28,000
Cash and bank balances	1,600	17,000
	£266,600	£184,000

(b) PROFIT AND LOSS ACCOUNT EXTRACTS
YEAR TO 30 JUNE 19X5

	£
Profit from ordinary activities	42,000
Less interest payable	8,400
Profit before tax	33,600
Less taxation	13,600
Profit before extraordinary item	20,000
Profit arising from sale of investments (less tax at £1,500)	3,500
Profit available for appropriation	23,500
Less proposed dividend	15,000
Retained profit for the year	£8,500

(c) The company purchased additional plant, costing £100,000 in the autumn of 19X4. The plant became fully operational on 1 January 19X5 and this resulted in profits from ordinary activities, in the second half of the financial year to 30 June 19X5, which were twice as high as in the previous six months.

(d) The bank loan is secured on the freehold property. The advance was made on 1 July 19X4 and is repayable by four quarterly instalments commencing 30 September 19X5. Interest is payable at the end of each quarter.

(e) The directors estimate that the freehold property, which is essential to the business, would fetch £75,000 on the open market.

(f) The proposed dividend is usually paid within two weeks of the annual general meeting which is held at the beginning of March.

(g) The investments were sold in December 19X4.

The directors estimate that, during the year to 30 June 19X6:

(a) profits from ordinary activities will accrue at the same rate as in the second half of the year to 30 June 19X5, and this will give rise to a tax liability of £18,000 for the full year;

(b) the depreciation charge will be the same as in the previous year;

(c) charges in the system of stock control will enable the level of investment in stock and work in progress to be reduced to £65,000;

(d) the levels of debtors and creditors will remain approximately the same;

(e) interest payable on the bank loan will amount to £5,250 and the directors again propose to pay a dividend of £15,000.

Required:

(a) A discussion of past performance based on:

    (i)   a statement of source and application of funds for the year to 30 June 19X5;
    (ii) the pre-tax rate of return on shareholders' equity;
    (iii) the liquidity ratio at 30 June 19X5.   (15 marks)

(b) A discussion so far as the information permits, of future prospects based on:

    (i)   an estimated source and application of funds for the year to 30 June 19X6;
    (ii) the estimated pre-tax rate of return on shareholders' equity;
    (iii) the estimated liquidity ratio at 30 June 19X6.   (15 marks)

Notes:

(1) Ignore advance corporation tax.

(2) For the purpose of calculating the rate of return, shareholders' equity is defined as share capital plus reserves at the beginning of the year.

(3) You may assume that the bank has agreed to provide overdraft facilities to meet any estimated cash deficiency during the year to 30 June 19X6. Interest payable on any overdraft needed may be ignored.

23. CHADWICK (30 marks)

The balance sheet of Chadwick, a trader, as at 1 January 19X4, was as follows:

	£	£
Fixed assets		
Plant and machinery at cost		27,500
Less accumulated depreciation		9,600
		17,900
Current assets		
Stock	7,800	
Trade debtors	5,300	
	13,100	
Current liabilities		
Trade creditors	3,500	
Bank overdraft	800	
	4,300	
Working capital		8,800
		£26,700
Capital		£26,700

The following information is provided for 19X4:

	£
Receipts from customers	63,500
Payments to suppliers	37,600
Depreciation charged	6,100
Loan from friend	2,000
Interest paid on loan	150
Purchase of plant	8,000
General expenses paid in cash	7,300
Cash drawings	12,000

At 31 December 19X4, £3,950 was owing to trade creditors and £5,900 owed from trade debtors. Stock on hand amounted to £11,000.

Required:

(a) Prepare the following financial statements for 19X4:

    (i)   receipts and payments of cash (the statement should reveal the net increase or decrease in the cash balance);

    (ii) trading and profit and loss account;

    (iii) sources and applications of working capital (the statement should reveal the net increase or decrease in working capital). (16 marks)

(b) Explain the difference between the profit (loss) for the year and the net change in the cash balance. You should base your explanation on an appropriate numerical reconciliation. (6 marks)

(c) What are the respective merits and demerits of the profit and loss account and the cash account as bases for assessing the performance of a business? (8 marks)

24. MR NIMMO (20 marks)

Mr Nimmo has produced estimates which show that his business will suffer from a cash shortage of £100,000 throughout the last six months of 19X7. Overdraft facilities are fully utilised and the bank believes that Nimmo should explore other means of meeting his cash deficiency. An old business acquaintance of Nimmo has suggested the following options.

(i)   A short-term loan of £100,000 could be raised from a finance company. The advance would be made at an annual interest rate of 20% and the fee for arranging the loan would be £1,000. The interest and the arrangement fee would both be paid on the same date as the loan is repaid.

(ii)   The purchase of plant costing £150,000, planned for 1 July 19X7, could be delayed to 1 January 19X8. Production requirement would be met by working overtime instead. This would result in an extra operating cost of £3,000 per month, payable at the end of each month.

(iii)   90 days credit to be taken from a company which supplies £120,000 of raw materials each month. Nimmo's business currently receives from this supplier a cash discount of 2½% of the invoiced price, provided payment is made within 30 days.

Nimmo and the bank have agreed that any cash raised in excess of the £100,000 required would be used to reduce the bank overdraft on which interest is charged at 1% per month.

Required:

(a)   A numerical analysis which shows the cost of each of the options (i), (ii) and (iii) above. Advise Nimmo which is cheapest.   (14 marks)

(b)   Inform Nimmo of any other considerations which should be taken into account when choosing between the options.   (6 marks)

Note: assume that the schemes are put into effect so as to make additional cash available for the period 1 July to 31 December 19X7.

25. OVEREND (30 marks)

Overend Ltd is to be incorporated on 1 June 19X7 with an authorised share capital of £500,000 divided into ordinary shares of £1 each. On the same day 300,000 shares will be issued at par, for cash, to the company's directors, Paul Smith and Phil Davies, who are experienced businessmen. The company intends to start trading on 1 July 19X7, and the following plans and estimates have been made:

(i)   Fixed assets costing £400,000 will be purchased and paid for in June. These assets will have a nine year life and a residual value of £40,000 at the end of that period.

(ii)   Sales will amount to £1,200,000 during the year to 30 June 19X8 and will accrue at an even rate.

(iii)   The gross profit margin will be 20% of sales.

(iv)   Each month sufficient purchases will be made to meet the following month's sales requirements, ie purchases will be made in June to meet July's sales requirements.

(v) Two months' credit will be allowed to customers and received from suppliers.

(vi) Fixed running expenses (other than depreciation) of £130,000 will be incurred and paid for during the first year of operations. This sum includes a remuneration of £20,000 for the services of each director, which is a reasonable rate for the work involved.

Required:

(a) A summarised cash statement for the period to 30 June 19X8 (a monthly analysis is not required) showing the estimated deficiency at the year end. (6 marks)

(b) The estimated trading and profit and loss account of Overend Ltd for the year to 30 June 19X8 and the estimated balance sheet at that date. (11 marks)

(c) An assessment of the forecast profitability and solvency position of Overend Ltd using relevant ratios based on the financial statements prepared under (a) and (b) above. (5 marks)

(d) Advise Overend's bank whether to finance the estimated deficiency. Base your advice on your own assessment, made in answer to (c) above, and the additional information that the estimated trading results are likely to be repeated in the following two years. (3 marks)

(e) Paul Smith has estimated that advertising expenditure of £8,000 would enable a substantial increase in sales to be made during the first year of operations. Assuming the directors decide to undertake and pay for the advertising campaign during June 19X7, calculate the level of sales which would result in a zero cash balance at 30 June 19X8 (ie there would be no cash surplus or deficiency). (5 marks)

Note: ignore taxation and any interest on the bank overdraft.

26. HAMMOND (30 marks)

Hammond Ltd was incorporated and started business, in rented accommodation, on 1 January 19X2. It is a small family company run by three brothers who, between them, own all the shares. The company manufactures a limited range of products using six identical machines. The summarised profit and loss account and summarised balance sheet of Hammond for 19X6 are as follows:

PROFIT AND LOSS ACCOUNT, 19X6

	£'000	£'000
Sales		1,500
Less: Manufacturing costs other than depreciation	1,050	
Depreciation	120	
Running expenses	180	
Directors' remuneration	75	
		1,425
Net profit		75

BALANCE SHEET AT 31 DECEMBER 19X6

	£'000
Machines at cost (£120,000 each)	720
Accumulated depreciation	380
	340
Working capital	240
	580
Financed by:	
Share capital	250
Retained profit	330
	580

Each machine has the capacity to manufacture goods with a sales value of £250,000 per annum, and all six machines were in full use during the whole of 19X6. The machines were purchased on the following dates:

    2 machines on 1 January 19X2
    2 machines on 1 January 19X4
    1 machine on 1 January 19X5
    1 machine on 1 January 19X6

Each machine has a useful working life of six years and a zero scrap value at the end of that period. They are depreciated on the straight line (equal annual instalment) basis. The demand for the company's products has increased steadily since incorporation and this trend is expected to continue. The following forecasts are prepared for the next four years:

(i)   Sales to increase by £300,000 per annum.

(ii)   Manufacturing costs other than depreciation to remain the same percentage of sales as in 19X6.

(iii) Running expenses to increase at the rate of £10,000 per annum.

(iv) Total directors' remuneration to be increased by £6,000 per annum.

(v)   Working capital requirements to increase by £48,000 each year. There is no cash surplus to current requirements in the figure for working capital shown in the balance sheet.

(vi) Machines to be acquired on 1 January each year, at a cost of £120,000 each, to replace any items worn out and to meet the expected increase in demand for the current year. The new machines will have the same capacity and life as the old machines.

Required:

(a)   A calculation of the number of machines to be purchased on 1 January in each of the years 19X7 to 19Y0 inclusive.   (6 marks)

(b)   Summarised profit and loss accounts for each of the years 19X7 to 19Y0 inclusive.   (9 marks)

(c)   Summarised funds flow statement for each of the years 19X7 to 19Y0 inclusive. (7 marks)

(d)   A discussion of the extent to which the directors are able to finance developments out of funds generated from operations, and proposals for dealing with any problems which emerge.

(8 marks)

Notes: (i)   Ignore taxation and dividends.
(ii)   Ignore interest for the purpose of requirements (b) and (c).
(iii)   Assume that you are making the required calculations in answer to this question on 1 January 19X7.

27. COMPTON (20 marks)

The following estimated profit and loss account and balance sheet for 19X7 has been prepared for Compton Ltd, a trading company.

FORECAST PROFIT AND LOSS ACCOUNT FOR 19X7

	£'000	£'000
Sales		900
Less: purchases	720	
stock decrease during 19X7	30	
Cost of goods sold		750
Gross profit		150
Less: depreciation	40	
other running expenses	50	
		90
Net profit		60

FORECAST BALANCE SHEET AT 31 DECEMBER 19X7

	£'000	£'000
Fixed assets		
Freehold property at cost less depreciation		200
Plant and machinery at cost less depreciation		125
		325
Current assets		
Stocks	110	
Trade debtors	150	
	260	
Current liabilities		
Trade creditors	60	
Bank overdraft	40	
	100	
Net current assets		160
		485
Financed by:		
Share capital (£1 ordinary shares)		300
Reserves		185
		485

It is to be assumed that 19X7 consists of twelve months, each of thirty days, and transactions take place at an even rate throughout the year.

The directors intend to undertake an expansion of business activity at the beginning of 19X8, and plan to approach the bank for finance at that time. The directors are worried that the bank manager is unlikely to be impressed by the figures above and are considering ways of improving the financial appearance of the company. The following ideas are put forward at a board meeting:

(i)   Restate the freehold property at its recent professional valuation of £300,000.

(ii)   Extend the period of credit taken from suppliers to 45 days for purchases made on and after 1 October 19X7. This charge will not affect the company's creditworthiness.

(iii)   Offer customers a cash discount of 2½% for payment within 30 days. This offer to take effect for sales made on and after 1 October 19X7. All the company's customers are expected to take advantage of this offer with the level of sales being unaffected.

(iv)   Arrange for a loan of £50,000 to be made to the company on 31 December 19X7. The loan will carry interest at 15% per annum and be repayable on 30 June 19X8.

(v)   Make a bonus (capitalisation) issue of two additional £1 shares, at par value, for every three shares held at present. The issue to be made during December 19X7.

(vi)   The average period for which stocks are held to be amended to 72 days. Additional purchases to be made during October to put this policy into effect.

Required:

Taking each course of action separately, set out a statement showing the following:

Course of action	Net profit for 19X7 £	Bank balance (or overdraft) at 31 Dec 19X7 £	Working capital at 31 Dec 19X7 £	Working capital (current) ratio at 31 Dec 19X7
(i)				
(ii)				
(iii)				
(iv)				
(v)				
(vi)				

For any items unaffected by a course of action, show the original figure derived from the accounts.

Notes: (i)   Ignore taxation.
        (ii)   Assume no course of action will alter the amount of bank interest payable.

28. THREE COMPANIES (20 marks)

The following information is provided in respect of three companies, of which one is a steel manufacturer, another is a grocery store chain and the third is a finance company. Extracts from the accounts of each of these companies are reproduced below.

PROFIT AND LOSS ACCOUNT EXTRACTS

	Company A £'000	Company B £'000	Company C £'000
Turnover/revenue	3,029	1,556	206
Net profit	45	67	43

SUMMARISED BALANCE SHEETS

	Company A £'000	Company B £'000	Company C £'000
Fixed assets at book value	257	1,094	6
Stock	236	241	-
Debtors	9	201	1,347
Other assets	66	286	413
	568	1,822	1,766
Shareholders' equity	320	1,200	410
Long-term liabilities	64	321	578
Current liabilities	184	301	778
	568	1,822	1,766

Required:

(a) Calculate the following accounting ratios for each of the three companies:
   (i) net profit percentage;
   (ii) total asset turnover;
   (iii) rate of return on gross assets;
   (iv) liquidity ratio (assume that the 'other assets' are non-current for the purpose of this calculation).

(12 marks)

(b) Indicate which company you believe is the steel manufacturer, which is the grocery store chain and which is the finance company.

Briefly explain your choice using clues obtained from calculating the accounting ratios and from examining the accounting information provided.

(8 marks)

29. GREYWELL AND KENDALL (20 marks)

Greywell plc and Kendall plc trade in the same industry but in different geographical locations. The following data are taken from the 19X2 annual accounts.

	Greywell	Kendall
	£'000	£'000
Turnover	40,000	60,000
Total operating expenses	36,000	55,000
Average total assets during 19X2	30,000	25,000

Required:

(a) Calculate the rate of return on total assets (profits as a percentage of total assets) for each company.   (4 marks)

(b) Analyse the rates of return in part (a) into the net profit percentage and the ratio of turnover to total assets.   (6 marks)

(c) Comment on the relative performance of the two companies insofar as the information permits. Indicate what additional information you would require to decide which company is the better proposition from the viewpoint of:

(i)   potential shareholders; and
(ii) potential loan creditors.   (10 marks)

Note: Ignore taxation.

30. COTFORD (30 marks)

You are considering the possibility of acquiring shares in Cotford plc, which brews beer, manufactures a range of spirits and soft drinks and is the owner of public houses and hotels. The information given below has been extracted from the company's published accounts.

PROFIT AND LOSS ACCOUNT EXTRACTS, YEAR TO 30 JUNE

	19X8	19X7
	£'000	£'000
Turnover	21,200	17,200
Operating profit	2,750	2,085
Interest payable	(800)	(550)
Profit before tax	1,950	1,535
Taxation	(590)	(395)
Profit after tax	1,360	1,140
Dividends paid and proposed	(500)	(315)
Retained profit	860	825

SUMMARISED BALANCE SHEET AT 30 JUNE

	19X8 £'000	19X7 £'000
Tangible assets at cost or valuation	28,900	16,300
Investments	880	700
	29,780	17,000
Current assets	3,850	3,150
Current liabilities	4,500	4,000
Net current liabilities	(650)	(850)
Total assets less current liabilities	29,130	16,150
Less: borrowing repayable after more than one year	7,520	5,100
	21,610	11,050
Financed by:		
Share capital: ordinary shares of £1 each fully paid	2,400	1,700
Revaluation reserve	9,000	-
Profit and loss account	10,210	9,350
	21,610	11,050

The company revalued its non-industrial freehold and leasehold properties on 30 June 19X8. No depreciation is provided on these assets, as it is the company's policy to maintain them, out of expenditure charged to revenue, to a standard which ensures that their estimated aggregate residual values exceed net book amounts.

The present market value of each Cotford share is £6.20. The typical price/earnings ratio of companies in Cotford's line of business is 10.

Required:

(a) Calculate the ratios listed below for 19X7 and 19X8. Base your calculations on the information provided in the accounts above. You should present the ratios in the following form:

	19X8	19X7
Working capital ratio	....	....
Interest cover	....	....
Debt/equity ratio	....	....
Total asset turnover	....	....
Operating profit percentage	....	....
Return on total assets	....	....
Return on equity	....	....

(14 marks)

(b) A report on the financial performance and position of Cotford in each of the following broad areas:

(i)   solvency and gearing;
(ii) asset utilisation; and
(iii) profitability.

You should base your analysis on the information provided, the ratios calculated under (a), and any other relevant calculations.   (16 marks)

31. SOMERTON (30 marks)

The directors of Somerton plc require £500,000 to invest in a new project. The directors intend to finance the project either by making a rights issue to existing shareholders or by raising a bank loan. Over the last twelve months shares have been purchased and sold at prices which have increased from £1.50 to £1.60 per share ex dividend. The directors therefore believe that a rights issue at £1.25 per share would prove attractive to existing investors. The directors have estimated that a 12% rate of interest would be charged on the bank loan which would be repayable by five equal annual instalments commencing 31 December 19X6. Extracts from the accounts for the last two years are reproduced below.

PROFIT AND LOSS ACCOUNT EXTRACTS
YEAR TO 31 DECEMBER

	19X3 £'000	19X4 1,000
Turnover	6,175	6,329
Operating profit	350	320
Less interest payable	30	30
Profit before tax	320	290
Less taxation	96	87
Profit after tax	224	203

SUMMARISED BALANCE SHEETS AT 31 DECEMBER

	19X3 £'000	19X4 £'000
Assets		
Fixed assets at cost less depreciation	901	1,064
Stocks	447	426
Debtors	308	321
Balance at bank	52	11
	1,708	1,822
Capital and liabilities		
Ordinary share capital, £1 shares	500	500
Reserves	557	678
Loans: 10% debentures repayable 19Y4	300	300
Trade creditors	205	207
Taxation payable	96	87
Dividends	50	50
	1,708	1,822

Required:

(a) For each year calculate the following:
    (i)   working capital ratio;
    (ii)   interest cover;
    (iii) price/earnings ratio;
    (iv) rate of return on gross assets;
    (v)   post-tax rate of return on shareholders' equity;
    (vii) debt/equity ratio.   (12 marks)

(b) Identify two ratios which you consider to be of particular interest to shareholders and two ratios of particular interest to the bank. Give reasons for your choice and assess the significance of the changes over the two-year period.   (8 marks)

(c) Advise the company's management which method of financing to adopt, basing your advice on calculations of:

    (i)   the immediate effect of the two schemes upon the company's gearing (debt/equity) ratio, assuming either scheme can be put into effect on 1 January 19X5;

    (ii)   forecasts of the interest cover and post-tax rate of return on shareholders' equity for 19X5, under each method of finance. Assume profit earned on existing assets during 19X4 will be repeated and that the new project will produce a profit of £200,000 before deducting interest and corporation tax. If the rights issue is made, the dividend for 19X5 will be increased to £100,000.   (10 marks)

Notes:

(1) Assume that there is no difference between accounting profit and taxable profit.

(2) The rate of corporation tax is 30%. Ignore advance corporation tax.

(3) Assume that you are making the calculations on 1 January 19X5 and work to one decimal place.

32. EASTHOPE AND QUILTER (20 marks)

The following are the summarised accounts of two trading companies, each of which has recently approached your bank requesting a loan of £150,000 to acquire the shares of a director who is about to retire.

REVENUE ACCOUNTS FOR 19X5

	Easthope Ltd £'000	*Easthope Ltd* £'000	*Quilter Ltd* £'000	*Quilter Ltd* £'000
Turnover		2,050		2,620
Less cost of sales		1,435		1,890
Gross profit		615		730
Less depreciation	50		120	
other indirect expenses	445		480	
		495		600
		120		130

BALANCE SHEET AT 31 DECEMBER 19X5

	£'000	£'000
Ordinary share capital	500	600
Retained profit	100	300
	600	900
Current liabilities	260	300
	860	1,200
Premises	50	430
Other fixed assets	355	245
Current assets	455	525
	800	1,200

You discover that neither company needs to replace fixed assets in the near future. The 19X5 results are expected to be repeated for the next few years and the directors plan to pay out the entire profits in the form of dividends.

Required:

(a) The following calculations, ratios and percentages presented in a tabular format for each company:

	Easthope	Quilter

Funds generated from operations,
Proprietorship ratio
Working capital ratio
Net profit as a percentage of sales
Return on year-end balance of shareholders' equity

(10 marks)

(b) Based on your findings under (a), state the areas in which Easthope appears to be stronger and the areas in which Quilter appears to be stronger. (4 marks)

(c) To which company would you be more willing to grant loan facilities? Give your reasons. (6 marks)

33. PUDSEY (20 marks)

The following is a summary of the accounts of Pudsey Limited, a trading company, for 19X3.

SUMMARISED PROFIT AND LOSS ACCOUNT FOR 19X3

	£'000	£'000
Sale		1,600
Less cost of goods sold		960
Gross profit		640
Less: running costs - variable	160	
fixed	300	
		460
		180

SUMMARISED BALANCE SHEET AT 31 DECEMBER 19X3

	£'000	£'000
Fixed assets at cost		1,000
Less: accumulated depreciation		200
		800
Current assets		
Stock	160	
Trade debtors	200	
Bank balance	10	
	370	
Current liabilities		
Trade creditors	80	
Working capital		290
		1,090
Financed by:		
Share capital		700
Retained profit		390
		1,090

The directors plan to expand the level of business activity in 19X4. There is a strong demand for the company's product, and there exists sufficient capacity to increase sales substantially. Any increase in sales will result in a proportionate increase in cost of goods sold, stock, trade debtors and trade creditors. The fixed running costs include depreciation of fixed assets, £50,000, computed on the straight line basis.

Required:

(a) A calculation of the level of sales required to increase net profit to £300,000.
(6 marks)

(b) The forecast balance sheet at 31 December 19X4 assuming that the level of sales calculated under (a) is achieved. The bank balance may be inserted as the balancing item in the balance sheet you prepare. (8 marks)

(c) An explanation for the difference between the net profit of £300,000 and the net change in the bank balance during 19X4. You should support your explanation with an appropriate numerical statement. (6 marks)

Note: Ignore dividends and taxation.

34. NEWHAVEN (30 marks)

Newhaven Photographics Ltd will have free space in one of its main retail outlets when a tenancy ends on 30 June 19X8. The company has had enquiries about the possible sale of the surplus premises, and has discovered that they would fetch £120,000 if sold at any time during the next five years.

The company's Projects Manager believes that they should instead use the space to market a Japanese personal computer (PC). The following financial forecasts have been prepared:

(a) The premises are to be refurbished at a cost of £30,000 to be paid for in June 19X8. The cost is to be written off over five years on the straight line basis.

(b) A stock of 80 PCs is to be purchased and paid for in June 19X8. Purchases, for cash, will subsequently be made at the end of each month, commencing July 19X8, to replace items sold.

(c) Sales, also on the cash basis, are expected to be at the rate of 60 PCs per month, commencing July 19X8.

(d) The sales price of each PC will be £600 and the purchase price £500.

(e) Annual running costs, other than depreciation, are estimated at £34,000.

(f) The company aims to achieve, annually, a target return of 20% on the initial investment in any project undertaken.

Required:

(a) Calculations of:

   (i)   The amount of the initial investment at 30 June 19X8.

   (ii)   The breakeven level of sales per annum, in units and value.

   (iii)   The forecast profit per annum.

   (iv)   The margin of safety.

   (v)   The level of sales required to achieve the target return of 20% on the initial investment. (22 marks)

(b) A discussion of the Projects Manager's proposal based on your calculations under (a) and the information provided. (8 marks)

Note: ignore the time value of money.

35. ALUMINEX (30 marks)

Ken Dowden and his two brothers are the three directors of a small company, Aluminex Limited, which manufactures aluminium widgets. The company has banked with you for a number of years and is financially sound. The summarised final accounts for 19X2 are set out below:

SUMMARISED PROFIT AND LOSS ACCOUNT FOR 19X2

	£	£
Turnover (100,000 units at £5 each)		500,000
Less: variable costs	300,000	
depreciation	20,000	
other fixed costs	120,000	
		440,000
Net profit		£60,000

SUMMARISED BALANCE SHEET AT 31 DECEMBER 19X2

	£
Fixed assets at cost	200,000
Less: accumulated depreciation	80,000
	120,000
Working capital	200,000
Bank deposit account	25,000
	£345,000
Financed by:	
Share capital	200,000
Retained profits	145,000
	£345,000

It is expected that during 19X3 production costs for the existing level of activity will remain unchanged; the selling price is also expected to remain the same. In 19X2 the company worked a day shift only, and existing plant was used to its full capacity. There is a heavy demand for the company's product and the three directors are planning to increase the level of activity. Ken Dowden's brothers believe that it will be possible to sell another 50,000 widgets, without reducing the sales price, but Ken believes that an increase of 30,000 is a more realistic estimate. Two alternative proposals for increasing the level of output are under consideration:

1   Work an evening shift. This would enable the company to produce additional output of up to 50,000 units. The variable cost per unit would be 50% higher than the rate for the day shift, the depreciation charge would remain unchanged and other fixed costs would increase by £2,000.

2   Purchase additional plant costing £120,000 with a capacity of 50,000 units. The plant would be depreciated on the straight line basis over ten years, assuming a nil residual value. The variable cost per unit and annual depreciation charge on the existing plant would remain unchanged but other fixed costs would increase by £40,000.

Under either alternative, working capital requirements would increase proportionately with the level of activity. The balance on the bank deposit account, in the balance sheet set out above, is surplus to operating requirements and could be used to help to finance the planned expansion of activity. Your bank has been approached to finance any shortfall.

Required:

(a) A summarised profit and loss account for 19X3 and a summarised balance sheet at 31 December 19X3, under alternative 1, assuming sales of widgets increase to 150,000 units.

(9 marks)

(b) A summarised profit and loss account for 19X3 and a summarised balance sheet at 31 December 19X3, under alternative 2, assuming sales of widgets increase to 150,000 units.

(9 marks)

(c) A full discussion of the two alternatives, including an assessment of the effect of the company failing to achieve additional sales of 50,000 units. You should support your discussion with calculations of the break even point on the additional sales (ie the amount of additional sales required to ensure that profits earned in 19X3 are equal to those earned in 19X2).

(12 marks)

Notes:
1   Assume that the calculations are being made on 1 January 19X3.
2   The balance on the bank account or the bank overdraft may be treated as the balancing item in the balance sheets you prepare.
3   Ignore interest payable, if any.

36. MARGINAL (30 marks)

Marginal Limited manufactures one standard product, the standard marginal cost of which is as follows:

	£
Direct materials	10.0
Direct wages	7.5
Variable production overhead	1.25
	£18.75

The budget for the year includes the following:

Output, in units	80,000
	£
Fixed overhead: production	1,000,000
administration	600,000
marketing	500,000
Contribution	2,500,000

Management, in considering this budget for the coming year, is dissatisfied with the results likely to arise. A board meeting held recently discussed possible strategies to improve the situation and the following ideas were proposed:

(a) the production director suggested that the selling price of the product should be reduced by 10%. This he feels could increase the output and sales by 25%. It is estimated that fixed production overhead would increase by £50,000 and fixed marketing overhead by £25,000;

(b) the finance director suggested that the selling price should be increased by 10%. It is estimated that if the current advertising expenditure of £100,000 were to be increased by £400,000, sales could be increased to 90,000 units. Fixed production overhead would increase by £25,000 and marketing overhead by £20,000;

(c) the managing director seeks a profit of £600,000. He asks what selling price is required to achieve this if it is estimated that:

(i) an increase in advertising expenditure of £360,000 would result in a 10% increase in sales; and

(ii) fixed production overhead would increase by £25,000 and marketing overhead by £17,000;

(d) the marketing director suggested that with an appropriate increase in advertising expenditure sales could be increased by 20% and a profit on turnover of 15% obtained. It is estimated that in this circumstance fixed production overhead would increase by £40,000 and marketing overhead by £25,000. What additional expenditure on advertising would be made to achieve these results?

You are required to compile a forecast profit statement for the year for each of the proposals given and comment briefly on each.

37. PRESBURY (20 marks)

The directors of Presbury Ltd have under consideration two alternative schemes for manufacturing a new product for which they believe there exists a strong demand. The details relating to the two schemes are as follows:

SCHEME A

The company will acquire plant costing £280,000. Fixed expenses (other than depreciation) would amount to £130,000 per annum and variable expenses per unit would be £150.

SCHEME B

The company will acquire plant costing £400,000. Fixed expenses (other than depreciation) would amount to £300,000 per annum and variable expenses per unit would be £120.

In both cases the plant is expected to last four years and then be worthless. The straight line method of depreciation is considered appropriate. The finished product will be marketed for £200 per unit irrespective of the level of sales. The forecast level of demand is 7,000 units per annum. The working capital requirement amounts to £60,000 under each scheme.

Required:

(a) For each scheme, A and B, calculate:

(i) the number of units which must be produced and sold each year to break even (ie where the total revenues exactly cover total costs);

(ii) the forecast profit per annum;

(iii) the margin of safety. (11 marks)

(b) Calculate the annual level of sales at which the same profit arises under each scheme.

(3 marks)

(c) A discussion of these two alternative schemes of production indicating the main factors to be taken into account when choosing between scheme A and scheme B. (6 marks)

Note: ignore the time value of money.

38. ROPER (30 marks)

Roper Limited intends to form a wholly-owned subsidiary. Bowman Ltd, to sell a variety of different types of industrial cleaning equipment manufactured by a range of UK suppliers. The directors need to choose between two different plans for organising the activities of Bowman.

Plan Y

(i) Bowman is to operate from premises specially acquired at a cost of £200,000. the company is to stock industrial cleaning equipment and employ a sales force to visit potential customers.

(ii) Items will be sold at a mark-up of 100% on cost, eg industrial cleaning equipment costing £50 will sell for £100.

(iii) An initial investment of £80,000 in working capital is required.

(iv) It is estimated that sales in excess of £240,000 will require an additional investment in working capital of £0.25 for each £1 of sales.

(v) Fixed cost per annum (including full allowance for interest will amount to £290,000; variable costs, other than the cost of the industrial cleaning equipment, will amount to £20 for every £100 of sales.

(vi) The company will be provided with an initial issued share capital of £100,000. A long-term loan of £450,000 will be raised at 15% per annum. The bank has aged to finance any shortfall by an overdraft.

Plan Z

(i) Bowman is to operate from a small office rented from Roper Ltd and sell industrial cleaning equipment on an agency basis. These goods are to be advertised in the press and despatched to customers, on Bowman's instructions, direct from the manufacturers.

(ii) Items will be at a mark-up of 25% on cost, eg industrial cleaning equipment costing £80 will sell for £100.

(iii) An investment in working capital of £0.19 for each £1 of sales will be required.

(iv) Fixed costs per annum (including full allowance for interest) will amount to £50,000; variable costs, other than the cost of the industrial cleaning equipment, will amount to £5 for every £100 of sales.

(v) The company will be provided with an initial issued share capital of £100,000. The bank has agreed to finance any shortfall by an overdraft.

The maximum potential annual sales under each plan is estimated at £2,000,000.

Required:

(a) Calculations of:

  (i) The value of sales, under each plan, at which a target profit of £100,000 is achieved.

  (ii) The profit at maximum sales under each plan.

  (iii) The value of sales (the same for each plan) at which profits earned under each plan are equal. (14 marks)

(b) Balance sheets at the end of the first year of operations, consistent with the calculations under (a) (i). If necessary, a bank overdraft or figure for cash surplus to working capital requirements should be inserted as the balancing item. (6 marks)

(c) A full discussion of the relative merits of the two plans, based on the results of (a) and (b) above and any other calculations you consider relevant. Advise Roper's management which plan (Y or Z) it should adopt. (10 marks)

39. BARENTS (20 marks)

Barents Limited began trading on 1 January 19X0. It acquired stock-in-trade costing £100,000 in 19X0, £105,000 in 19X1 and £135,000 in 19X2. Balance sheet figures for stock at 31 December, under different valuation methods, are given below.

Stock valuation for balance sheet under various cost flow assumptions

31 December	LIFO	FIFO	Lower of FIFO cost and net realisable value
19X0	£40,200	£40,000	£37,000
19X1	£36,400	£36,000	£34,000
19X2	£41,800	£44,000	£44,000

Required:

Answers to the following questions, clearly indicating how each answer is deduced:

(a) Assuming that in any one year, prices moved only up or down, but not both, in the same year:
   (i) did prices go up or down in 19X0?
   (ii) did prices go up or down in 19X2?
(b) Which inventory method, LIFO or FIFO, would show the highest profit for 19X0?
(c) Which would show the highest profit for 19X2?
(d) Which would show the lowest profit for all three years combined?
(e) For 19X2 how much higher or lower would profit be on the FIFO basis than it would be on the lower of FIFO cost or net realisable value basis?

40. PURCHAS (20 marks)

Purchas Limited is a construction company which has been in business for a number of years. The company makes up its annual accounts to 30 September and the following information is provided in respect of one of its long-term contracts:

(a) Contract price: £4,000,000

(b) Date commenced: 30 June 19X1

(c) Expected completion date: 31 March 19X4

(d) Costing details as at 30 September:

	19X1 £'000	19X2 £'000	19X3 £'000
Costs to date	250	2,000	3,100
Estimated costs to completion	3,300	1,560	520
Value of work certified	400	2,500	3,400
Progress payments received and receivable	–	2,000	3,000

An explosion occurred on site on 30 September 19X3 and this is expected to cause the company to incur additional costs of £490,000 not included in the costings prepared under (d) above. The company is insured against damage occurring on site, but the insurance company believes that essential safety precautions were not taken and has not yet admitted the claim.

Required:

Calculations, in accordance with the provisions of SSAP9 'Stocks and work in progress', of:

(a) the attributable profit or foreseeable loss, if any, on the contract for each of the years to 30 September 19X1, 19X2 and 19X3;   (11 marks)

(b) the balance sheet value of the contract as at 30 September 19X1, 19X2 and 19X3.
                                                                (9 marks)

Calculations should be made for 19X3 on the alternative assumptions that the insurance company (i) accepts and (ii) rejects the claim for damages. For the purposes of part (b) you may ignore the new provisions of SSAP 9 (revised).

41. KESTER & CO (30 marks)

Kester, Wang, Pollins & Fraser carry on business in partnership as Kester & Co. They are all in their late fifties or early sixties and decide to sell the firm and retire. They believe that there are several firms who would be willing to take over their business assets and assume responsibility for paying their trade creditors but, before entering into negotiations, they wish to have some idea of the value of the firm. They approach you for advice.

The balance sheet of the firm, prepared on the historical cost basis as at 30 June 19X4, is as follows:

BALANCE SHEET 30 JUNE 19X4

	£'000	£'000
Fixed assets at cost less depreciation		350
Current assets:		
Stocks at the lower of cost and net realisable value	210	
Debtors net of provision for bad debts	145	
	355	
Current liabilities:		
Bank overdraft	75	
Trade creditors	105	
	180	
Net current assets		175
		525

	Capital Account £'000	Current Account £'000	
Kester	150	10	160
Wang	100	15	115
Pollins	100	50	150
Fraser	100	–	100
	450	75	525

The following details have been extracted from the profit and loss accounts for the last three years.

PROFIT AND LOSS ACCOUNT EXTRACTS YEAR TO 30 JUNE

	19X2 £'000	19X3 £'000	19X4 £'000
Interest charged on bank overdraft	4	8	10
Depreciation charged	50	50	50
Net profit	125	150	145

In the course of discussions, the partners make the following comments:

Kester: 'The balance sheet has been prepared by a reputable firm of accountants and is based on objective facts. I think that we should value the business at what it shows.'

Wang: 'The fixed assets were purchased three years ago and the policy of writing them off by ten equal annual instalments is proving to be realistic. The balance sheet value is, however, out of date. It would cost £490,000 to replace the fixed assets with items of a similar age and condition. In addition, raw material costs have recently risen quite rapidly and it would cost £250,000 to replace the stocks held at 30 June. These facts should be taken into account in arriving at the valuation.'

Pollins: 'The business exists to earn profits and should be valued as a whole. I am told that companies in our line of business have a price/earnings ratio of 8:1. I think that we should apply this ratio to our average net profit as shown in the accounts for the last three years, after taking account of our drawings which averaged £100,000 per annum.'

Fraser: 'On the open market we could, in a quick sale, get £295,000 for our fixed assets and £220,000 for our stocks. This is what I think is important.'

Required:

(a) Valuations of the firm on each of the bases suggested by the four partners. For the purpose of your calculations, assume that the buyer is to accept responsibility for paying the trade creditors but will not take over the bank overdraft.   (12 marks)

(b) In the context of this question, comment briefly on the merits, if any, of each valuation.
                                                                                        (8 marks)

(c) Prepare an earnings yield valuation based on average 'maintainable profits' for the last three years and assess the merit of this basis. For the purpose of this valuation, you should take account of the fact that £60,000 per annum is adequate remuneration for the services provided by the four partners. In addition, enquiries reveal that the opening stock for the year to 30 June 19X2 was overvalued by £32,000.   (10 marks)

Notes:
1 Assume that you are making the valuations on 30 June 19X4
2 Ignore taxation.

42. CONNECTICUT (30 marks)

The directors of Connecticut plc, who own 50% of the company's ordinary shares, have approached the bank, requesting a renewal of the overdraft facility of £50,000 for a further twelve months. Connecticut's share quotation was suspended last month because of irregularities concerning the purchase and sale of the company's shares by one of its directors. The director has since resigned and it is expected that the Stock Exchange will resume dealing in the company's shares in the near future.

The following historical cost information has been extracted from previously published accounts:

BALANCE SHEET AT 31 DECEMBER 19X2

	£'000	£'000
Fixed assets		
Equipment at cost less depreciation		800
Current assets		
Stocks	810	
Debtors	580	
	1,390	
Current liabilities		
Trade creditors	316	
Proposed dividends	100	
Bank overdraft	24	
	440	
Net current assets		950
		1,750
Capital and reserves		
Ordinary shares (£1 each)		1,000
Reserves		550
		1,550
10% preference shares		200
		1,750

PROFIT AND LOSS ACCOUNTS

	19X0	19X1	19X2
Net profit for the year	126	210	240
Less: dividends - ordinary shares	80	80	80
- preference shares	20	20	20
	100	100	100
Retained profit for the year	26	110	140

The following additional information is provided:

1   Depreciation of £60,000 per year has been charged on the equipment during each of the last three years. The equipment is old and in need of replacement; annual depreciation based on current replacement cost would be in the region of £76,000.

2   On investigation, the stock in the balance sheet shown above was found to be overvalued by £14,000.

3   The profit for 19X0 was arrived at after deducting an exceptional loss of £56,000 arising from the liquidation of a major customer.

4   It is estimated that the equipment and stocks possess respective liquidation values of £240,000 and £600,000. The debtors would be collected in full and liquidation costs would amount to £52,000.

5   A recent article in the financial press estimated a dividend yield of 12% and an earnings yield of 20% for other companies in Connecticut's industry.

Required:

(a)   A table, completed in the following form, showing valuations for the entire ordinary share capital of Connecticut plc.

Valuation

1   Earnings yield basis (based on average earnings for the last three years, after making appropriate adjustments).

2   Liquidation (break-up basis)

3   Dividend yield basis

(18 marks)

(b)   Comments on the significance of the above-mentioned valuations, paying particular attention to the request for a renewal of the overdraft facility.

(12 marks)

Notes:
1   Assume that you are making the valuations at 31 December 19X2
2   Ignore taxation.

43. BOLMIN (20 marks)

The directors of Bolmin plc have decided to make an offer to purchase all the shares of Tooden Repairs Limited. They have decided to value the company at eight times its average adjusted pre-tax profits for 19X1 and 19X2. To make the adjustment they have asked that depreciation be calculated on a replacement cost basis and that a reduction of 50% be made in the figure shown for directors' remuneration.

The chief accountant of Bolmin plc has now to calculate the value placed on Tooden Repairs Limited by this method, but he has suggested that before making a decision the directors should consider other methods of valuation and their relative merits. In particular he has pointed out that similar companies have an average earnings yield of 8%.

He has access to Tooden's accounts for 19X1 and 19X2 which show the following figures.

PROFIT STATEMENTS

	19X1 £	19X1 £	19X2 £	19X2 £
Sales		250,000		280,000
Less:				
Materials used	156,000		176,000	
Depreciation of equipment	5,000		5,000	
Directors' remuneration	20,000		24,000	
Other expenses	54,000		64,000	
		235,000		269,000
Net profit before tax		15,000		11,000
Taxation		6,000		4,000
Net profit after tax		£9,000		£7,000

BALANCE SHEETS

	End of 19X1 £	End of 19X1 £	End of 19X2 £	End of 19X2 £
Fixed assets				
Freehold property		80,000		80,000
Equipment (net book value)		35,000		30,000
		115,000		110,000
Current assets				
Stock	32,000		36,000	
Debtors	60,000		68,000	
Bank	3,000		1,000	
	95,000		105,000	
Current liabilities				
Trade creditors	22,000		25,000	
Taxation	6,000		4,000	
	28,000		29,000	
		67,000		76,000
		£182,000		£186,000

Financed by:

	£	£
Issued share capital		
(£1 ordinary shares)	50,000	50,000
Reserves	132,000	136,000
	£182,000	£186,000

In addition to the accounts the chief accountant of Bolmin has obtained the following information:

1   Equipment has been depreciated at an annual rate of 10% on cost but no depreciation has been provided against the freehold property.

2   At the end of 19X2 the estimated realisable values of the freehold property and equipment were £169,000 and £24,000 respectively.

3   The original cost of equipment was £50,000 but its replacement value at the end of 19X2 was £80,000.

4   At the end of 19X2 it was estimated that the stock could be disposed of for £17,000 in a forced sale on closure.

Required:

In order to guide the directors of Bolmin plc:

(a) calculate the value per share and the total value of Tooden Repairs Limited using the directors' multiple of average profits method;   (5 marks)

(b) calculate:

  (i)   the unadjusted balance sheet value per share of Tooden Repairs at the end of 19X2;

  (ii)   the break-up value per share of Tooden Repairs at the end of 19X2; and

  (iii) the unadjusted yield value per share at the end of 19X2 based on the earnings of similar companies;   (7 marks)

(c) comment on the different methods of valuation used in sections (a) and (b) of these requirements.   (8 marks)

44. GURNEY (30 marks)

Gurney Ltd is an unlisted company; all the ordinary shares, but none of the preference shares, are held by the directors and their families. The directors have decided to retire and move to the south of France. They wish to discover the likely value of their shares before entering into discussions with potential purchasers. They have been told by friends that, for the purpose of sale as a going concern, the business should be valued on the 'earnings yield' basis. If they fail to agree a price with a buyer, the company will be liquidated.

The following facts and information are provided:

(i)   BALANCE SHEET OF GURNEY LTD AT 31 DECEMBER 19X6

	£'000	£'000
Plant and equipment at cost less depreciation		2,605
Current assets		
Stocks	1,372	
Debtors	896	
Bank	57	
	2,325	
Less: *current liabilities*		
Creditors	509	
Proposed dividends (including £40,000 for preference shares)	240	
	749	
Net current assets		1,576
		4,181
Financed by:		
Ordinary share capital		2,000
8% preference share capital issued 19X0		500
Reserves		1,681
		4,181

(ii)   Net reported profits:

	£'000
19X4	715
19X5	483
19X6	572

(iii) The company changed from the marginal cost to the total cost basis for valuing stock when preparing the accounts for 19X4, but failed to re-state opening stock on the new basis. The relevant values for the opening stock at 1 January 19X4 are:

	£'000
Marginal cost basis	826
Total cost basis	966

(iv)   The plant and equipment would fetch £1,800,000 in the second-hand market and the stocks would realise £1,406,000 in a forced sale.

(v)   A re-examination of the debtor balances at 31 December 19X6 shows £30,000 to be doubtful or bad.

(vi)   In December 19X4 the company sold a section of its activities which had contributed £85,000 towards the reported profit for that year.

(vii) The depreciation charges averaged £200,000 for the years 19X4-X6. The replacement cost of fixed assets in similar condition is significantly lower than book value and would require an annual depreciation charge of £165,000.

(viii) The cost of liquidating the company is estimated as £31,000.

(ix) The typical earnings yield of listed companies, engaged in a similar line of business to Gurney Ltd, is 12%.

Required:

(a) Valuations of the ordinary shareholders' interest in Gurney Ltd on:

    (i) The earnings yield basis. This should be based on 'maintainable' profits, defined as average reported profits for the last three years after making appropriate adjustments.
    (ii) The liquidation basis.   (16 marks)

(b) A full discussion of the merits and demerits of the two methods used above to value Gurney.   (14 marks)

Notes: (i) Assume you are making the valuations at 31 December 19X6.
       (ii) Ignore taxation.

45. RICHARDS (20 marks)

Richards plc suffered a series of trading losses in the first half of the 19X0s, which resulted in management changes and a substantial re-organisation of the company's activities between November 19X5 and February 19X6. This produced an encouraging improvement in the results reported for 19X6: profits for the year amounted to £2,000,000 and a dividend of 10 pence per share was paid on 31 December 19X6. The balance sheet at 31 December 19X6 contained the following information:

BALANCE SHEET AT 31 DECEMBER 19X6

	£'000
Freehold property at cost less depreciation	5,000
Plant and machinery at cost less depreciation	3,350
	8,350
Current assets	6,750
Current liabilities	2,900
Net current assets	3,850
	12,200
Financed by:	
Share capital (£1 ordinary shares)	8,000
Reserves	4,200
	12,200

During August 19X7, Hadlee plc made an unwelcome takeover bid for the company at a price of £2.90 per share. The directors have advised the shareholders not to sell and informed them that, during the first half of 19X7, sales were 15% higher than in the first half of 19X6. They have forecast profits of £2,720,000 for 19X7 and a leading firm of accountants has approved these figures.

A recent article in the financial press drew attention to the fact that the replacement value of Richards' freehold property is £10,000,000 and the replacement value of the plant and machinery is £6,000,000.

The shares of Richards have, in recent months, been purchased and sold at a price of £2.60 per share. Shares in quoted companies in the same industry as Richards have an average price/earnings ratio of 10 and a dividend yield of 5%.

Required:

(a) Valuations of one £1 ordinary share in Richards' plc. Set out these valuations in the following manner:

Valuation of one £1 ordinary share

(i)	Book value basis	___
(ii)	Replacement cost basis	___
(iii)	Dividend yield basis	___
(iv)	Price/earnings basis – 19X6 profits	___
(v)	Price/earnings basis – 19X7 forecast profits	___

(10 marks)

(b) Discuss the relevance of your valuations to the shareholders in the light of the take-over bid by Hadlee plc. Advise the shareholders whether or not to sell. (10 marks)

Note: ignore taxation.

46. HANSARD (20 marks)

The following information relates to an investment project under consideration by Hansard Limited.

(a) Initial investment – fixed assets: £100,000
    – working capital: £ 40,000

(b) Forecast annual profit for the five year life of the project, after charging depreciation of £18,000 per annum: £13,000.

(c) At the end of the project, the fixed assets are expected to be sold for £10,000 and the working capital disinvested.

The company's cost of capital is 14%.

Required:

Calculate the DCF yield (internal rate of return) of the project set out above to the nearest whole percent. Based on this calculation, advise management whether it should undertake this project.

Notes:

1   The initial investment will be made at the outset of the project, and the annual cash flows from operations may be assumed to arise at the year end.

2   Ignore taxation.

TABLE OF FACTORS FOR THE PRESENT VALUE OF £1

1	0.909	0.900	0.893	0.885	0.877	0.870	0.862	0.855	0.847	0.840	0.833
2	0.826	0.812	0.797	0.783	0.769	0.756	0.743	0.731	0.718	0.706	0.694
3	0.751	0.731	0.712	0.693	0.675	0.658	0.641	0.624	0.609	0.593	0.579
4	0.683	0.659	0.636	0.613	0.592	0.572	0.552	0.534	0.516	0.499	0.482
5	0.620	0.594	0.567	0.543	0.519	0.497	0.476	0.456	0.437	0.419	0.402

47. BURLEY (20 marks)

The directors of Burley Limited are considering two mutually exclusive investment projects in respect of which the following information is provided:

		Project A £	Project B £
Initial capital outlay		80,000	100,000
Net cash inflows, year	1	40,000	20,000
	2	60,000	30,000
	3	10,000	50,000
	4	5,000	50,000
	5	5,000	50,000

The initial capital outlay will occur immediately and you may assume that the net cash inflows will arise at the end of each year.

Burley's estimated cost of capital over the five year period is 12%.

Required:

(a) Numerical assessments of the two projects based on the following methods of investment project appraisal.
 (i) payback;
 (ii) net present value (NPV) (12 marks)

(b) Comment on the relative merits of the two methods of investment project appraisal in the light of your findings under (a). (8 marks)

Note: ignore taxation.

FACTORS FOR THE PRESENT VALUE OF £1 APPLYING A DISCOUNT RATE OF 12%

Year	Factor
1	0.893
2	0.797
3	0.712
4	0.636
5	0.567

48. CATALAN

The directors of Catalan plc are considering a plan for the manufacture and sale of widgets. This requires an immediate investment in plant of £200,000 and in working capital of £60,000.

The estimated annual net cash flows, from the purchase and sale of widgets at May 19X8 prices, are as follows:

Year	£
1	80,000
2	90,000
3	90,000
4	50,000
5	30,000

In addition the plant will be sold for £12,000 and working capital disinvested at the end of year 5. The following further assumptions should be made:

(a) Annual cash flows arise at the year end.

(b) The general rate of inflation is 8% per annum.

(c) The company's *money* cost of capital is 19%.

Required:

(a) Calculate the payback period of the project. (3 marks)

(b) Calculate the net present value of the project using the *real* cost of capital for discounting purposes. (12 marks)

(c) List the main advantages of each of the above methods of investment appraisal. (5 marks)

Note: ignore taxation.

Table of factors for the present value of £1

Years	1	2	3	4	5
7%	0.935	0.873	0.816	0.763	0.713
8%	0.926	0.857	0.794	0.735	0.680
9%	0.917	0.842	0.773	0.709	0.651
10%	0.909	0.826	0.751	0.683	0.620
11%	0.900	0.812	0.731	0.659	0.594
12%	0.893	0.797	0.712	0.636	0.567
13%	0.885	0.783	0.693	0.613	0.543
14%	0.877	0.769	0.675	0.592	0.519
15%	0.870	0.756	0.658	0.572	0.497
16%	0.862	0.743	0.641	0.552	0.476
17%	0.855	0.731	0.624	0.534	0.456
18%	0.847	0.718	0.609	0.516	0.437
19%	0.840	0.706	0.593	0.499	0.419
20%	0.833	0.694	0.579	0.482	0.402

49. VETCH (20 marks)

The directors of Vetch Limited are considering whether to undertake either of two mutually exclusive investment projects at a cost of £500,000. It is intended to finance the project as follows:

	£'000	Cost
Equity finance	300	20%
Bank loan	200	12%
	500	

The cash flows associated with the two projects have been estimated as follows:

		Project A £'000	Project B £'000
Cash flows:			
Initial investment		500	500
Cash inflows:	Year 1	200	400
	Year 2	300	200
	Year 3	200	200
	Year 4	400	200

Required:

(a) Calculate the weighted average cost of capital for either of these projects to the nearest whole per cent. (6 marks)

(b) Calculate the net present value of each project. (10 marks)

(c) Advise management which project it should undertake. (4 marks)

Notes:
(i) The initial investment will occur immediately and you may assume that cash inflows occur at the end of each year.
(ii) Ignore taxation.

TABLE OF FACTORS FOR THE PRESENT VALUE OF £1

Year	12%	13%	14%	15%	16%	17%	18%	19%	20%	21%	22%
1	0.893	0.885	0.877	0.870	0.862	0.855	0.847	0.840	0.833	0.826	0.820
2	0.797	0.783	0.769	0.756	0.743	0.731	0.718	0.706	0.694	0.683	0.671
3	0.712	0.693	0.675	0.658	0.641	0.624	0.609	0.593	0.579	0.564	0.551
4	0.636	0.613	0.592	0.572	0.552	0.534	0.516	0.499	0.482	0.467	0.451
5	0.567	0.543	0.519	0.497	0.476	0.456	0.437	0.419	0.402	0.386	0.370

QUESTIONS

50. BARRON (20 marks)

Barron Limited owns a small warehouse which has recently become vacant. The warehouse is reported in the company's balance sheet at a written down value of £160,000 (£200,000 cost, less £40,000 accumulated depreciation). A firm has offered to rent the premises from Barron for the next five years at a rental of £12,000 per annum payable in advance.

However, Barron Ltd is considering whether to purchase and re-sell widgets, using this warehouse. Barron has already spent £9,000 on a feasibility study and has discovered that this activity would produce a positive cash flow, before charging depreciation, of £25,000 per annum for the next five years. Demand for widgets would cease after five years. If this option is chosen, Barron needs to spend £30,000 immediately on new fittings.

The warehouse could be sold immediately for £275,000 or in five years' time for £500,000.

Barron's estimated cost of capital over the five year period is 14%.

FACTORS FOR THE PRESENT VALUE OF £1
APPLYING A DISCOUNT RATE OF 14%

Year	Factor
1	0.877
2	0.769
3	0.675
4	0.592
5	0.519

Required:

(a) A numerical assessment of the available options based on the information provided above.
(16 marks)

(b) Advise the directors of Barron which course they should follow, basing your advice on the calculations in (a) above and any other relevant considerations.   (4 marks)

Notes:
1.   You may assume that the annual cash flow from the sale of widgets arises at the year end.
2.   Ignore taxation.

51. DORMAN (20 marks)

The directors of Dorman Limited are considering a new investment project for which the following estimates are available:

Capital investment	£100,000
Life of project	5 years
Net annual cash inflow	£ 40,000

The capital investment would be made at the outset and the annual cash inflows may be assumed to arise at the year end.

The directors know that the company's cost of capital is 12%, and they are confident that the capital investment is estimated correctly. They are doubtful about the accuracy of the estimates made of the life of the project and the amount of the net annual cash inflow.

Required:

(a) Calculate the net present value (NPV) of the project based on the estimates given above and state whether it should be undertaken. (8 marks)

(b) Calculate the approximate minimum acceptable life of the project, assuming all the other estimates are correct. (6 marks)

(c) Calculate the minimum acceptable average net annual cash inflow, assuming all the other estimates are correct. (6 marks)

Note: ignore taxation

FACTORS FOR PRESENT VALUE OF £1 APPLYING A DISCOUNT RATE OF 12%

Year	Present value of £1	Present value of £1 per year
1	0.893	0.893
2	0.797	1.690
3	0.712	2.402
4	0.636	3.038
5	0.567	3.605

52. BARBICAN (20 marks)

The summarised trial balance of Barbican Ltd at 31 March 19X8 contained the following information:

TRIAL BALANCE AT 31 MARCH 19X8

	£'000	£'000
Retained profit at 1 April 19X7		260
Operating profit for the year before tax		450
Trade creditors and accruals		372
Share capital: shares of £1 each		1,000
Deferred tax account		54
Fixed assets at cost	1,250	
Accumulated depreciation at 31 March 19X8		820
Interim dividend paid	73	
Advance corporation tax (ACT)	85	
Overprovision for corporation tax in previous year		10
Stock, debtors and cash	1,558	
	2,966	2,966

The following information is provided in respect of the year to 31 March 19X8:

(a) Taxable profits amount to £400,000 and net originating timing differences, expected to reverse at a future date, amount to £50,000.

(b) The directors propose to pay a final dividend of 15p in the £.

(c) A corporation tax rate of 25% should be used and advance corporation tax may be taken as $\frac{25}{75}$ for the purpose of your calculations.

Required:

The profit and loss account of Barbican Ltd for the year to 31 March 19X8 and the balance sheet at that date, not necessarily in a form suitable for publication, but complying with the provisions of SSAP 8 and SSAP 15.

53. MAWDSLEY (20 marks)

Mawdsley Ltd was incorporated and commenced business on 1 April 19X5. The following information is taken from the accounts for the year ended 31 March 19X6 and from the forecasts for the year ending 31 March 19X7.

	19X6	19X7
Plant purchased on 1 April (£000)	160	–
Depreciation charge for the year (£000)	30	30
Proposed dividend for the year, net (£000)	21	15
Taxable profit before deducting capital allowances (£000)	140	110
Annual writing-down allowance on plant for tax purposes, based on tax written-down value	25%	25%
Rate of mainstream corporation tax	25%	25%
Rate of advance corporation tax	25/75	25/75

The proposed dividend for each year is paid during July following the accounting year end. It is the company's policy to make full provision for deferred taxation, ie all originating 'timing' differences are expected to reverse in due course.

Required:

For each of the years to 31 March 19X6 and 31 March 19X7 calculate:

(a) The taxable profit for the year, after deducting capital allowances.

(b) The mainstream corporation tax charge for the year debited to the profit and loss account.

(c) The transfer to/from the deferred tax account to be debited/credited to the profit and loss account.

(d) The advance corporation tax payable reported in the balance sheet.

(e) The balance on the deferred tax account.

(f) The mainstream corporation tax liability reported in the balance sheet for payment on the following 1 January.

You should present your answer in the form of a schedule as below:

Year to 31 March	19X8	19X7
	£	£
Taxable profit	–	–
Mainstream corporation tax charge	–	–
Transfer to (from) the deferred tax account	–	–
Advance corporation tax payable	–	–
Balance on the deferred tax account	–	–
Mainstream corporation tax liability	–	–

Note: show workings where appropriate.

54. **EASY** (20 marks)

Extracts from the draft accounts of Easy Limited show:

	£'000	£'000
Balances brought forward at 1.1.19X8		
19X7 proposed final dividend		15
ACT payable on proposed final dividend		5
Corporation tax payable (being the estimated tax charge for 19X7)		102
Deferred taxation:		
Provision for timing differences	22	
Less ACT on proposed final dividend	(5)	
Net balance		17

During 19X8 the following transactions occurred:

(a) the final dividend for 19X7 was duly paid. An interim dividend for 19X8 of £21,000 (net) was also paid;

(b) debenture interest of £7,500 (net) was received;

(c) the 19X7 tax charge was finally agreed at £98,000 and was paid in October.

The proposed final dividend for 19X8 is £10,500 and the estimated tax charge for 19X8 is £112,000. A transfer of £5,000 is to be made to the deferred taxation account in respect of timing differences arising during 19X8.

You are required to prepare extracts from Easy Limited's 19X8 profit and loss account and balance sheet, showing all figures affected by the above information.

Assume an ACT rate of 25/75 of the net dividend paid.

55. ANGLO (30 marks)

Anglo Limited is a well established private company which over a number of years built up a large balance of liquid resources surplus to operating requirements. The decision was taken, late in 19X2, to use these resources to diversify the company's activities and substantial shareholdings were subsequently acquired in Bangle Limited and Carmen plc. The latter acquisition caused Anglo to arrange for a bank overdraft secured on its freehold property.

The following information is provided in respect of the three companies:

(a)   SUMMARY OF BALANCES AT 31 DECEMBER 19X3

	Anglo £'000	Bangle £'000	Carmen £'000
Assets			
Goodwill at cost	–	–	104
Freehold property at cost less depreciation	200	180	700
Plant and equipment at cost less depreciation	756	107	1,113
Investments:			
Bangle Ltd (180,000 shares)	440	–	–
Carmen plc (500,000 shares)	760	–	–
Current assets	521	351	976
	2,677	638	2,893
Share capital, reserves and liabilities			
Issued share capital (£1 ordinary shares)	1,000	200	2,000
Retained profit at 1 January 19X3	950	210	128
Net profit for 19X3	247	90	236
Bank overdraft	374	–	–
Other current liabilities	106	138	529
	2,677	638	2,893

(b)   The shares in Carmen were purchased on 1 January 19X3 and in Bangle on 31 December 19X3.

(c)   Following the share acquisition, directors were appointed to the boards of both Bangle and Carmen to take an active part in their financial and operating decisions.

(d)   The freehold property of Bangle possessed a fair value of £300,000 on 31 December; there were no other significant differences between the fair values and book values of the assets of Bangle and Carmen at the acquisition dates.

(e)   Anglo's freehold property was recently valued at £230,000. This valuation is not to be written into the books.

Required:

(a) A consolidated balance sheet of the group at 31 December 19X3, not necessarily in a form for publication but complying so far as the information permits with the requirements of SSAPs 1 and 14. You may ignore the requirement of SSAP22 to eliminate or amortise goodwill arising on consolidation. (25 marks)

(b) A discussion of the uses and limitations of consolidated accounts from the viewpoint of Anglo's bank. (5 marks)

56. PARK AND GATE (20 marks)

The following balances relate to Park and Gate Limited at 31 December 19X4.

	Park Ltd £	Gate Ltd £
Issued share capital (£1 ordinary shares)	200,000	80,000
Retained profits at 31 December 19X3	45,100	37,500
Profit for 19X4	17,600	28,500
Unsecured loan repayable 19X9	-	30,000
Current liabilities	53,700	26,000
	£316,400	£202,000
Freehold property, net of depreciation	-	99,000
Other fixed assets, net of depreciation	182,300	35,000
48,000 shares in Gate Limited at cost	72,000	-
Current assets	62,100	68,000
	£316,400	£202,000

Park Limited acquired its shares in Gate Limited on 31 December 19X3.

The board of directors of Park Limited require £400,000 to finance a new project and have approached the bank to borrow this amount.

Required:

(a) The consolidated balance sheet of the group at 31 December 19X4 presented in good style so far as the information permits. (16 marks)

(b) Briefly advise the bank on security for the requested advance, based on the accounts of the companies. (4 marks)

57. MARTENS (30 marks)

The draft balance sheets at 30 June 19X3 of three companies, Martens plc, Tasman Limited and Wood Limited, who together carry on group activities, are set out below:

	Martens £'000	Tasman £'000	Wood £'000
Ordinary share capital	800	200	100
General reserve	438	64	64
9% debentures	-	-	40
Current account - Martens plc	-	-	42
- Tasman Limited	30	-	-
Creditors (including taxation)	88	15	15
Overdraft (Midshire Bank)	-	25	-
	1,356	304	261
Property	350	114	-
Plant and machinery	380	58	-
Investment in Tasman Limited	200	-	-
Investment in Wood Limited	50	-	-
Current account - Martens plc	-	36	-
- Wood Limited	42	-	-
Stocks and work in progress	152	32	50
Debtors and prepayments	153	64	51
Bank/cash	29	-	27
	1,356	304	261

Martens plc purchased 150,000 of the 200,000 ordinary £1 shares of Tasman Limited on 1 July 19X2 when the general reserve of Tasman Limited stood at £16,000.

Also on 1 July 19X2 the directors of Martens plc agreed with the board of Wood Limited (a materials supplier) that periodic loans would be made by Martens plc to help Wood Limited to maintain its activities and that Martens plc would be represented on the board of directors of Wood Limited to assist in the implementation of a mutually acceptable corporate strategy. On the same day Martens plc purchased 22,000 of the 100,000 £1 shares of Wood Limited when there was £10,000 in the general reserve of Wood Limited.

The following items have not yet been taken into account:

(i) A cheque for £6,000 drawn by Tasman Limited in favour of Martens plc has been lost in the post. It will be cancelled and redrawn in the new year.
(ii) Wood Limited has agreed to accept a charge of £4,000 from Martens plc to compensate for sub-standard materials supplied during the year.

Required:

(a) Prepare the consolidated balance sheet of the group at 30 June 19X3 in good style suitable for publication supported by your working sheets for checking if necessary.

(26 marks)

(b) Say, giving reasons, what changes, if any, would be necessary in your treatment of the group's interest in Wood Limited if Martens plc had purchased only 19,000 shares in Wood Limited.

(4 marks)

You may ignore the requirement of SSAP22 to eliminate or amortise goodwill arising on consolidation.

58. HAKLUYT (20 marks)

Hakluyt plc, a carpet manufacturer and wholesaler, purchased 300,000 of the 400,000 issued ordinary shares of a much smaller company Cook Limited on 1 January 19X1 when the retained earnings account of Cook Limited had a credit balance of £36,000.

The latest accounts of the two companies are:

SUMMARY PROFIT AND LOSS ACCOUNTS FOR THE YEAR TO 30 SEPTEMBER 19X2

	Hakluyt plc £'000	Cook Ltd £'000
Credit sales	7,220	880
Cost of sales and production services	2,380	420
Gross profit	4,840	460
Expenses, taxation and dividends	4,744	320
Profit retained	96	140
Brought forward from last year	800	96
Carried forward to next year	896	236

SUMMARISED BALANCE SHEET AT 30 SEPTEMBER 19X2

	Hakluyt plc £'000	Cook Ltd £'000
Fixed assets at cost less depreciation	2,833	364
Investment in Cook Limited	350	-
Current account with Hakluyt plc	-	50
Stock	396	103
Debtors	1,500	185
Bank	60	12
	5,139	714
Share capital	4,000	400
Retained earnings	896	236
Current account with Cook Limited	45	-
Creditors for goods and services	198	78
	5,139	714

On 28 September 19X2 Hakluyt plc sent a cheque for £5,000 to Cook Limited. This was not received until 2 October 19X2. The directors of the group wish to replace some of the plant and machinery of Cook Limited. The accountant has told them that there would be ample funds available for this if the gross profit percentage of Cook Limited was as good as that of Hakluyt plc and if the levels of stock, debtors and creditors of Cook Limited could be maintained at the same proportions to the activity as is currently being achieved by Hakluyt plc.

Required:

(a) Prepare the consolidated balance sheet of Hakluyt plc and its subsidiary Cook Limited at 30 September 19X2.   (10 marks)

(b) Comment on the validity of the accountant's assertion, giving an estimate of the amount of funds (if any) that could be available if the assertion were correct.   (10 marks)

59. A AND B (20 marks)

The share capital of B Limited consists of 200,000 ordinary shares of £1 each, of which A Limited bought 150,000 on the first day of the accounting period to which the profit and loss account below relates.

DRAFT PROFIT AND LOSS ACCOUNTS
FOR YEAR ENDED 31 DECEMBER 19X0

	A Limited		B Limited	
	£	£	£	£
Turnover (excluding intra- group sales)		1,000,000		2,000,000
Cost of sales (excluding intra-group purchases)		600,000		1,500,000
		400,000		500,000
Expenditure				
General administration etc	98,000		91,000	
Depreciation	29,000		20,000	
Audit fees	1,200		1,100	
Debenture interest (gross)	–		5,000	
		(128,200)		(417,100)
		271,800		82,900
Investment income				
Dividend received from B Ltd (net)		7,500		–
Dividend receivable from B Ltd (net)		15,000		–
Debenture interest from B Ltd (gross)		2,000		–
		296,300		82,900
Less: taxation				
Corporation tax		108,720		33,160
Profit for the financial year		187,580		49,740
Profits b/f		82,000		26,000
		269,580		75,740
Less: Transfer to capital reserve	30,000		15,000	
Dividends paid (net)	–		10,000	
Dividends proposed (net)	190,000		20,000	
		220,000		45,000
		£49,580		£30,740

During the last month of the financial year, A Limited sold goods to B Limited and made a profit of £6,000 thereon. These goods are included in the stocks of B Limited at invoice value. The dividends paid and proposed are all out of current profits.

You are required to prepare the consolidated profit and loss account of A Limited and its subsidiaries for the year ended 31 December 19X0.

(*Note to students.* You will not be required in the examination to prepare a consolidated profit and loss account, but you are expected to understand the principles involved in its construction. This question is included to test your understanding).

60. APPLE BANANA AND CHERRY (30 marks)

The summarised balance sheets of Apple Ltd, Banana Ltd and Cherry Ltd are as follows:

SUMMARISED BALANCE SHEETS AT 31 DECEMBER 19X5

	Apple £'000	Banana £'000	Cherry £'000
Fixed assets at book value	800	600	700
Shares in Banana at cost	1,500	–	–
Shares in Cherry at cost	–	850	–
Net current assets	270	470	310
Total assets less current liabilities	2,570	1,920	1,010
Less 12% long-term loans	650	500	250
	1,920	1,420	760
Share capital	1,200	1,000	600
Retained profit at 1 January 19X5	563	300	100
Profit for 19X5	157	120	60
	1,920	1,420	760

Apple purchased 60% of the share capital of Banana, and Banana purchased the entire share capital of Cherry on 1 January 19X5.

At 1 January 19X6 the 'book' value of Banana's fixed assets was £750,000, while their 'fair' value was estimated to be £1,200,000. The amount of depreciation charged in the accounts of Banana for 19X5 was £150,000; and appropriate charge based on the 'fair' valuation would be £240,000. the remaining assets of Banana and all the assets of Cherry were stated in the balance sheets of those companies at 1 January 19X5 at figures which were approximately equal to their 'fair' values.

Required:

(a) Prepare the consolidated balance sheet of Apple Ltd and its subsidiaries at 31 December 19X5, complying as far as the information permits, with the requirements of SSAP14.

(22 marks)

(b) Calculate the debt/equity ratio for each individual member of the group and for the group as a whole. (4 marks)

(c) Discuss the differences between the debt/equity ratio, calculated under (b), for each individual company and for the group as a whole. (4 marks)

Notes:

(i) Ignore taxation.
(ii) No dividends were paid by any of the companies during 19X5 or proposed at the year end.

61. DINOS AND NIVIS (30 marks)

The balance sheets of Dinos Ltd and Nivis Ltd at 31 December 19X7 were as follows:

	Dinos £'000	Nivis £'000
Fixed assets at book value	2,465	920
Net current assets	1,218	265
	3,683	1,185

Financed by:

Share capital (£1 shares)	3,000	600
Reserves at 1 January 19X7	540	300
Profit for 19X7	143	285
	3,683	1,185

The following additional information is provided:

(a) Dinos purchased the entire share capital of Nivis on 1 January 19X7 and issued 400,000 of its own shares in exchange. Dinos shares were valued at £3.50 each at the date of this transaction. The acquisition has not been entered in the books of Dinos, and is not reflected in the balance sheet above.

(b) The fair value of Nivis's fixed assets at 1 January 19X7 was £1,200,000 compared with a book value of £930,000 at that date. There were no material differences between the book values and fair values of its current assets.

(c) Depreciation charged by Nivis for 19X7 was £87,000. An appropriate charge, based on the fair value of its assets as at 1 January 19X7 and additions during the year, is £116,000.

(d) Any goodwill arising on consolidation is to be written off against reserves.

Required:

(a) The consolidated balance sheet of Dinos Ltd and its subsidiary at 31 December 19X7. Use the acquisition method described in SSAP 14. (15 marks)

(b) The consolidated balance sheet of Dinos Ltd and its subsidiary at 31 December 19X7. Use the merger method as described in SSAP 23. (8 marks)

(c) Outline the conditions which must be satisfied before the merger method may be adopted. Explain the purpose of these conditions. (7 marks)

62. ACCOUNTING POLICIES (20 marks)

A recent conference of businessmen listened to a lecture on 'accounting policies' and were surprised to discover the extent to which the level of reported profit depends on the accounting procedures chosen for the purpose of valuing assets and liabilities. One of the participants suggested that this was a good reason for adopting a prudent approach when measuring profit, and there was some support for this view, though others argued that it was important to adopt a realistic approach rather than a pessimistic approach when preparing company accounts.

Required:

Indicate which accounting policy is likely to produce the more conservative figure for reported profit in each of the circumstances listed below. You should explain your choice:

(a) using first in, first out (FIFO) or last in, last out (LIFO) as the basis for valuing stock, assuming prices are rising and there is no change in the volume of stock held;

(b) using marginal or total cost as the basis for valuing stock, assuming prices are stable and the volume of stock held is increasing;

(c) using marginal or total cost as the basis for valuing stock at the end of the first year of a company's operations;

(d) applying the lower of cost and net realisable value rule to separate items of stock and work in progress or to groups of similar items;

(e) using the reducing balance or straight line method of depreciation during the early years of a particular asset's life;

(f) valuing freehold property at historical cost less depreciation or current cost less depreciation when prices are rising.

63. HATFIELD (30 marks)

The accounts of Hatfield Limited for the year ended 30 June 19X4 are being prepared for publication. The following information is provided:

A *Stock*

Groups of similar items	Marginal cost	Total cost	Net realisable value
	£	£	£
Group A	16,000	25,000	36,000
Group B	9,000	12,000	4,000
Group C	63,000	71,000	94,000
Group D	46,000	51,000	67,000

B *Long-term contract work in progress*

The company has one long-term contract in respect of which costs incurred to 30 June 19X4 amount to £51,000. Estimates suggest that, on completion, the contract will show a total profit of £30,000. Architects have certified the contract to be 60% complete on 30 June 19X4.

C *Tangible fixed assets*

These include:

(i) Freehold land and a building purchased on 1 July 19W3 for £380,000 (including £80,000 for the land). The building has been depreciated at the rate of 4% per annum on cost for each of the ten years to 30 June 19X3. The property was professionally revalued at £800,000 (including land £200,000) on 1 July 19X3 and the directors have decided to write this figure into the books. It is now estimated that the building has a remaining useful life of 20 years and a residual value of £100,000 at the end of that period.

(ii) A machine which was shown in the 19X3 accounts at cost, £100,000 less accumulated depreciation, £30,000. The machine has been depreciated on the straight line basis assuming a zero residual value after ten years. The directors now believe that the reducing balance method will provide users of accounts with a fairer presentation of the financial results and position of the company. The directors consider a depreciation rate of 30% to be appropriate. They do not expect any change in the useful life of the machine.

D *Research and development expenditure*

Expenditure incurred during the year is as follows:

Research expenditure	£1,500
Development expenditure	£5,000

The expenditure has been incurred in an attempt to develop a new product line. The directors are not entirely confident that a new product line will eventually materialise but a minority are fairly hopeful.

E   *Taxation*

	£
Balance at the credit of the deferred tax account at 1 July 19X3 relating entirely to originating timing differences	80,000
Taxable profit for the year	300,000
Originating timing differences, net of reversing timing differences for the year	25,000
Corporation tax rate: 30%	

There were no transactions giving rise to permanent differences between reported profit and taxable profit during the year.

Required:

For each of the items A-E, calculations of the balances for inclusion in accounts prepared in accordance with the Companies Acts 1985 and relevant Statements of Standard Accounting Practice. It is not necessary to give the exact location of each item in the balance sheet and profit and loss account, but the balances should be suitably described. In respect of balance sheet items it should be made clear whether the balance is an asset or a liability and, in respect of profit and loss account items, whether the balance is a revenue or an expense. You may, if necessary, explain the treatment you have adopted.

Notes:

1   For the purpose of your calculations, treat each item in isolation.
2   Comparative figures for the previous year are not required.

64. GUYON   (20 marks)

The published accounts of Guyon Ltd for the year ended 31 March 19X8 are being prepared. The following information is provided:

(a)   The company purchased the business assets of T Rayner, a trader, on 1 January 19X8. The assets acquired included goodwill valued at £52,000.

(b)   Guyon Ltd purchased 40,000 ordinary shares in Tours Ltd for £110,000 on 1 April 19X7. The issued share capital of Tours then, and now, consisted of 100,000 ordinary shares of £1 each. Tours reported profits totalling £36,000 for the year to 31 March 19X8, but paid no dividends. Guyon plays a full part in the financial and operating policies of Tours through representation on its board of directors.

(c)   The company manufactures five different types of goods. The following information is provided in respect of closing stocks of each of them:

Type	Prime cost	Total cost	Net realisable value
	£	£	£
V	35,000	61,000	92,000
W	12,500	16,000	5,000
X	21,100	23,200	36,500
Y	13,300	22,200	15,600
Z	30,500	41,200	63,800

(d) Guyon's issued share capital consists of 1,000,000 ordinary shares of 25p each. The directors propose to pay a final dividend of 5p per share subject to the approval of the annual general meeting. The current rate of advance corporation tax is 25/75.

(e) The company sold a freehold property, surplus to requirements, for £300,000 on 1 March 19X8. The amount received was credited to a fixed asset disposal account. The book value of the property is £140,000. The company is subject to mainstream corporation tax at 35%.

Required:

Explain fully how each of the items, listed under (a) - (e), should be treated in the accounts to comply with the Companies Act 1985 and relevant SSAPs. Where appropriate you should calculate, as far as the information permits, the balances to be disclosed.

65. PORTLAND (30 marks)

The financial director of Portland Limited has prepared the following information with a view to drawing up the company's profit and loss account for the year to 30 June 19X3:

	£
Retained profit at 1 July 19X2	7,200
Turnover	17,500
Cost of sales (note 1)	10,800
Loss on closure of factory in Scotland	760
Administration expenses (note 2)	3,660
Distribution costs	1,200
Taxation (note 3)	635
Dividends paid and proposed	100

Notes:

1 The calculation of cost of sales includes opening stock of £1,000,000 and closing stock of £1,200,000, each valued on the marginal cost basis. The directors have since decided that the total cost basis gives a fairer presentation of the company's results and financial position, and the auditors agree with this assessment. Using the total cost basis, opening stock should be valued at £1,425,000 and closing stock at £1,840,000. You may ignore the effect on tax payable of this change in the method of stock valuation.

2 Administration expenses include bad debts of £850,000. Bad debts are normally in the region of £100,000 per annum, whereas the figure for the current year includes a loss of £750,000 incurred when a major customer went into liquidation.

3 The figure for taxation is made up of the following items:

	£'000	£'000
Tax payable on normal trading profit		1,180
Less: Tax relief on bad debt arising from liquidation of a major customer	375	
Tax relief arising from loss on closure of factory in Scotland	170	
		545
		635

97

QUESTIONS

Required:

(a) Define exceptional items and extraordinary items in accordance with the provisions of SSAP 6. Give two examples of each. (8 marks)

(b) Prepare the profit and loss account and statement of retained earnings of Portland Limited, not necessarily in a form suitable for publication but in accordance with good accounting practice and complying with the provisions of SSAP 6. (22 marks)

66. SELHURST (30 marks)

The accounts of Selhurst Limited for the year ended 31 December 19X4 are being prepared, and the balances extracted from the books include the following items:

	£	£
Turnover		6,174,000
Dividends – amount received		9,000
Dividends paid and proposed		64,000
Loss arising on closure of factory in South Wales, net of tax		126,500
Administrative expenses:		
Chairman's fee	5,000	
Directors' emoluments	29,000	
Rates	6,400	
Office salaries	248,600	
Auditors' remuneration	32,000	
Auditors' expenses	1,900	
Light, heat and cleaning	41,800	
Depreciation of office furniture	9,300	
Depreciation of motor vehicles	27,200	
Bad debts	18,700	
General expenses	108,200	
		528,100
Distribution costs		135,600
Interest payable on bank overdraft		22,300
Cost of sales		4,850,000
Retained profit at 1 January 19X4		736,400

The following additional information is provided:

(1) The company closed the South Wales factory on 1 January 19X4, and the result of the board's decision to concentrate production at its factory in the West Midlands.

(2) One of the company's major customers went into liquidation during December 19X4 owing Selhurst Limited £144,000. It is now estimated that a payment of £0.25 in the £ will eventually be made.

(3) The directors have now decided to depreciate the company's freehold office buildings which have been carried at cost, £250,000, since they were acquired at the beginning of 19W5. At 1 January 19X5 it was estimated that the buildings had a remaining useful life of 20 years, after which they would possess a realisable value of £10,000.

(4) Directors' emoluments consist of annual fees paid to the company's three executive directors of £3,000 each, and a salary of £20,000 pa payable to the managing director. The chairman is non-executive.

(5) Distribution costs include the sales director's salary of £16,000.

(6) Cost of sales includes the salary of the production director, £18,000 and depreciation of plant and machinery, £124,000.

(7) The corporation tax charge for the year has been estimated at £180,000. In addition, a transfer of £34,000 is to be made to the deferred tax account.

(8) It is the directors' policy to make an annual transfer of £30,000 to the preference share redemption reserve.

Required:

(a) A calculation of Selhurst's operating profit for 19X4.   (6 marks)

(b) The profit and loss account and appropriation account of Selhurst for 19X4, together with relevant notes, complying with the minimum requirements of the Companies Acts and relevant statements of standard accounting practice so far as the information permits.
                                                                    (24 marks)

Notes:

(i) The headings contained in profit and loss account format 1 are reproduced below.

(ii) Advance corporation tax should be taken as 25/75 for the purpose of any calculation.

COMPANIES ACT 1985: FORMAT 1 - PROFIT AND LOSS ACCOUNT

1   Turnover
2   Cost of sales
3   Gross profit or loss
4   Distribution costs
5   Administrative expenses
6   Other operating income
7   Income from shares in group companies
8   Income from shares in related companies
9   Income from other fixed asset investments
10 Other interest receivable and similar income
11 Amounts written off investments
12 Interest payable and similar charges
13 Tax on profit or loss on ordinary activities
14 Profit or loss on ordinary activities after taxation
15 Extraordinary income
16 Extraordinary charges
17 Extraordinary profit or loss
18 Tax on extraordinary profit or loss
19 Other taxes not shown under the above items
20 Profit or loss for the financial year

67. SHEPPARTON (30 marks)

Shepparton Ltd was incorporated on 1 October 19X7. The books were balanced as at 30 September 19X8 and a trial balance was extracted. A profit and loss account was then prepared and the remaining balances, together with the balance from the profit and loss account, are listed below:

	£
Share capital	280,000
Freehold property at cost	305,000
Retained profit at 30 September 19X8	26,500
Plant and machinery at cost	100,000
Bank loan	80,000
Shares in Megon Ltd	6,200
Accumulated depreciation: freehold property	10,100
plant and machinery	20,000
Balance at bank	1,300
Stocks	153,400
Debtors	78,500
Trade creditors	32,100
12% debentures	150,000
Interest payable accrued due	21,300
National Insurance payments outstanding	4,800
Corporation tax due 30 June 19X9	7,700
Prepaid expenses	3,100
Proposed dividend	15,000

The following additional information is provided:

(a) The balance of share capital consists of the proceeds arising from the issue of 200,000 ordinary £1 shares on 1 October 19X7.

(b) The bank loan was raised on 31 December 19X7 and is repayable in four equal annual instalments commencing 31 December 19X8.

(c) The shares in Megon Ltd were acquired as a temporary investment on 5 September 19X8, using cash surplus to immediate operating requirements.

(d) Advance corporation tax may be taken as $\frac{25}{75}$ for the purpose of your calculations.

Required:

(a) The balance sheet of Shepparton Ltd at 30 September 19X8 together with relevant notes complying with the requirements of the Companies Act 1985 so far as the information permits. (14 marks)

Note: an outline balance sheet format, complying with the requirements of the Companies Act 1985, is given overleaf.

(b) A general discussion of the limitations of published accounts from the viewpoint of 'external' users of accounting information. (16 marks)

COMPANIES ACT 1985 BALANCE SHEET FORMAT 1

A. Called up share capital not paid

B   Fixed assets

    I   Intangible assets
    II   Tangible assets
    III   Investments

C. Current assets

    I   Stocks
    II   Debtors
    III   Investments
    IV   Cash at bank and in hand

D. Prepayments and accrued income

E. Creditors: amounts falling due within one year

F. Net current assets (liabilities)

G. Total assets less current liabilities

H. Creditors: amounts falling due after more than one year

I. Provisions for liabilities and charges

J. Accruals and deferred income

K. Capital and reserves

    I   Called up share capital
    II   Share premium account
    III   Revaluation reserve
    IV   Other reserves
    V   Profit and loss account

68. MALHAM (30 marks)

The following balances have been extracted from the books of Malham Limited, a trading company, as at 31 March 19X4:

	£'000
Issued share capital 800,000 ordinary shares of £1 each	800
Bank loan	140
Retained profit at 1 April 19X3	573
Net profit for the year to 31 March 19X4	229
Freehold properties at cost	780
Fixtures and fittings at cost	217
Accumulated depreciation on fixtures and fittings at 31 March 19X4	76
Creditors	206
Trade debtors	391
Prepaid expenses	13
Stocks at cost	464
Balance of cash at bank	75
Cash in hand	24
Goodwill at cost	60

The following additional information is provided:

1 The freehold properties, purchased 20 years ago, were revalued at £1,050,000 on 31 March 19X4. The valuation was made by Collins & Co, a firm of chartered surveyors, and the directors have decided to use this figure for the purpose of the accounts.

2 The company purchased fixtures and fittings costing £67,000 during the year to 31 March 19X4. The depreciation charge for the year amounted to £22,000. There were no sales of fixed assets.

3 The figure for creditors includes advance payments of £15,000 from a customer who was not supplied with the goods ordered until 5 April 19X4.

4 The following information is provided in respect of groups of similar items of stocks:

Group	Cost	Net realisable value
	£000	£000
W	127	186
X	35	7
Y	209	352
Z	93	184

5 The goodwill arose on the purchase of the business assets of Tarn Limited, a small private company, on 1 April 19X3. The goodwill is believed to have a useful economic life of five years.

6 A bank loan of £160,000 was raised to help to finance the acquisition of Tarn's business assets. The loan carries interest at a fixed rate of 12% and is repayable by eight equal annual instalments. The first instalment was paid on 31 March 19X4 together with interest accrued to that date.

7 The directors propose to recommend to the annual general meeting the payment of a dividend of eight pence per ordinary share.

Required:

The balance sheet of Malham Limited at 31 March 19X4 together with relevant notes complying with the minimum requirements of the Companies Acts so far as the information permits.

Notes:
1 The main headings contained in balance sheet format 1 are reproduced below.
2 Ignore depreciation of freehold properties and taxation.
3 Show your calculation of the profit and loss account balance for inclusion in the balance sheet.

COMPANIES ACT 1985 : BALANCE SHEET FORMAT 1

A Called up share capital not paid

B Fixed assets:
   i   Intangible assets
   ii   Tangible assets
   iii Investments

C Current assets:
   i   Stocks
   ii   Debtors
   iii Investments
   iv   Cash at bank and in hand

D Prepayments and accrued income

E Creditors: amounts falling due within one year

F Net current assets (liabilities)

G Total assets less current liabilities

H Creditors: amounts falling due after more than one year

I Provisions for liabilities and charges

J Accruals and deferred income

K Capital and reserves:

   i   Called up share capital
   ii   Share premium account
   iii Revaluation reserve
   iv   Other reserves
   v   Profit and loss account

69. MILFORD (30 marks)

The final accounts of Milford Limited are in the course of preparation and it is intended to publish them in accordance with the formats prescribed by the Companies Act 1985. The draft profit and loss account and balance sheet, both of which comply with format 1, are set out below.

PROFIT AND LOSS ACCOUNT
FOR THE YEAR ENDED 31 DECEMBER 19X2

	£	£
Turnover		862,150
Less cost of sales		484,500
Gross profit		377,650
Less: distribution costs	25,000	
administration expenses	185,700	
		210,700
Operating profit		166,950
Less interest payable		12,000
Profit on ordinary activities before taxation		154,950
Tax on profit on ordinary activities		77,000
Profit on ordinary activities after taxation		77,950
Retained profit as at 1 January 19X2		96,800
Retained profit as at 31 December 19X2		£174,750

BALANCE SHEET AS AT 31 DECEMBER 19X2

	£	£
Fixed assets		
Intangible assets		
Development costs	24,100	
Goodwill	33,000	
		57,100
Tangible assets		
Land and buildings	85,000	
Plant and machinery	126,600	
		211,600
		268,700
Current assets		
Stocks	139,400	
Debtors	91,200	
Cash at bank and in hand	14,000	
	244,600	
Creditors: amounts falling due within one year		
Trade creditors	57,100	
Current corporation tax	77,000	
	134,100	
Net current assets		110,500
Total assets less current liabilities		379,200
Creditors: amounts falling due after more than one year		
12% debenture		(100,000)
		£279,200

Capital and reserves
Called up share capital 100,000
Share premium account 4,450
Profit and loss account 174,750
£279,200

The following additional information is provided:

1   Development costs £24,100 are made up of: £

    Research costs 15,000
    Development expenditure 9,100
    £24,100

The development expenditure relates to a separately identifiable project which will undoubtedly produce a significant improvement in the quality of one of the company's product lines.

2   The figure for goodwill is stated at cost, and arose as the result of purchasing the business of a former competitor on 1 January 19X2. It is thought that the goodwill possesses an economic life of five years.

3   Stock is valued at total cost in the balance sheet set out above. Stock was valued at prime cost £75,000 for the purpose of the 19X1 accounts, and this amount was used when computing the cost of sales figure appearing in the profit and loss account. The corresponding total cost valuation of stock at 31 December 19X1 is £98,300 made up as follows:

    £
Prime cost 75,000
Production overheads 23,300
£98,300

4   It has recently come to light that an invoice for £4,900 received from a supplier, has been erroneously omitted from the books. The goods referred to in the invoice were included in the physical stock-take.

5   The company's land and buildings are stated in the balance sheet at cost less depreciation. They were professionally revalued at £120,000 on 1 January 19X2. It has now been decided to use this figure for the purpose of the accounts. Administration expenses include a depreciation charge of £2,000 which should be revised to £3,500 to take account of the revaluation.

Required:

(a) The profit and loss account of Milford Limited for 19X2 and the balance sheet at 31 December 19X2 redrafted, as necessary, to take account of the additional information. The revised accounts should comply, so far as the information permits, with the requirements of the Companies Act 1985 and statements of standard accounting practice.

(26 marks)

(b) A calculation of the profit available for distribution according to the requirements of s263 CA 1985. (4 marks)

Assume that the adjustments you make do not alter tax payable.

70. BOLT (20 marks)

The summarised balance sheet of J Bolt, a sole trader, contained the following information at 30 June 19X6.

BALANCE SHEET AT 30 JUNE 19X6

	£	£
Fixed assets at book value		25,000
Current assets		
Stocks	12,000	
Debtors	9,600	
Cash at bank	1,400	
	23,000	
Current liabilities	7,000	
		16,000
		41,000
Capital		41,000

Briston Ltd has offered J Bolt £60,000 in cash for the assets of his business other than the cash at bank. It is thought that the fair values of fixed assets and stocks are £21,600 and £14,700 respectively. The debtors figure includes £500 due from a customer recently declared bankrupt.

Required:

(a) A calculation of the value of goodwill in J Bolt's business based on the above information.
(4 marks)

(b) Explain the difference between 'purchased' and 'non-purchased' goodwill and outline the ways in which these items should be accounted for to comply with SSAP 22 entitled 'Accounting for goodwill'.
(8 marks)

(c) Discuss the advantages and disadvantages of the procedures prescribed by SSAP 22 to account for purchased goodwill.
(8 marks)

71. HERAPATH AND BLACKWALL (30 marks)

Herapath Ltd and Blackwall Ltd are companies in the same line of business but in difference geographical areas; each was incorporated on 1 January 19X4. The summarised balance sheets and abstracts from the statements of accounting policies for 19X4 and 19X5 are given below.

SUMMARISED BALANCE SHEETS AT 31 DECEMBER

	Herapath		Blackwall	
	19X4	19X5	19X6	19X7
	£'000	£'000	£'000	£'000
Plant at cost	200	200	300	300
Accumulated depreciation	20	40	90	153
	180	160	210	147
Stocks	100	140	130	175
Net liquid funds	30	70	45	105
	310	370	385	427
Share capital	250	250	375	375
Profit 19X4	60	60	10	10
19X5	-	60	-	42
	310	370	385	427

Abstracts from statements of accounting policies:

	Herapath	Blackwall
Depreciation	10% on cost	30% reducing balance
Stock valuation	First in first out (FIFO)	Last in first out (FIFO)

FIFO gives the following valuations for Blackwall's stock at 31 December:

    19X4 £150,000
    19X5 £210,000

Required:

(a) Summarised balance sheets for Blackwall Ltd as at 31 December 19X4 and 31 December 19X5, in the same form as the above presentation, adjusted to comply with the accounting policies used by Herapath. You must show clearly any changes which you make to the reported profit figures. (16 marks)

(b) Calculations of the rate of return on shareholders' equity for each company for each year on the basis of the information provided in the question and, in the case of Blackwall Ltd, on the basis of the statements prepared in answer to part (a). (6 marks)

(c) Explain why it is important for companies to adopt similar accounting policies. You should use the information prepared in answer to parts (a) and (b) to support your explanation. (8 marks)

Notes:

(i) Ignore taxation
(ii) No dividends were paid or proposed for 19X4 or 19X5
(iii) For the purposes of calculations under (b) use year-end balances for shareholders' equity.

72. GURNEY (20 marks)

Gurney Ltd was incorporated on 1 January 19X4 with an authorised share capital of £1,000,000 divided into ordinary shares of £1 each. On the same date 400,000 shares were issued at par for cash. Long-term prospects are excellent, but profits are expected to fluctuate owing to changes in trading conditions. The estimated profits (loss) and planned dividend per share for each of the next six years are as follows:

	Profits (Loss) £'000	Dividend pence
19X4	110	15
19X5	20	16
19X6	95	17
19X7	30	18
19X8	200	19
19X9	(20)	20

The dividend to be paid each year is the lower of the planned payment for the year and the maximum legal distribution.

The directors plan to finance a modest rate of expansion over the next six years out of retained profit and, for this reason, they have decided to capitalise the balance of undistributed profits at the end of 19X9.

Required:

(a) Calculate the planned dividend payment for each of the years 19X4 - X9.

(3 marks)

(b) For each of the years 19X4-X9 prepare a statement showing the profit available for distribution, the amount of the distribution and the amount of retained profits carried forward. You should give effect to any legal restrictions on the amount of dividend payable in the year in question. You should explain the treatment you adopt.

(15 marks)

(c) Indicate the amount of the capitalisation issue on 31 December 19X9.

(2 marks)

Note: ignore taxation.

73. NEWTON (30 marks)

The following balances have been extracted from the books of Newton Ltd as at 31 March 19X7:

	£'000
Issued share capital	950
12% debentures	600
Bank loan	200
Plant and machinery at cost	1,800
Accumulated depreciation to 31 March 19X6	900
Creditors	375
Debtors	719
Stock at cost	584
Cash at bank and in hand	35
Research and development expenditure	84
Goodwill at cost	72
Debenture redemption reserve at 31 March 19X6	120
200,000 ordinary shares in Norfolk Ltd	430
Retained profit at 1 April 19X6	108
Balance of profit for year to 31 March 19X7	471

The following additional information is provided:

(i) The balance of issued share capital is made up of the proceeds from 500,000 ordinary shares issued at par (£1) on incorporation, and a further 300,000 ordinary shares issued in January 19X7.

(ii) The bank loan is repayable by five equal annual instalments commencing 31 December 19X7. Interest due on the bank loan has been paid up to date.

(iii) Debenture interest due for the year to 31 March 19X7 has not yet been paid or provided for. It is the directors' policy to make an annual transfer of £20,000 to the debenture redemption reserve.

(iv) The plant and machinery were purchased on 1 April 19X0 and have been depreciated on the straight-line basis assuming a twelve-year life and zero residual value at the end of that period. The condition of the fixed assets was reviewed in April 19X6 and it is now estimated that they have a remaining useful life of four years from that date. The depreciation for the year to 31 March 19X7 has not yet been provided for.

(v) The cost and net realisable value of the company's stock, analysed in groups of similar items, are as follows:

Group	Cost	Net realisable value
	£'000	£'000
X	107	90
Y	326	502
Z	151	206

(vi) The balance of research and development expenditure, all incurred during the year ended 31 March 19X7, is made up as follows:

	£'000
Research expenditure	25
Development expenditure	59

The expenditure has been incurred in respect of a new product which, it is hoped, will be marketed for the first time in 19Y0. The majority of the directors have substantial reservations concerning the prospects for the new product, but the managing director says, "It is a great idea and we need to give it a try".

(vii)   The goodwill arose on the purchase of the trading assets of a small firm on 2 April 19X6. The goodwill is believed to have a useful economic life of four years.

(viii)   The shares in Norfolk Ltd were purchased some years ago. Norfolk, which supplies Newton with essential raw materials, has a total issued share capital of 250,000 ordinary shares of £1 each.

Required:

(a)   A calculation of the balance of retained profit of Newton Ltd at 31 March 19X7.
(7 marks)

(b)   The balance sheet of Newton Ltd at 31 March 19X7 together with relevant notes, so as to comply, as far as the information permits, with the Companies Act 1985 and relevant statements of standard accounting practice.   (19 marks)

(c)   An explanation of your accounting treatment of goodwill and research and development expenditure in (a) and (b) above.   (4 marks)

Notes: (i)   Ignore dividends and taxation.
       (ii)   The main headings contained in balance sheet format 1 are as follows:

COMPANIES ACT 1985, BALANCE SHEET FORMAT 1

A. Called up share capital not paid.

B. Fixed assets
    I   Intangible assets
    II   Tangible assets
    III Investments

C. Current assets
    I   Stocks
    II   Debtors
    III Investments
    IV   Cash at bank and in hand

D. Prepayments and accrued income

E. Creditors: amounts falling due within one year

F. Net current assets (liabilities)

G. Total assets less current liabilities

H. Creditors: amounts falling due after more than one year

I. Provisions for liabilites and charges

J. Accruals and deferred income

K. Capital and reserves
    I   Called up share capital
    II   Share premium account
    III Revaluation reserve
    IV   Other reserves
    V   Profit and loss account

74. KYLSANT (20 marks)

The summarised balance sheet of Kylsant Ltd as at 31 March 19X7 is as follows:

SUMMARISED BALANCE SHEET
AS AT 31 MARCH 19X7

	£
Ordinary shares of £1 each	200,000
8% convertible preference shares of £1 each	100,000
Share premium account	60,000
Retained profits (all distributable)	685,000
	1,045,000
Fixed and net current assets	1,045,000

The company's freehold property, currently included in the balance of fixed and net current assets at £300,000, has been professionally valued at £620,000.

Required:

Starting from the summarised balance sheet above, prepare five revised balance sheets which take *separate* account of each of the following schemes:

(a)   The freehold property to be recorded and reported at the new valuation. (3 marks)

(b)   The company to make a bonus issue to existing ordinary shareholders of three new ordinary shares, fully paid, for each share currently held.   (3 marks)

(c)   The company to make a rights issue of one new ordinary share at £3 per share for every ordinary share currently held.   (3 marks)

(d)   The preference shareholders to exercise their right to exchange their shares for 80,000 ordinary shares of £1 each.   (5 marks)

(e)   50,000 of the ordinary shares are redeemable. The company to redeem these at a price of £1.50 per share. The shares were issued at par some years ago.   (6 marks)

75. GOWER (30 marks)

Gower Ltd was incorporated in December 19X5 to manufacture and sell 'widgets'. The company commenced business operations on 1 January 19X6 and the trial balance at the end of its first year of trading contained the following information:

TRIAL BALANCE AT 31 DECEMBER 19X6

	£'000	£'000
Share capital (ordinary shares of £1 each)		1,000
Trade creditors		106
Sales		1,650
Manufacturing costs, other than depreciation	1,100	
Trade debtors	350	
Cash at bank	36	
Administration, selling and distribution expenses	216	
Research and development expenditure	54	
Plant and machinery at cost	1,000	
	2,756	2,756

The company's directors have to decide how to value stock, plant and machinery, and research and development expenditure, for the purpose of the published accounts.

The company's accountant has produced the following information:

(i)   Valuations for closing stock:

First in first out basis	£220,000
Average cost basis	£200,000

(ii)   The plant and machinery has an expected working life of four years and can be reduced to its estimated disposal value of £240,000, using either the straight line method or applying a rate of 30% on the reducing balance basis.

(iii) The research expenditure (£14,000) and development expenditure (£40,000) have been incurred in respect of a new process for manufacturing widgets. The new process, which has produced significant savings, became operational on 1 January 19X7.

Required:

(a) On the basis of the above information and the regulations contained in relevant SSAPs, explain how Gower should account for stocks, plant and machinery, and research and development, if the directors wish to report the lowest possible profit figure for 19X6.
(6 marks)

(b) Prepare a profit and loss account for 19X6 and a balance sheet at 31 December 19X6, using conventionally acceptable accounting policies which produce the *lowest* measure of reported profit for the year. (7 marks)

(c) Prepare a profit and loss account for 19X6 and a balance sheet at 31 December 19X6, using conventionally acceptable accounting policies which produce the *highest* measure of reported profit for the year. (7 marks)

(d) Discuss fully the effect of the alternative accounting policies, used in (b) and (c) above, on the levels of profit reported for 19X6 and for future years. (10 marks)

Note: ignore taxation

76. DEXTER (30 marks)

The summarised profit and loss appropriation account and summarised balance sheet of Dexter Ltd for 19X6 are as follows:

PROFIT AND LOSS ACCOUNT, 19X6

	£'000
Net profit before tax	200
Less: Corporation tax	60
	140
Less: Dividends	100
	40

BALANCE SHEET AT 31 DECEMBER 19X6

	£'000
Fixed assets and net current assets	1,070
Financed by:	
Share capital (£1 shares)	1,000
Retained profits	70
	1,070

The directors plan to expand the level of operations by acquiring the assets of an existing business, engaged in similar activity, for £1,000,000 on 1 January 19X7. The directors need to decide whether to raise £1,000,000 by making a rights issue to existing shareholders or issuing a 12% debenture. The terms of the rights issue would be to issue shares at £2.50 each on the basis of two additional shares for every five shares currently held.

Forecast profits of the expanded company before interest charges, if any, for the next three years are as follows:

	£'000
19X7	520
19X8	240
19X9	600

The directors plan to pay out the entire post-tax profit of each of the years in the form of a cash dividend.

Mainstream corporation tax should be charged at the rate of 30% on profits before tax.

Required:

(a) Forecast profit and loss accounts for each of the years 19X7 to 19X9 inclusive and the forecast balance sheet at the end of that period, assuming the expansion is financed by a rights issue. (6 marks)

(b) Forecast profit and loss accounts for each of the years 19X7 to 19X9 inclusive and the forecast balance sheet at the end of that period, assuming the expansion is financed by issuing a 12% debenture. (6 marks)

(c) Calculations of the debt: equity ratio and the rate of return on shareholders' equity. Base your calculations on the figures given for 19X6 and your answers under (a) and (b) above. (8 marks)

(d) A discussion of the advantages and disadvantages of the alternative methods of financing the expansion (as in (a) and (b) above). Your discussion should make reference to the position of (i) the shareholders of Dexter Ltd and (ii) the management of Dexter Ltd. (10 marks)

Notes: (i) Assume that you are making the required calculations in answer to this question on 1 January 19X7.

(ii) In the balance sheets you prepare in answer (a) and (b) above, insert the figure for fixed assets and net current assets as the balancing figure.

77. GARNER (20 marks)

The following information is provided for Garner Ltd respect of the year to 30 June 19X7:

	£'000
Turnover	37,200
Cost of sales *(Note 1)*	24,600
Loss on closure of manufacturing division *(Note 2)*	7,300
Distribution costs	3,600
Administration expenses	6,200
Bad debts write off arising from fundamental error *(Note 3)*	2,140
Retained profit at 1 July 19X6	12,600

Notes:

1. The cost of sales figure includes closing stock of finished goods valued at £2,370,000. The company's auditors have drawn attention to the fact that £520,000 of this stock is obsolete and should be written off.

2. In the past the company's activities consisted of a manufacturing division and a service division. The service division has been making healthy profits in recent years but the manufacturing division has been making losses. The manufacturing division was closed down during the year to 30 June 19X7.

3. It has been discovered that last year's accounts were wrongly prepared. Owing to a clerical error, a debt due to Garner of £2,140,000, which was known to be bad, was wrongly classified as cash at bank.

Required:

(a) Define exceptional items and extraordinary items in accordance with the provisions of SSAP 6. (4 marks)

(b) Prepare the profit and loss account and statement of retained earnings of Garner Ltd in accordance with good accounting practice and comply with the provisions of SSAP 6. You are not required to produce statements in a form suitable for publication. (16 marks)

Notes: (i) Ignore taxation
(ii) No dividends were paid or proposed for the year to 30 June 19X7.

78. LANGOSTA

The draft balance sheet of Langosta Ltd as at 31 December 19X7, together with comparative figures for the previous year, is as follows:

	19X6	19X5
	£000	£000
Tangible fixed assets at cost or valuation	1,360	940
Less: accumulated depreciation	98	72
	1,262	868
Current assets		
Stock and work in progress	346	338
Debtors	175	150
Cash at bank and in hand	7	-
	528	488
Creditors: amounts falling due within one year		
Creditors and accruals	106	101
Bank overdraft	-	37
Taxation due 30 September 19X6	-	65
Taxation due 30 September 19X7	91	-
Proposed dividends	36	55
	233	258
Net current assets	295	230
Total assets less current liabilities	1,557	1,098
Creditors falling due after one year		
Debentures redeemable 19X9	(200)	(200)
	1,357	898
Capital and reserves		
Ordinary share capital (£1 each)	500	400
Preference share capital (£1 each)	-	250
Share premium account	80	-
Property revaluation reserve	310	-
Capital redemption reserve	70	-
Debenture redemption reserve	140	120
Plant replacement reserve	75	52
Profit and loss account	182	76
	1,357	898

The following additional information is provided:

(a) The balances of tangible fixed assets are made up as follows:

	Land and buildings	Plant and achinery	Total
Cost or valuation	£'000	£'000	£'000
Balance at 31 December 19X5	700	240	940
Additions	-	110	110
Revaluation	310	-	310
Balance at 31 December 19X6	1,010	350	1,360

Accumulated depreciation

Balance at 31 December 19X5	-	72	72
Charge for the year	-	26	26
Balance at 31 December 19X6	-	98	98

(b) 100,000 ordinary shares were issued on 1 January 19X6 at £1.80 per share. All the preference shares were redeemed at par on the following day.

Required:

(a) A reconstruction of the profit and loss account for 19X6 so as to disclose the figure for profit before tax.   (9 marks)

(b) The statement of source and application of funds for 19X6 prepared in accordance with the provisions of SSAP 10 as far as the information permits.   (11 marks)

(c) An explanation of how the balances on the share premium account and capital redemption reserve have arisen.   (4 marks)

(d) State, giving your reasons, whether the balances on each of the following accounts are distributable as dividends:

    Property revaluation reserve
    Capital redemption reserve
    Debenture redemption reserve.   (6 marks)

Notes:
(i) Ignore advance corporation tax
(ii) Land and buildings are not depreciated
(iii) An interim dividend was not paid for 19X6.

79. HOLFORD (20 marks)

The summarised profit and loss account of Holford Limited for 19X2 prepared under the historical cost convention was as follows:

PROFIT AND LOSS ACCOUNT FOR 19X2

	£'000	£'000
Turnover		360,000
Less: opening stock	35,000	
purchases	200,000	
closing stock	(50,000)	
cost of goods sold		185,000
Gross profit		175,000
Less: depreciation	20,000	
other running costs	126,000	
		146,000
Operating profit		29,000
Interest payable		5,000
Profit on ordinary activities before taxation		24,000
Taxation		10,000
Profit after tax		14,000
Dividends		7,000
Retained profits for the year		£7,000

The following additional information is provided:

1   Relevant indices for stocks are as follows:

Average for October/December 19X1	120
At 31 December 19X1	124
Average for 19X2	135
Average for October/December 19X2	142
At 31 December 19X2	145

On average the company holds stock for three months.

2   All the company's fixed assets were purchased when the company was incorporated six years ago. Their original cost was £200,000,000 and they are being depreciated over a ten year period assuming a nil residual value. The original estimate of these assets' lives is still considered appropriate. The following current cost valuations are provided.

	£'000
At 1 January 19X2	310,000
Average for 19X2	330,000
At 31 December 19X2	355,000

3   Net borrowings were approximately one third of net operating assets throughout 19X2.

Required:

A summarised profit and loss account for 19X2 prepared on the current cost basis in accordance, so far as the information permits, with the principles contained in SSAP 16.

Notes: (i)   All calculations are to be made to the nearest £'000.
        (ii) Ignore the monetary working capital adjustment.

80. BELL (20 marks)

The summarised trading and profit and loss account of Bell plc for the year ended 31 December 19X4 prepared under the historical cost convention is as follows:

TRADING AND PROFIT AND LOSS ACCOUNT

	£'000	£'000
Sales		2,000
Less: opening stock	300	
purchases	1,200	
closing stock	(360)	
cost of goods sold		1,140
Gross profit		860
Less: depreciation	150	
other running costs	550	
		700
Net profit		160

The following price indices are provided for the company's stock and fixed assets:

	Stock	Fixed assets
At 1 January 19X0	100	100
Average for October/December 19X3	120	130
At 31 December 19X3	120	132
Average for 19X4	124	134
Average for October/December 19X4	126	136
At 31 December 19X4	128	136

The company's stock turns over, on average, once every three months; fixed assets were purchased on 1 January 19X0.

Required:

(a) The current cost profit and loss account of Bell plc, containing a cost of sales adjustment and a depreciation adjustment. (10 marks)

(b) Outline the main arguments for and against changing from the historical cost basis to the current cost basis for preparing company accounts. (10 marks)

Note: calculations to the nearest £'000.

81. NORWICH (20 marks)

The following information has been extracted from the accounts of Norwich plc prepared under the historical cost convention for 19X6.

PROFIT AND LOSS ACCOUNT EXTRACTS, 19X6

	£m
Turnover	200
Operating profit	15
Less interest payable	3
Net profit	12

SUMMARISED BALANCE SHEET AT 31 DECEMBER 19X6

	£m	£m
Fixed assets at cost less depreciation		60
Current assets:		
Stocks	20	
Debtors	30	
Bank	2	
	52	
Less current liabilities	30	
Net current assets		22
Total assets less current liabilities		82
Less 15% debentures		20
		62
Capital and reserves		62

119

The company's accountant has prepared the following current cost data:

	£m
Current cost adjustments for 19X6:	
Depreciation adjustment	3
Cost of sales adjustment	5
Replacement cost at 31 December 19X6	
Fixed assets, net of depreciation	85
Stocks	21

Required:

(a) A calculation of the current cost operating profit of Norwich plc for 19X6 and the summarised current cost balance sheet of the company at 31 December 19X6, so far as the information permits.   (6 marks)

(b) Calculations of the following ratios from both the historical cost accounts and current cost accounts:
  (i)   interest cover;
  (ii) rate of return on shareholders' equity;
  (iii) debt/equity ratio   (6 marks)

(c) A discussion of the significance of the ratios calculated under (b) and of the reasons for differences between them.   (8 marks)

Note: ignore taxation.

SUGGESTED SOLUTIONS

1. **BASIC**

    Tutorial note. This question is designed to revise your knowledge of (a) depreciation and (b) the accruals concept. Remember that the accruals concept states that the profit and loss account for a year should include all expenses relating to that year, whenever paid. Note how in (b), (c) and (e) each payment is analysed between amounts relating to 19X4 and amounts relating to 19X3 or 19X5. Only the former amounts are charged to profit and loss account in 19X4.

    (a) *Depreciation of office equipment*

	£
Cost at 1.1.X4	13,500
Less accumulated depreciation at 1.1.X4	4,700
Net book value at 1.1.X4	8,800
Less net book value of disposals in year	1,700
	7,100
Add cost of additions in year	7,200
NBV of assets in use at 31.12.X4	£14,300

    $$\therefore \text{Depreciation charge} = 10\% \times £14{,}300$$
    $$= £1{,}430$$

    (b) *Telephone expenses*

	£	£
Quarter to 31.1.X4	180	
Less: relating to year ended 31.12.X3	112	
		68
Quarter to 30.4.X4		190
Quarter to 31.7.X4		195
Quarter to 31.10.X4		210
Quarter to 31.1.X5	216	
Less: relating to year ended 31.12.X5*	72	
		144
Amount charged to 19X4 P & L account		£807

    *This is an estimated figure. Of the three months to 31 January 19X5 only two fall in 19X4. One third of the quarter's bill is therefore allocated to 19X5.

    (c) *Rates*

	£	£
Six months to 31.3.X4	1,200	
Less three months to 31.12.X3	600	
Balance – three months to 31.3.X4		600
Six months to 30.9.X4		1,400
Six months to 31.3.X5	1,400	
Less three months 1.1.X5 - 31.3.X5	700	
Balance – three months 1.10.X4 - 31.12.X4		700
Amount charged to 19X4 P & L account		£2,700

(d) *Bad and doubtful debts*

	£	£
Bad debts written off during year		130
Less recovery of debt previously written off		90
Profit and loss charge for bad debts		40
Provision for doubtful debts at 31.12.X4:		
Balances specifically provided for	300	
General provision for remainder of		
balances (2% x (£24,800 - £300))	490	
	790	
Less already provided at 1 January 19X4	380	
Profit and loss charge for doubtful debts		410
Total charge to 19X4 P & L account		£450

(e) *Rental income*

	£	£
Quarter to 28.2.X4	240	
Less amount relating to Dec 19X3		
(one third)	80	
Balance (1.1.X4 - 28.2.X4)		160
Quarter to 31.5.X4		240
Quarter to 31.8.X4		270
Quarter to 30.11.X4		270
Quarter to 28.2.X5	270	
Less amount relating to Jan, Feb 19X5		
(two thirds)	180	
Balance (1.12.X4 - 31.12.X4)*		90
Amount charged to 19X4 P & L account		£1,030

* It does not matter that this amount was not received until 19X5. The £90 would be included as a debtor in the balance sheet at 31.12.X4 (or, more properly, the balance sheet would show a debtor of £270 (amount receivable from tenant) and a creditor of £180 (19X5 income received in advance)).

2. TREND

Tutorial note. This question tests your understanding of depreciation by asking you in effect to work backwards: given the amounts of depreciation charged, to calculate the method being used. The most common method (straight line) is ruled out, because accumulated depreciation does not increase evenly over years 1 and 2.

(a) *Depreciation method*

19X1 depreciation charge is £16,000, 20% of £80,000.

19X2 depreciation balance is £28,800. No new assets have been purchased so:

	£
Original cost of assets	80,000
19X1 depreciation	(16,000)
	64,000
19X2 depreciation (28,800-16,000)	(12,800)
	51,200

$\frac{12,800}{64,000}$ = 20%. Therefore method is 20% reducing balance.

(b) *Depreciation schedule*

19X1	Charge to 31 March 19X1	16,000
	Balance at 31 March 19X1	16,000
19X2	Charge to 31 March 19X2	12,800
	Balance at 31 March 19X2	28,800
	Disposal during year to March 19X3 *(working 1)*	(5,400)
	Depreciation charge	13,320
19X3	Balance per question	36,720
	Disposal *(working 2)*	(14,640)
	Depreciation charge *(working 3)*	17,584
	Closing balance 31 March 19X4	£39,664

(c) *Year ended 31 March 19X4*

		£
A	Plant at cost (90 - 30 + 50)	110,000
B	Depreciation accumulated (part b)	(39,664)
C	Net written down value	£70,336

125

Workings

First disposal		£
1	Original purchases year to 19X1	15,000
	Depreciation	(3,000)
		12,000
	Depreciation to March 19X2	(2,400)
	Written down value	£9,600

Therefore loss on disposal £(8,000 - 9,600) = (£1,600) (see below).

Second disposal		£
2	Purchase year to 19X1	30,000
	Depreciation 19X1	(6,000)
		24,000
	Depreciation 19X2	4,800
		19,200
	Depreciation 19X3	(3,840)
	Written down value	£15,360

Therefore profit on disposal £(21,000 - 15,360) = £5,640 (see below).

3	Depreciation charge 19X4	£
	Written down value 19X3	53,280
	Disposal at WDV *(from working 2)*	(15,360)
	Purchase	50,000
		£87,920
	20% reducing balance	£17,584

(d) *Profit on disposal*

	First disposal £	Second disposal £
Cash received	8,000	21,000
WDV *(workings 1,2)*	9,600	15,360
Profit/(loss)	£(1,600)	£5,640

3.   LAURA

TRADING AND PROFIT AND LOSS ACCOUNT
FOR THE YEAR ENDING 31 DECEMBER 19X0

	£	£
Sales		72,000
Cost of sales		
Opening stock	8,900	
Purchases	36,600	
	45,500	
Less closing stock	10,800	
		34,700
Gross profit		37,300
Expenses		
Wages and salaries £(19,800 - 2,400 - 600)	16,800	
Rates and insurance £(1,510 - 260)	1,250	
Motor expenses £(400 + 600)	1,000	
Sundry expenses £(1,500 + 120)	1,620	
Depreciation - factory 2% (£20,000 - £4,000)	320	
plant	480	
cars	650	
		22,120
Net profit		£15,180

BALANCE SHEET AS AT 31 DECEMBER 19X0

	Cost £	Dep'n £	NBV £
Fixed assets			
Factory	20,000	2,240	17,760
Plant	4,800	2,080	2,720
Cars	2,600	1,850	750
	£27,400	£6,170	21,230
Current assets			
Stocks		10,800	
Debtors £(3,600-60)	3,540		
Less provision £(280-60)	220		
		3,320	
Prepayment (rates)		260	
Cash at bank		11,490	
		25,870	
Current liabilities			
Trade creditors	4,200		
Accruals (sundry expenses)	120		
		4,320	
Net current assets			21,550
			£42,780
Capital			
Opening balance			30,000
Add: net profit for year		15,180	
less drawings		2,400	
retained profit for year			12,780
Closing balance			£42,780

4. EXPLAIN

(a) (i) A bonus issue occurs when a company decides to turn some of its reserves into share capital. In such an issue existing ordinary shareholders will be *given* new shares in proportion to their existing shareholdings. No cash changes hands: the shareholders do not pay for the new shares, nor does the 'bonus' they receive consist of cash. It is purely an exercise in bookkeeping, a reclassification of reserves as share capital.

(ii) The share capital of a company shown in its balance sheet is the *nominal* value of its issued shares. In practice, shares are often issued at a price above their nominal value. In such a case, the excess cash (share premium) received by the company is credited to a share premium account which is a reserve forming part of shareholders' funds. The reserve is not distributable and may only be used for certain limited purposes, one of which is to fund a bonus issue of shares.

(iii) A capital redemption reserve arises when shares are redeemed out of profits. It is a general principle of company law that such redemptions should not reduce the 'creditors' buffer', the amount of funds from which, in a liquidation, creditors' claims can be met. The Companies Act 1985 provides that when shares are redeemed out of profits (ie the redeemed shares are not replaced by a new issue of shares) a transfer should be made from profit and loss account to a capital redemption reserve (CRR). The amount of the transfer should equal the nominal value of the shares redeemed. Since the CRR is not a distributable reserve, this procedure has the effect that the company's fixed capital remains the same after the redemption as it was before.

(b) (i) EXTRACT FROM PROFIT AND LOSS ACCOUNT
FOR THE YEAR ENDED 31 MARCH 19X5

	£	£
Operating profit		200,000
Less debenture interest (12% x £20,000)		2,400
Profit for the financial year		197,600
Appropriations of profit:		
Transfer to CRR *(working 4)*	10,000	
Bonus issue *(working 5)*	30,000	
Preference dividend (10% x £30,000)*	3,000	
Ordinary dividend (10% x £270,000)**	27,000	
		70,000
Retained profit for the financial year		127,600
Retained profits brought forward		430,000
Retained profits carried forward		£557,600

*Since an ordinary dividend is proposed, the preference dividend must first be paid.

** See *working 1*

(ii)   EXTRACT FROM BALANCE SHEET AT 31 MARCH 19X5

		£
540,000 ordinary shares of 50p each *(working 1)*		270,000
20,000 10% preference shares of £1 each *(working 2)*		20,000
Capital redemption reserve *(working 4)*		10,000
Retained profits ((i) above)		557,600
Shareholders' funds		857,600
12% debentures		20,000
		£877,600

Workings

1   Ordinary share capital

	No	£
At 31 March 19X4	400,000	200,000
New issue on 1 June	50,000	25,000
	450,000	225,000
Bonus issue (1 for 5) on 1 July	90,000	45,000
At 31 March 19X5	540,000	£270,000

2   Preference shares

	£
At 31 March 19X4	30,000
Redemption on 1 April	(10,000)
At 31 March 19X5	£20,000

3   Share premium account

	£
At 31 March 19X4	10,000
Premium on ordinary shares issued on 1 June (50,000 x 10p)	5,000
	15,000
Less used to fund bonus issue	15,000
At 31 March 19X5	£ -

4   Capital redemption reserve

	£
Transfer from profit and loss account on 1 April	£10,000

5   Bonus issue

	£
Nominal value of bonus shares *(working 1)*	45,000
Less: funded from share premium account *(working 3)*	15,000
Balance funded from retained profits	£30,000

5. **GRAFTON**

(a) A limited company may, if authorised to do so by its articles, issue shares which are (or at the option of the company are to be liable) to be redeemed, provided that:

   (i) no redeemable shares may be issued at any time when there are no issued shares of the company which are not redeemable. In other words, a company must always have in issue at least *some* non-redeemable shares;

   (ii) redeemable shares may not be redeemed unless they are fully paid;

   (iii) the terms of redemption must provide for payment on redemption;

   (iv) redeemable shares may only be redeemed:

      (1) out of distributable profits of the company; or
      (2) out of the proceeds (including any premium obtained) of a fresh issue of shares made for the purposes of the redemption;

   (v) any premium on redemption *must be paid out of distributable profits* of the company. The exception to this rule relates to the redemption of shares originally issued at a premium. This is dealt with later.

   The purpose of the rules is to prevent the erosion of the company's capital base. If a company redeems shares (ie pays back capital to shareholders) the 'creditors' buffer' of fixed capital at first might appear to be reduced. To prevent this, the amount paid to redeem shares must either:

   (i) be matched by the proceeds of a new share issue so that the company's fixed capital is immediately restored to at least its former level; or

   (ii) be paid from *distributable profits*. This means that the payment must come from assets not regarded as part of the fixed capital but available for distribution to shareholders.

   If the redemption is not financed (or is only partly financed) from a new share issue the procedure is to reclassify some of the company's distributable reserves as an undistributable reserve, called the *capital redemption reserve* (CRR).

   There are similar rules regulating the purchase by a company of its own shares.

(b) The permanent capital of Grafton plc is as follows:

	£
Ordinary shares	500,000
Share premium account	150,000
	650,000

(c) *Revised balance sheet extracts at 1 September 19X8*

	(i)	*(ii)*	*(iii)*
	£'000	£'000	£'000
Ordinary shares	300	300	380
Preference shares	-	100	-
Share premium account	150	150	190
Capital redemption reserve (CRR)	200	100	40
Profit and loss account	50	150	250
	700	800	860

Notes

(i) No new issue of shares takes place and therefore the entire nominal value (£200,000) of the shares redeemed must be transferred from profit and loss account. The profit and loss account is also reduced by £120,000 in respect of the redemption premium.

(ii) The £100,000 received on the issue of new shares means that the transfer to CRR is limited to only £100,000 (not the full £200,000). Again, the premium on redemption must also be charged to profit and loss account.

(iii) In this case, the transfer to CRR is reduced by the £160,000 proceeds received from the new share issue. The transfer from profit and loss account is therefore only £40,000.

Because the shares to be redeemed were originally issued at a premium, it is possible to charge some of the premium on redemption against the share premium account, instead of charging it all against profit and loss account. However, the amount treated in this way must not exceed the premium received on the original issue (here 200,000 x 20p = £40,000). The remainder of the premium on redemption (£80,000, ie £120,000 - £40,000) must be charged against profit and loss account in the normal way.

The following calculations show how the balance sheet figures are derived.

	£'000
Ordinary shares (500 + 80 - 200)	380
Share premium account (150 + 80 - 40)	190
CRR (200 - 160)	40
Profit and loss account (370 - 40 - 80)	250
	860

6. TRAFFORD

(a) When shares are redeemed it is normally necessary to maintain the level of undistributable funds in a company by reclassifying distributable reserves as an undistributable 'capital redemption reserve'(CRR). In this case shares with a nominal value of £200 are redeemed and cancelled by the company. £200 of distributable profits are therefore reclassified as CRR. The resulting balance sheet is as follows:

	£
Ordinary shares of £1 each £(1,000 - 200)	800
Share premium account	400
Capital redemption reserve	200
Undistributable funds	1,400
Distributable profits £(600 - 200)	400
Net assets	£1,800

Net assets have fallen by £200 being the amount paid to shareholders to redeem their shares. Undistributable funds have remained constant at £1,400.

(b) In this case there is a premium payable on redemption of the shares (200 x 30p = £60). Such premiums must be charged against distributable profits. (The one exception to this rule is discussed in (d) below.) Distributable profits must also be reduced by a £200 transfer to CRR, as in (a) above.

The resulting balance sheet is as follows:

	£
Ordinary shares of £1 each	800
Share premium account	400
Capital redemption reserve	200
Undistributable funds (unchanged)	1,400
Distributable profits £(600 - 60 - 200)	340
Net assets	£1,740

Net assets have fallen by £260 being the amount (200 x £1.30) paid to shareholders to redeem their shares.

(c) The premium on redemption (200 x 20p = £40) must again be charged against distributable profits.

The new issue of shares boosts the level of undistributable funds in the company by 100 x £1.05 = £105. The required transfer to CRR is correspondingly reduced and therefore amounts to £(200 - 105) = £95.

The resulting balance sheet is as follows:

	£
Ordinary shares of £1 each £(1,000 - 200 + 100)	900
Share premium account £(400 + 100 x 5p)	405
Capital redemption reserve	95
Undistributable funds (unchanged)	1,400
Distributable profits £(600 - 95 - 40)	465
Net assets	£1,865

Net assets have fallen by £(200 x 1.20) = £240, but risen by £(100 x 1.05) = £105, a net reduction of £135.

(d) There is one exception to the rule that a premium payable on redemption of shares should be charged against distributable profits. This is the case where:

(i) a new share issue is made to finance the redemption, wholly or in part; and also

(ii) the shares being redeemed were themselves originally issued at a premium.

In this case, and subject to a maximum amount explained below, the premium payable may be charged against share premium account.

The amount charged to share premium account must not exceed either of the following two amounts:

(i) the premium received on the original issue of the shares (here 200 x 25p = £50);

(ii) the balance on share premium after the new issue is made. Here the balance is:

	£
Before new issue	400
New issue (100 x 10p)	10
	£410

The maximum amount chargeable against share premium account is therefore £50. The total premium payable is 200 x 40p = £80. If £50 is charged against share premium account, the balance of £30 must be charged against distributable profits.

Again, a transfer to CRR is required, calculated as follows:

	£
Nominal value of shares redeemed	200
Less proceeds of new issue £(100 x 1.1)	110
Transfer to CRR	£90

The resulting balance sheet is as follows:

	£
Ordinary shares of £1 each £(1,000 - 200 + 100)	900
Share premium account £(400 + 10 - 50)	360
Capital redemption reserve	90
Undistributable funds	1,350
Distributable profits £(600 - 90 - 30)	480
Net assets	£1,830

Net assets have fallen by £(200 x 1.40) = £280, but risen by £(100 x 1.10) = £110, a net reduction of £170.

Notice that the undistributable funds of the company have fallen by the amount of premium charged against share premium account.

7. RIVERSIDE AND ORLANDO

(a) The rate of return on shareholders' equity is equal to:

$$\frac{\text{profit available for equity shareholders}}{\text{equity shareholders' funds}}$$

(i) Profit available for equity shareholders

	Riverside £'000	Orlando £'000
Profit before loan interest	600	900
Loan interest: 15% x £500	(75)	
15% x £4,000		(600)
	525	300

(ii) Equity shareholders' funds

	£'000	£'000
Share capital	2,000	1,000
Reserves	1,500	1,000
	3,500	2,000

	Riverside	Orlando
∴ Rate of return =	$\frac{525}{3,000}$	$\frac{300}{2,000}$
=	15%	15%

(b) Orlando is a much more highly geared company than Riverside. Its ratio of debt capital: equity capital is 2:1 compared with 0.14:1 in the case of Riverside. This makes it a much more risky investment. Whereas Riverside's profits need only amount to £75,000 to cover its loan interest, Orlando's profits must exceed £600,000 before any distribution can be made to shareholders.

From the shareholder's point of view this makes Orlando a much more volatile investment. On the one hand, he will receive no dividend at all if profits fall 50% below the 19X2 level; on the other hand, any increase in profits above the 19X2 level will lead to a more than proportionate increase in the earnings available for equity.

Suppose in 19X3 Orlando's profits were to rise by 50% to £1,350,000. After paying loan interest of £600,000 this would leave earnings available for equity of £750,000, a return on equity of $\frac{750}{2,000} = 37.5\%$.

This is an increase of 150% over the 19X2 rate of return. The range of possible returns for Orlando is therefore from zero to 37.5%.

For Riverside the range is much less.

	50% decrease in profits £'000	50% increase in profits £'000
Profit before loan interest	300	900
Loan interest	(75)	(75)
	225	825
Rate of return =	$\frac{225}{3,500}$	$\frac{825}{3,500}$
=	6.4%	23.6%

For management, Riverside is a less demanding company to run. Only a major disaster could lead to profits falling below interest payable. With Orlando, the directors must be constantly aware of the receiver at their back.

8. ALLERTON

(a) *Piecemeal liquidation*

	£'000	£'000
Amounts realised for assets		630
Paid to:		
(i) Secured creditors (bank)	70	
(ii) Liquidation expenses	10	
(iii) Preferential creditors	30	
(iv) Shipley plc (floating charge)	400	
		510
Balance for other creditors		£120
Other creditors consist of:		
Bank overdraft (195-70)		125
Sundry creditors (205-30)		175
		300

Payment to other creditors will amount to $\frac{120}{300} =$ 40p in the £

	£'000
The bank will therefore receive:	
In respect of fixed charge	70
Balance at 40p in the £ (125 x 0.4)	50
	120

Sale of company to Shipley plc

	£'000
Bank would receive:	
Immediate payment of 20p in the £(195 x 0.2)	39
After one year - 75% x (195 - 39)	117
	156

(b) The second option appears clearly preferable to the bank in terms of cash received, but most of the cash is not received until one year later. A truer comparison would be as follows:

	Liquidation	Sale to Shipley
	£	£
Cash received immediately	120,000	39,000
Interest earned at 12% for one year	14,400	4,680
	134,400	43,680
Cash received after one year	-	117,000
Value of proceeds after one year	£134,400	£160,680

The sale to Shipley still appears more valuable to the bank. Against this should be set the reasonable certainty, under the liquidation option, of receiving the amount calculated. If the company is sold as a going concern, the amount eventually realised may be affected by events in the coming year. Since Shipley is a public company much financial information about it should be available, enabling an assessment to be made of the likelihood of any default on its undertaking.

9. LION

(a) DISTRIBUTION STATEMENT AT 1 MAY 19X6

	£'000
Amounts realised from sale of assets	
Freehold property	120
Plant and machinery	18
Stocks	57
Debtors	50
	245
Distributions	
Gulf: secured debenture	50
Bank: secured overdraft*	70
Liquidation expenses	5
Preferential creditors (20 + 10)	30
Unsecured creditors: balance remaining**	90
	245

* The bank has a second charge on the freehold property. However, the property realises only £120,000 and after paying the debenture holders £50,000 only £70,000 is left for the bank. The remainder of the overdraft (£35,000) is unsecured and ranks with the other unsecured liabilities.

* Unsecured creditors include trade creditors of £85,000 (ie £95,000 less £10,000 preferential) and the unsecured portion of the overdraft (£35,000). Only £90,000 is available to meet these total claims of £120,000, and unsecured creditors will therefore receive 75p in the pound. In total, therefore, the bank receives (£70,000 + 0.75 x £35,000) £96,250.

(b) If the company is liquidated, the bank received £96,250 immediately (see part (a)).

If the company is sold to Gulf, the bank will receive the full £105,000, but will have to wait one year. The present value of this amount can be calculated by discounting at 12%:

$$\frac{£105,000}{1.12} = £93,750$$

On these figures, it appears that the bank does better to press for immediate liquidation. This view is strengthened by a consideration of the risks involved in each option. The realisable values of the company's assets in an immediate liquidation should be relatively easy to discover, and the figures quoted are therefore likely to be reliable. But the ability of the company to repay all its debts in full after a further year's trading must be very doubtful. The doubt might be reduced if Gulf plc itself guaranteed the debts, so that their repayment was not conditional on the performance of Lion.

Although there are good reasons for preferring the liquidation option, the bank should also consider factors which point the other way.

(i) If Lion Ltd remains in business, and manages to trade successfully, the company may become a valuable customer.

(ii) If the bank presses for liquidation it may forfeit the goodwill of unsecured creditors, some of whom may be customers or potential customers.

(iii) If the bank accepts Gulf plc's scheme, there may be a chance of selling bank services to Gulf.

(iv) Once the debentures are converted to share capital, the bank's own charge over the freehold property would be promoted to become a first charge. This would reduce the risk associated with the going concern option.

The difference in the cash receivable under each option is small (the present values differ by only £2,500) and the bank might well conclude that the going concern option is preferable.

10. SUTHERLAND

Tutorial note Part (a) requires a re-organised balance sheet, for which most of the revised asset values are given. The main difficulty is the new share capital - see W2. Part (b) is a popular type of question: it requires students to realise firstly that book values of assets are irrelevant in this context and secondly that any loss suffered by shareholders has already occurred and is not made worse by any re-organisation.

Suggested solution

(a)   REVISED BALANCE SHEET AS AT 1 JANUARY 19X6

	£	£
Fixed assets		
Intangible asset		
Development costs		85,000
Tangible assets		
Land and buildings	320,000	
Plant and machinery	125,000	
		445,000
		530,000
Current assets		
Stocks	210,000	
Debtors	500,000	
Cash at bank *(working 1)*	233,000	
	943,000	
Creditors: amounts falling due within one year		
Creditors (£393,000 – £180,000)	213,000	
Net current assets		730,000
Total assets less current liabilities		1,260,000
Creditors: amounts falling due after more than one year		
Bank loan (secured)		(600,000)
		£660,000
Capital and reserves		
Called up share capital *(working 2)*		£660,000

(b)   REPORT TO SHAREHOLDERS OF SUTHERLAND LIMITED

Introduction
As at 31 December 19X5 Sutherland Limited has net current liabilities of £123,000 and accumulated losses of £232,000. Total liabilities are £1,080,000 of which £687,000 is owed to the bank. A scheme for financial reorganisation of the company has been drawn up for the consideration of shareholders and creditors. Details of the proposed scheme are set out in an appendix to this report.

Discussion of the scheme
Under the proposed reorganisation, the bank and the trade creditors will receive cash and securities equal (in nominal value) to the full amount of their debts. The nominal value of equity belonging to existing shareholders will fall from £618,000 to £160,000.

At first sight this may appear inequitable but there are two reasons why such an assumption would be wrong:

(i) unlike shareholders, creditors have had no right to share in the profitability of the company, and it would be unfair if they now had to bear its losses;

(ii) the fall in nominal value of the shareholders' investment merely recognises a fall in real value which has already occurred. The point of a reorganisation scheme is to state the assets at what they are actually worth, rather than at their book value.

The only obvious alternative to accepting the scheme would be to liquidate the company. If this happened, the assets could be sold for £1,120,000. After paying off creditors this would have £40,000 for shareholders.

If the scheme is accepted, existing shareholders will retain nearly 73% of the company (480,000/660,000 - *working 2*). The company is expected to be profitable in the future (otherwise shareholders would not consent to subscribe a further £320,000 in a rights issue) and will be able to pay dividends because the accumulated losses will have been eliminated.

Conclusion
Shareholders should accept the proposed reorganisation.

(c) REPORT TO X BANK PLC: PROPOSED RE-ORGANISATION OF SUTHERLAND LTD

Introduction
Sutherland Ltd owes the bank £687,000 and has recently suffered badly from a fall in demand for its products. Accumulated losses of the company amount to £232,000 as at 31 December 19X5. A scheme of financial re-organisation has been drawn up for consideration by shareholders and creditors, including the bank.

Possible courses of action
The options now open to the bank are:

(i) to oppose the scheme and the liquidation of the company. An offer of £1,120,000 has been received for the business assets and if this amount were realised all creditors, including the bank, could be paid in full;

(ii) to support the scheme. In this case the bank would receive an immediate payment of £87,000 and the remaining indebtedness of £600,000 would be consolidated into a loan carrying interest at 13% per annum. The loan would be secured by a fixed charge on the company's land and buildings and a floating charge on the company's remaining assets;

(iii) to propose a revised scheme of re-organisation including more favourable terms for the bank.

The most prudent course appears to be to press for liquidation since this would lead to immediate recovery of the full amount owing to the bank. Before doing this the bank would need to obtain assurance that the £1,120,000 offered for the company's assets would be forthcoming. It would also require assurance that the balance sheet discloses all the liabilities of the company, ie that there are no undisclosed creditors who might also have a claim on the £1,120,000.

But pressing for liquidation may be excessively prudent. The bank is currently earning 10% interest on the £400,000 loan advance. there is a chance now to earn 13% interest on a £600,000 advance. This may well be a good lending proposition, but again certain assurances are needed:

(i)   The bank needs to know the true market values of the company's assets, particularly the land and buildings. This will permit an assessment of the extent to which the principal sum is at risk.

(ii)   The bank needs to investigate the claim that the company now has a profitable future ahead.

Conclusion
Assuming that the necessary assurances are obtained, it seems likely that the scheme of re-organisation may represent a good lending proposition for the bank.

Workings

1.   *Cash at bank*

The £80,000 £1 shares in issue are to be written down to 800,000 20p shares. The shares will then be consolidated: 800,000 20p shares will become 800,000/5 £1 shares, ie 160,000 £1 shares. The rights issue will be 160,000 x 2 ie 320,000 £1 shares, issued at par.

	£
Proceeds of rights issue (320,000 x £1)	320,000
Less payment to bank	87,000
Cash remaining at bank	£233,000

2.   *Called up share capital*

	£
Before rights issue *(working 1)*	160,000
Rights issue	320,000
Issued to creditor	180,000
	£660,000

11. GRASSINGTON

(a) Creditors' payment period $= \dfrac{160}{1,800} \times 360$ days

$= \underline{32 \text{ days}}$

Debtors collection period $= \dfrac{300}{2,700} \times 360$ days

$= \underline{40 \text{ days}}$

Stock turnover period $= \dfrac{305}{1,830} \times 360$ days

$= \underline{60 \text{ days}}$

(b) The cash operating cycle can be shown as follows:

Day 1 - purchase goods
Day 32 - pay supplier (creditors' payment period = 32 days)
Day 60 - sell goods (stock turnover period = 60 days)
Day 100 - collect cash (debtors collection period = 40 days)

Thus cash is collected from the customer on day 100, 68 days after the goods were paid for.

∴ Cash operating cycle = $\underline{68 \text{ days}}$

(c) To achieve a reduction of £20,000 in the overdraft the directors have the options of running down the investment in stocks or in debtors by the required amount, or increasing the credit taken from suppliers.

To show the effects of this procedure, debtors will be taken as an example, ie it is assumed that the directors will reduce the average debtors outstanding from £300,000 to £280,000.

This would mean enforcing a collection period of:

$\dfrac{280}{2,700} \times 360$ days $= 37.3$ days

This would lead to a reduction in the cash operating cycle of 2.7 days.

12. MANUFACTURING COMPANY

Tutorial note. The company is expecting changes in its working capital requirements to arise for two reasons:

(a) a reduction in credit periods and stockholding periods;
(b) an inflationary increase.

The procedure needed to calculate the revised working capital is:

(a) calculate the new credit periods and stockholding periods; then
(b) apply these periods to the inflation - adjusted figures for purchases and sales.

WORKING CAPITAL STATEMENT AS AT 30 JUNE 19X2

	£	£
Stock of raw materials *(working 1)*		86,770
Stock of finished goods *(working 2)*		48,773
		135,543
Debtors *(working 3)*		1,189,598
Bank/cash balances		50,000
Total current assets		1,375,141
Trade creditors *(working 4)*	86,770	
Expense creditors	15,000	
Provision for dividend (£40,000 x 115%)	46,000	
		147,770
Net working capital		£1,227,371

Workings

1 *Stock of raw materials*

Average days' stock for 19X0 and 19X1	30
10% reduction	3
No of days' stock for 19X2	27

Budgeted material purchases in 19X2	= £1,020,000
Revised for inflation (x 115%)	= £1,173,000
∴ Material stock at 30.6.X2	= 27/365 x £1,173,000
	= £86,770

2 *Stock of finished goods*

Average days' stock for 19X0 and 19X1	10
10% reduction	1
No of days' stock for 19X2	9

	£'000
Budgeted variable cost of sales for 19X2:	
Materials/labour	1,200
Variable overheads	520
	1,720
Inflation adjustment (15%)	258
	1,978

∴ Finished goods stock at 30.6.X2	= 9/365 x £1,978,000
	= £48,773

3   *Debtors*

Average days' sales in debtors for 19X0 and 19X1	80
10% reduction	8
No of days' sales in debtors at 30.6.X2	72

Budgeted sales for 19X2	=	£5,244,000
Revised for inflation	=	£6,030,600
∴ Debtors at 30.6.X2	=	72/365 x £6,030,600
	=	£1,189,598

4   *Trade creditors*

Average days in creditors for 19X0 and 19X1	30
10% reduction	3
Average days in creditors at 30.6.X2	27

Budgeted raw material purchases (inflation adjusted) for 19X2	=	£1,173,000 *(working 1)*
∴ Trade creditors at 30.6.X2	=	27/365 x £1,173,000
	=	£86,770

13.   DEEPDALE

Tutorial note. Deepdale Limited is planning to tie up funds both in additional working capital and in new fixed assets. Both elements need to be considered in assessing the additional investment required by the company. The planned increase in sales is 25%.

(a)   (i)   *Additional investment required*

	£'000	£'000
Working capital:		
Stocks (25% x £108,000)		27
Debtors: at 31.3.X6		
(125% x 150% x £80,000)	150	
at 31.3.X5	(80)	
increase		70
Cash (25% x £12,000)		3
Creditors (25% x £60,000)		(15)
		85
Fixed assets		110
		195

(ii)   *Funds generated from operations*

	£'000
Profit before interest charges	
(10% x £1,000,000)	100
Less interest (10% x £100,000)	(10)
Profit before tax	90
Adjustment for item not involving the movement of funds: depreciation	50
	140

(b) The planned build-up in working capital will presumably take place gradually over the year, but the new investment in fixed assets of £110,000 is scheduled to take place early in the year. A large proportion of the £195,000 additional investment is therefore required very soon. Since the company's £12,000 cash at bank is needed for day-to-day operations the only immediate source of finance is the temporary investments, which have a market value of £19,000.

Possible alternative sources of finance include:

(i)   the shareholder directors;
(ii) outside investors (including, possibly, a bank overdraft);
(iii) an increase in the credit period taken from suppliers.

The shareholder directors are presumably convinced that the expansion will be profitable and could contribute finance either gradually (by drawing lower salaries) or immediately (perhaps by a rights issue).

Outside investors would need to be convinced that the project would be profitable. The budgeted profit before tax and interest is £100,000 from which interest of £10,000 is currently being paid. With interest cover at a comfortable ten times one possibility would be the issue of further 10% debentures.

An issue of £60,000 would lead to a debt/equity ratio of 1:1 beyond which the company might consider it inadvisable to go. The interest payable is allowable for tax and the after-tax cost of the new finance would therefore be only 6%. Alternatively a new share issue might be tempting to outside investors who wished for an equity share in the profitable expansion. From the directors' point of view this would have the disadvantage of diluting their control of the company.

An increase in the credit period taken from suppliers carries the risk that the suppliers may find it unacceptable and withhold supplies completely. Nevertheless, the investment in working capital as a whole is an area which might bear further investigation. The directors have simply assumed an increase in proportion to the increase in sales but it may be that the current levels of stocks and debtors are higher than necessary and could be reduced without detriment.

The budgeted cash profit of £140,000 will of course contribute only gradually to the additional investment required.

14. GREENHAYES

(a) CASH BUDGET FOR THE SIX MONTHS TO 31 MARCH 19X5

	◄——19X4——►			◄——19X5——►		
Receipts	Oct £	Nov £	Dec £	Jan £	Feb £	Mar £
Sales			10,000	10,000	10,000	10,000
Payments						
Purchases	4,000	4,000	4,000	4,000	4,000	4,000
Wages	3,000	3,000	3,000	3,000	3,000	3,000
Salaries	1,300	1,300	1,300	1,300	1,300	1,300
Factory overhead	500	500	500	500	500	500
Office and selling expenses	100	100	100	100	100	100
Total	8,900	8,900	8,900	8,900	8,900	8,900
Surplus/(shortfall)	(8,900)	(8,900)	1,100	1,100	1,100	1,100
Opening balance	6,400	(2,500)	(11,400)	(10,300)	(9,200)	(8,100)
Closing balance	£(2,500)	£(11,400)	£(10,300)	£(9,200)	£(8,100)	£(7,000)

(b)

FORECAST MANUFACTURING TRADING AND PROFIT AND LOSS ACCOUNTS FOR THE SIX MONTHS ENDED 31 MARCH 19X5

	£	£
Raw materials		
Purchases (7 x £4,000)	28,000	
Closing stock	(4,000)	
		24,000
Direct wages (6 x £3,000)		18,000
Prime cost (= £14 per unit produced)		42,000
Indirect factory expenses		
Depreciation of plant (£8,000 x 25% x 6/12)	1,000	
Factory rental (£1,600 x 3/4)	1,200	
Production director's salary	4,800	
Factory overhead	3,000	
		10,000
Factory cost of goods produced		£52,000
Sales (5 x £10,000)		50,000
Cost of sales		
Factory cost of goods produced	52,000	
Closing stock of finished goods (500 x £14)	(7,000)	
		45,000
Gross profit		5,000
Expenses		
Office rental (£1,600 x 1/4)	400	
Managing director's salary	3,000	
Office and selling expenses	600	
		4,000
Net profit		£1,000

144

FORECAST BALANCE SHEET
AS AT 31 MARCH 19X5

	£	£
Fixed assets		
Plant at net book value		7,000
Current assets		
Stocks (£4,000 + £7,000)	11,000	
Debtors (March sales)	10,000	
		21,000
		28,000
Current liabilities		
Bank overdraft	7,800	
Trade creditors (March purchases)	4,000	
		(11,000)
Total assets less current liabilities		£17,000
Share capital and reserves		
Share capital		16,000
Profit and loss account		1,000
		£17,000

(c) The company is forecast to achieve a profit of £1,000 on turnover of £50,000 for the six month period. The rate of return on capital employed is 1,000/16,000 x 12/6 = 12.5% per annum. This is despite a very low rate of gross profit (5,000/50,000 = 10% on sales).

If the stock of finished goods were valued in accordance with SSAP 9, a proportion of the production expenses would be included in the valuation. The new stock value would be £4,000 + 500/3,000 x £52,000 = £12,667 compared with £11,000, an increase in forecast profit of £1,667. The new rate of gross profit (£6,667 ÷ £50,000) would be 13.3%, the new net profit would be £2,667 and the rate of return on capital employed would be £2,667/£16,000 x 12/6 = 33.3%. The raised stock valuation would of course have no effect on the overdraft position since it is purely a bookkeeping adjustment.

The maximum overdraft level would be £11,400, occurring at the end of November. Assuming the correctness of the forecasts and that the same pattern continued beyond March this level would then reduce steadily at the rate of £1,100, except that in April and October payments will presumably have to be made for rent.

15. KENDAL

(a)

FORECAST BALANCE SHEET
AS AT 31 MARCH 19X5

	£'000	£'000
Fixed assets		
Cost (920 + 270)		1,190
Depreciation (170 + 130)		300
		890
Current assets		
Stocks (350 x 150%)	525	
Trade debtors (320 x 150% x 125%)	600	
	1,125	
Current liabilities		
Bank overdraft (balancing figure)	90	
Trade creditors (200 x 150%)	300	
Corporation tax* (180 + 16)	196	
	586	
Net current assets		539
Total assets less current liabilities		1,429
Capital and reserves		
Share capital		1,000
Profit and loss account:		
Balance at 1 April 19X4	205	
Profit for year	224	
		429
		1,429

*The tax liability brought forward at 1 April 19X4 will have been paid on 1 January 19X5. The tax liability at 31 March 19X5 is assumed to be equal to the tax charge for the year, which consists of £180,000 on trading operations and £16,000 on the extraordinary gain on disposal of investments.

(b) The overdraft requirement at 1 June 19X4 can be computed by calculating the amount of additional investment required in both fixed assets (new plant to be purchased in May) and working capital (assumed to take effect from 1 June). This additional investment will be financed from four sources:

(i)   funds generated from operations;
(ii)   proceeds of sale of investments in May;
(iii) the existing bank balances;
(iv)   bank overdraft.

The calculation is as follows:

	£'000	£'000
Purchase of plant		270
Investment in working capital:		
Stocks (525 - 350)	175	
Debtors (600 - 320)	280	
Creditors (200 - 300)	(100)	
		355
Additional investment required		625
Less funded from:		
Operations	60	
Sale of investments (70+24+16)	110	
Existing bank balance	35	
		205
Balance to be funded from overdraft		£420

It is clear that the company's overdraft will be at its maximum on 1 June. Afterwards the increased profits generated will enable the overdraft to be gradually run down, to the level of £90,000 on 31 March 19X5 if the forecasts are correct.

The position disclosed by the forecast balance sheet at 31 March 19X5 appears satisfactory. The current ratio is 1.9:1 (1,125/586) and the quick ratio is 1.0:1. The forecast return on capital employed is a healthy 15.7% (224/1,429), although this does not take account of the interest payable on bank overdraft.

This assessment of course depends on the accuracy of the assumptions used in the forecast. In particular:

(i) is it certain that the market exists for the additional 50% capacity which is scheduled to be produced?

(ii) has it been ascertained that the additional labour requirement will be available by 1 June? If part or all of the additional labour is to be supplied by the existing workforce, has account been taken in the profit forecast of any overtime premium which may be payable? If new employees are to be taken on, has consideration been given to the need for staff training and any delays which it may cause?

(iii) is it certain that the investments can be realised (at short notice) for £40,000 in excess of their cost?

16. BLAIR

Tutorial note. The main difficulty in this question concerns the cost of sales. We know from note (d) to the question that the cost of sales = 2/3 x sales.

	£	£	£	£	£	£
Sales	3,000	6,000	6,000	10,500	10,500	10,500
∴ Cost of sales	2,000	4,000	4,000	7,000	7,000	7,000

Each month's purchases amount to the cost of sales for that month (note (b)) and are paid for in the following month.

(a)   CASH FORECAST FOR THE SIX MONTHS ENDING 31 MARCH 19X4

	Oct £	*Nov* £	*Dec* £	*Jan* £	*Feb* £	*Mar* £
Payments						
Suppliers	5,000	2,000	4,000	4,000	7,000	7,000
Running expenses	1,600	1,600	1,600	1,600	1,600	1,600
Drawings	1,000	1,000	1,000	1,000	1,000	1,00
	7,600	4,600	6,600	6,600	9,600	9,600
Receipts						
Debtors	-	-	3,000	6,000	6,000	10,500
Surplus/(shortfall)	(7,600)	(4,600)	(3,600)	(600)	(3,600)	900
Opening balance*	7,000	(600)	(5,200)	(8,800)	(9,400)	(13,000)
Closing balance	£(600)	£(5,200)	£(8,800)	£(9,400)	£(13,000)	£(12,100)

*The opening balance for October consists of the £15,000 building society money, less £8,000 expended on fixed assets in September.

(b)   FORECAST TRADING AND PROFIT AND LOSS ACCOUNT
FOR THE SIX MONTHS ENDING 31 MARCH 19X4

	£	£
Sales £(3,000 + (2 x 6,000) + (3 x 10,500))		46,500
Cost of sales (2/3 x £46,500)		31,000
Gross profit		15,500
Expenses:		
Running expenses (6 x £1,600)	9,600	
Depreciation (£8,000 x 20% x 6/12)	800	
		10,400
Net profit		£5,100

FORECAST BALANCE SHEET AT 31 MARCH 19X4

	£	£
Fixed assets (£8,000 - £800)		7,200
Current assets:		
Stocks	5,000	
Debtors (Feb, March sales)	21,000	
	26,000	
Current liabilities:		
Bank overdraft	12,100	
Trade creditors (March purchases)	7,000	
	19,100	
		6,900
		£14,100
Proprietor's interest:		
Capital introduced		15,000
Profit for the period	5,100	
Less drawings	6,000	
		(900)
		£14,100

(c) The results for Blair's first six months of trading do not seem encouraging. His overdraft requirement reaches its highest level (£13,000) at the end of February, by which time the 'capital' provided by the bank will very nearly equal the amount originally contributed by Blair himself. Profits for the period are only £5,100 which is exceeded by the amount Blair expects to withdraw from the business.

The reduction in the overdraft predicted for March points the way to a silver lining. If sales are maintained at the level of £10,500 per month the figures for the first year of trading look more hopeful.

FORECAST TRADING AND PROFIT AND LOSS ACCOUNT
FOR THE YEAR ENDED 31 MARCH 19X4

	£	£
Sales:		
Oct–March	46,500	
April–Sept (6 x £10,500)	63,000	
		109,500
Cost of sales (2/3 x £109,500)		73,000
Gross profit		36,500
Expenses:		
Running expenses (12 x £1,600)	19,200	
Depreciation (£8,000 x 20%)	1,600	
		20,800
		£15,700

Of this £12,000 will have been withdrawn by Blair and of course no account has been taken of any overdraft interest payable. In March and each subsequent month cash inflows will exceed outflows by £900, leading to elimination of the overdraft by May 19X5.

17. KEHL

Tutorial note. As usual, it is important not to skimp on the discussion part of the question (part (c)). Preparing the financial statements is only the beginning: students must show that they can interpret their significance to a potential lender.

(a) QUARTERLY CASH FORECAST FOR 19X6

	Qtr 1 £	Qtr 2 £	Qtr 3 £	Qtr 4 £
Cash receipts				
Advance payments (1)	15,000	15,000	15,000	15,000
Completion payments (2)	20,000	45,000	45,000	45,000
New capital	6,000	-	-	-
	41,000	60,000	60,000	60,000
Cash payments				
Raw materials (3)	20,000	18,000	18,000	18,000
Other direct costs (4)	27,000	27,000	27,000	27,000
Other indirect costs (5)	3,000	3,000	3,000	3,000
Directors' remuneration (6)	7,500	7,500	7,500	7,500
Taxation (7)	-	-	1,800	-
	57,500	55,500	57,300	55,500
(Deficit)/surplus for quarter	(16,500)	4,500	2,700	4,500
Opening balance	2,000	(14,500)	(10,000)	(7,300)
Closing balance	£(14,500)	£(10,000)	£(7,300)	£(2,800)

Notes:

1   125% x 3 months x £20,000 per month

2.   1st quarter : 50% x £40,000
     2nd, 3rd and 4th quarters : 75% x 3 months x £20,000 per month

3.   1st quarter : £4,000 (creditor b/f) + £10,000 (January purchases)
          plus £6,000 (February purchases)
     2nd, 3rd and 4th quarters : 3 x £6,000

4.   3/12 x £108,000

5.   3/12 x £12,000

6.   3/12 x £30,000

7.   Taxation: the only tax payable during the year is the £1,800 19X5 liability, payable on 1 October 19X6. The 19X6 liability will be paid in 19X7.

(b)

FORECAST BALANCE SHEET AS AT 31 DECEMBER 19X6

	£	£
Fixed assets		
Plant and equipment £(20,000 - 2,000)		18,000
Current assets		
Stocks of materials	12,000	
Work in progress	45,000	
	57,000	
Current liabilities		
Bank overdraft	2,800	
Trade creditors (December purchases)	6,000	
Taxation (30% x £11,000)	3,300	
Advance payments from customers	15,000	
	27,100	
Net current assets		29,900
Total assets less current liabilities		£47,900
Capital and reserves		
Share capital £(30,000 + 6,000)		36,000
Retained profit:		
Balance at 1 January 19X5	4,200	
Retained profit for year £(11,000 - 3,300)	7,700	
Balance at 31 December 19X5		11,900
		£47,900

(c)

REPORT TO X BANK PLC : KEHL LIMITED FORECAST ACCOUNTS

Introduction

In 19X5, its first year of trading, Kehl Ltd made a net profit of £6,000 after charging directors' remuneration of £20,000. The directors are now proposing a change in the payment terms offered to customers which they hope will lead to a substantial increase in sales. A quarterly cash forecast for 19X6, a forecast profit and loss account for 19X6, and a forecast balance sheet at 31 December 19X6 have been submitted to the bank.

Assessment of Kehl's proposals and prospects

The forecast financial statements show a significant improvement on the results for 19X5: a profit before directors' remuneration of £41,000 compared with £26,000 in 19X5.

The proposals will lead initially to a large increase in work in progress (arising from the more generous payment terms) and a smaller increase in materials stocks. The effect of this will be to create an adverse cash position of £20,500 by the end of March 19X6, of which £6,000 will be made good by a new injection of capital from the directors. An overdraft of £14,500 is therefore expected at 31 March.

From April onwards the increased volume of business will lead to large receipts in completion payments and the overdraft position will improve, falling to £2,800 by the end of the year. If forecasts are met, the overdraft will be eliminated early in 19X7.

Conclusion

If the directors' assumptions are well founded the company's forecast position appears very healthy. Only two unfavourable points need to be made:

(i)   If a more generous payment profile is offered to customers an increase in bad debts may result.

(ii) An additional cost of £6,500 per annum for rates will be incurred for the first time in 19X7.

18. DODD

Tutorial note. This is a confusing question; students are apparently required *not* to deduct loan interest payable from net profit because it is not paid until 31 December. In other words, the question requires us to calculate the surplus funds generated by 31 December from which the interest is to be paid.

The phrase 'cash generated surplus to working capital requirements' is difficult to understand but apparently means the same as 'increase in net liquid funds' in a conventional funds statement.

(a)   FORECAST FUNDS STATEMENT FOR 19X6

	£	£
Net profit (£20,000 x 160%)		32,000
Adjustment for non-cash items: depreciation		8,000
Total generated from operations		40,000
Other source of funds: bank loan		35,000
Total sources of funds		75,000
Application of funds		
Purchase of fixed assets	24,000	
Increase in working capital	11,000	
Drawings	28,000	
		63,000
Cash generated surplus to working capital requirements		12,000

(b) The £12,000 cash surplus is said to accrue evenly over the year. Therefore the average balance on deposit account throughout the year is £6,000. Interest earned at 8% is therefore £480.

(c)   FORECAST BALANCE SHEET AS AT 31 DECEMBER 19X6

	£	£
Fixed assets		
£(40,000 + 24,000 - 8,000)		56,000
Working capital		36,000
Deposit account £(12,000 + 480 - 12% x 35,000)		8,280
Total assets		100,280
Bank loan		(35,000)
		£65,280

Capital		
At 1 January 19X6		65,000
Profit for year:		
From trading	32,000	
Interest receivable less payable £(480 - 4,200)	3,720	
	28,280	
Less drawings	28,000	
Retained profit for year		280
At 31 December 19X6		£65,280

(d) Bank borrowing is the cheaper option for Dodd. The bank loan carries interest at only 12%, whereas the cost of selling his private assets is the 15% interest that he would forfeit. The saving amounts to 3% x £35,000 - £1,050.

19. LISTER

Tutorial note. Part (a) is a straightforward funds statement but it is less easy to see that a forecast funds statement can also be used as a simple approach to part (c). In part (b) you should begin by calculating appropriate ratios and then build up a discussion based on your ratios and on your answer to part (a).

(a)
STATEMENT OF SOURCE AND APPLICATION OF FUNDS
FOR THE YEAR ENDED 30 JUNE 19X6

	£'000	£'000	£'000
Profit before tax			295
Adjustment for items not involving the movement of funds:			
Depreciation (1,100 - 800)		300	
Amortisation of advertising costs		50	
			350
Total generated from operations			645
Other source of funds: loan			800
Total source of funds			1,445
Application of funds			
Payment of tax (77 + 88 - 88)		77	
Payment of dividends (100 + 150 - 150)		100	
Purchase of fixed assets		1,000	
			1,177
			268
Movements in working capital			
Increase in stock and work in progress		140	
Increase in debtors		563	
Increase in creditors and accruals		(107)	
		596	
Movement in net liquid funds:			
Decrease in cash at bank and in hand	35		
Increase in overdraft	293		
		328	
			268

(b) *Solvency ratios*

	19X6		*19X5*
Interest cover:	472/177	= 2.67 times	–
Current ratio:	1,603/858	= 1.87	2.36
Quick ratio :	1,163/858	= 1.36	2.27
Gearing:	800/(800 + 1,945)	= 29.1%	–

Asset turnover ratio

Fixed asset turnover	6,750/1,900	= 3.6 times	3.75 times
Stock turnover	6,750/440	= 15.3 times	15 times

Discussion

Profit before interest and tax has more than doubled in 19X6 (£472,000 compared with £225,000) and profit after tax also shows a healthy 40% increase (£207,000 compared with £148,000). This has enabled a 50% increase in dividends to be paid, while still remaining the level of retained profits. Interest payments are covered by profits before interest nearly three times.

The company's internally generated funds amount to £645,000 for the year which amply covers its tax and dividend payments. Eventually generated funds comprise the £800,000 loan which has been used to finance most of the fixed assets purchases (£1,000,000 in the year). The funds statement shows a comfortable increase of £268,000 in working capital.

The company's net liquid funds have fallen from a credit position of £35,000 at 30 June 19X5 to an overdraft of £293,000. The overdraft in effect has financed much of the very large investment in debtors. Debtors' balances have risen by £563,000 over the year as a consequence of the increased volume of business.

The expansion in the company's activities has transformed its balance sheet. Of the long-term capital tied up in the business, 29.1% is now provided externally. The large overdraft also represents external financing. In 19X5, all long-term finance had been provided by shareholders. The current ratio and quick ratio have also been affected: down from 2.36 to 1.87 and from 2.27 to 1.36 respectively. But neither ratio is at a dangerous level.

The new assets purchased have been worked almost as hard as those already held in 19X5. Fixed asset turnover has shown a slight fall from 3.75 times to 3.6 times, but stock turnover has increased from 15 times to 15.3 times.

(c) The simplest way to approach this part of the question is to prepare an estimated funds statement for the year ending 30 June 19X7.

ESTIMATED STATEMENT OF SOURCE AND APPLICATION OF FUNDS
FOR THE YEAR ENDED 30 JUNE 19X7

	£'000	£'000
Funds generated from operations		645
Application of funds		
Tax	88	
Dividends	150	
Purchase of fixed assets	120	
		359
Increase in working capital		287

Assuming there are no significant changes in the levels of stock, debtors and creditors this £287,000 would represent the improvement in Lister Ltd's cash position. In that case it would very nearly have repaid the £293,000 overdraft by 30 June 19X7. But there are several reservations to this:

(i) It has been assumed that the 19X6 level of sales can be maintained without repeating the £150,000 of advertising expenditure incurred during June 19X5.

(ii) It has been assumed that interest payable will be the same as in the year to June 19X6. The 12% loan interest of course is constant, but the overdraft interest may be more or less than in the previous year.

(iii) On 1 July 19X7 the company must make a £200,000 loan repayment and will presumably require a new overdraft to finance it.

20. ROKER

(a)

CASH BUDGET FOR THE TWELVE MONTHS ENDING 30 JUNE 19X6

	Jul £	Aug £	Sept £	Oct £	Nov £	Dec £	Jan £	Feb £	Mar £	Apr £	May £	Jun £
Cash payments												
Purchases		6,000	4,500		4,500		4,500		4,500		4,500	
Advertising	150	150	150	150	150	150	150	150	150	150	150	150
Rate	150			300						300		
Other operating expenses	200	200	200	200	200	200	200	200	200	200	200	200
Drawings	700	700	700	700	700	700	700	700	700	700	700	700
	1,200	7,050	5,550	1,350	5,550	1,050	5,550	1,050	5,550	1,350	5,550	1,050
Cash receipts												
Sales	—	—	2,000	2,000	5,000	5,000	5,000	5,000	5,000	5,000	5,000	5,000
Net (deficit)/ surplus	(1,200)	(7,050)	(3,550)	650	(550)	3,950	(550)	3,950	(550)	3,650	(550)	3,950
Opening balance	2,000	800	(6,250)	(9,800)	(9,150)	(9,700)	(5,750)	(6,300)	(2,350)	(2,900)	750	200
Closing balance	£ 800	(6,250)	(9,800)	(9,150)	(9,700)	(5,750)	(6,300)	(2,350)	(2,900)	750	200	4,150

SUGGESTED SOLUTIONS

(b) **ESTIMATED PROFIT STATEMENT FOR THE YEAR TO 30 JUNE 19X6**

	£	£
Sales (2 x £2,000) + (9 x £5,000)		49,000
Less cost of sales:		
Purchases £(6,000 + (6 x 4,500)	33,000	
Less closing stock (bal fig)	8,500	
		24,500
Gross profit (100/200 x £49,000)		24,500
Less expenses:		
Amortisation of lease (1/10 x £15,000)	1,500	
Depreciation of van (1/4 x £3,000)	750	
Advertising	1,800	
Rates	600	
Other operating expenses	2,400	
		(7,050)
Net profit for the year		£17,450

(c) **RECONCILIATION BETWEEN ESTIMATED CASH SURPLUS AND ESTIMATED PROFIT**

	£	£
Net profit for the year		17,450
Add back items not involving cash expenditure:		
Amortisation		1,500
Depreciation		750
Cash generated from operations		19,700
Increase in credit taken from suppliers		4,500
		24,200
Applied as follows:		
Drawings	8,400	
Increase in debtors	5,000	
Increase in prepayments	150	
Increase in stock	8,500	
		22,050
Increase in cash (£4,150 - £2,000)		£2,150

(d) Roker's estimates suggest a profitable enterprise with net profits amounting to over £17,000 in the first year. His overdraft requirement peaks at £9,800 in September and from December onwards begins to fall quickly. By the end of his first year's trading he expects to be £4,150 in the black, although this does not allow for bank charges and overdraft interest.

Many of Roker's assumptions would need to be looked at closely before the required overdraft facility was granted. In particular, the increase in sales which he expects from November onwards does not arise from any increase in the advertising budget and it is not clear what justification he has for assuming a sudden jump from £2,000 to £5,000.

Roker's drawings are at the rate of £700 per month, less then half of the average monthly net profits. This retention of profits in the business will lead to a reasonably strong balance sheet position at the end of the year. The net worth of the business at that stage will be as follows:

		£	£
Opening capital			20,000
Add: net profit for the year		17,450	
less drawings		8,400	
			9,050
			£29,050

21. SHEDFORD

(a) CASH BUDGET FOR 19X7

	Qtr 1 £	Qtr 2 £	Qtr 3 £	Qtr 4 £
Receipts				
From customers (W1)	202,500	218,000	247,000	241,000
Payments				
To City Council	60,000	–	–	–
To suppliers (W2)	132,000	155,000	165,000	155,000
Wages	18,500	19,500	19,500	20,500
Directors' remuneration	7,500	7,500	7,500	7,500
Other expenses	36,000	33,000	35,000	32,000
	254,000	215,000	227,000	215,000
Surplus/(deficit) for the month	(51,500)	3,000	20,000	26,000
Opening balance b/f	1,500	(50,000)	(50,000)	(30,000)
	(50,000)	(47,000)	(30,000)	(4,000)
Interest charges:				
12% x $\frac{6}{12}$ x £50,000		(3,000)		
12% x $\frac{6}{12}$ x £30,000				(1,800)
Closing balance c/f	(50,000)	(50,000)	(30,000)	(5,800)

(b) FORECAST PROFIT AND LOSS ACCOUNT
FOR THE YEAR ENDING 31 DECEMBER 19X7

	£	£
Sales		910,000
Opening stock	172,000	
Purchases	615,000	
	787,000	
Less closing stock	180,000	
Cost of goods sold		607,000
Gross profit		303,000
Directors' remuneration	30,000	
Wages	78,000	
Depreciation	31,000	
Bank interest	4,800	
Other expenses	136,000	
		279,800
Profit before tax		23,200
Tax @ 30%		6,960
Retained profit for the year		16,240
Profits brought forward		379,000
Profits carried forward		395,240

(c) FORECAST BALANCE SHEET AS AT 31 DECEMBER 19X7

	£	£
Fixed assets		
Cost less depreciation at 1 January 19X9	425,000	
Two new shops	120,000	
Less depreciation charge for the year	(31,000)	
Cost less depreciation at 31 December 19X9		514,000
Current assets		
Stock	180,000	
Debtors (W1)	24,000	
	204,000	
Creditors: amounts falling due within one year		
Bank overdraft	5,800	
Trade creditors ($\frac{1}{3}$ x £150,000)	50,000	
Taxation	6,960	
City Council	60,000	
	122,760	
Net current assets		81,240
Total assets less current liabilities		595,240
Capital and reserves		
Share capital		200,000
Reserves		395,240
		595,240
Capital and reserves		
Share capital		200,000
Reserves		395,240
		595,240

(d) The best approach to this part of the question is to continue the cash budget into 19X8.

CASH BUDGET FOR 19X8

	Qtr 1 £	Qtr 2 £	Qtr 3 £	Qtr 4 £
Receipts				
From customers (W3)	204,000	218,000	247,000	241,000
Payments				
To City Council	60,000	–	–	–
To suppliers (W4)	140,000	155,000	165,000	155,000
Wages	18,500	19,500	19,500	20,500
Directors' remuneration	7,500	7,500	7,500	7,500
Other expenses	36,000	33,000	35,000	32,000
	262,000	215,000	227,000	215,000
Surplus/(deficit) for the month	(58,000)	3,000	20,000	26,000
Opening balance b/f	5,800	(63,800)	(64,628)	(44,628)
	63,800	(60,800)	(44,628)	(18,628)
Interest charges:				
12% x $\frac{6}{12}$ x £63,800		(3,828)		
12% x $\frac{6}{12}$ x £44,628				(2,678)
Closing balance c/f	63,800	(64,628)	(44,628)	(21,306)

At the end of 19X8, the overdraft will be £21,306. This will be reduced in 19X9 as follows:

	£
Quarter 1 cash surplus (no £60,000 payment)	2,000
Quarter 2 cash surplus (excluding interest)	3,000
Quarter 3 cash surplus	20,000
	25,000

Even allowing for interest charges in June 19X9, it is clear that the overdraft will be repaid approximately by the end of September 19X9.

Workings

1. *Cash receipts in 19X7*

	Qtr 1 £	Qtr 2 £	Qtr 3 £	Qtr 4 £
Opening balance due from credit card companies	22,500	20,000	22,000	25,000
Sales in period (A)	200,000	220,000	250,000	240,000
	222,500	240,000	272,000	265,000
Closing balance due from credit card companies (10% x A)	20,000	22,000	25,000	24,000
∴ Cash received in period	202,500	218,000	247,000	241,000

2. *Payments to suppliers in 19X7*

	£
Quarter 1: £(42,000 + ⅓ x £135,000)	132,000
Quarter 2: £(⅓ x £135,000 + ⅔ x £165,000)	155,000
Quarter 3: £(⅓ x £165,000 + ⅔ x £165,000)	165,000
Quarter 4: £(⅓ x £165,000 + ⅔ x £150,000)	155,000
	607,000

3. *Cash receipts in 19X8*

	Qtr 1 £	Qtr 2 £	Qtr 3 £	Qtr 4 £
Opening balance due from credit card companies	24,000	20,000	22,000	25,000
Sales in period (A)	200,000	220,000	250,000	240,000
	224,000	240,000	272,000	265,000
Closing balance due from credit card companies (10% x A)	20,000	22,000	25,000	24,000
∴ Cash received in period	204,000	218,000	247,000	241,000

4. *Payments to suppliers in 19X8*

	£
Quarter 1: £(50,000 + ⅓ x £135,000)	140,000
Quarter 2: as for 19X7	155,000
Quarter 3: as for 19X7	165,000
Quarter 4: as for 19X7	155,000
	615,000

22. SHELTON

Tutorial note. The main problem with the funds statement for 19X4/X5 is the treatment of the extraordinary item. In most cases it would be appropriate to add the extraordinary profit (net of tax) to the figure for profit before tax in arriving at the total generated from operations. In this case, however, the extraordinary profit is an item not involving the movement of funds, being the profit on disposal of fixed assets and investments:

	£
Disposal proceeds (balancing figure)	16,000
Less cost	11,000
Gross gain on disposal	5,000
Less taxation	1,500
Net gain on disposal	£3,500

The disposal proceeds will of course be shown as a source of funds. The net gain on disposal, £3,500 may be either:

(a) excluded from the statement altogether; or

(b) added to profit before tax and later deducted as an item not involving the movement of funds. This method is more informative and should be preferred.

(a) (i)   **STATEMENT OF SOURCE AND APPLICATION OF FUNDS**
           FOR THE YEAR ENDED 30 JUNE 19X5

	£	£
Source of funds		
Profit before tax		33,600
Add extraordinary item		3,500
		37,100
Adjustment for items not involving the movement of funds:		
Depreciation of plant £(75,000−40,000)	35,000	
Profit on disposal of fixed assets	(3,500)	
		31,500
Total generated from operations		68,600
Other sources of funds		
Bank loan	60,000	
Proceeds from sale of investments	16,000	
		76,000
Total source of funds		144,600
Application of funds		
Taxation paid *(working 1)*	10,000	
Dividend paid *(working 2)*	15,000	
Purchase of plant	100,000	
		(125,000)
Increase in working capital		£19,600
Movements in working capital		
Increase in stock and work in progress	31,000	
Increase in debtors and prepayments	13,000	
Increase in creditors and accruals	(9,000)	
		35,000
Movement in net liquid funds:		
Decrease in bank balance		(15,400)
Increase in working capital		£19,600

(ii)   Pre-tax rate of return on shareholders' equity

$$\frac{£33,600}{£144,000} = 23.3\%$$

(iii) Liquidity ratio at 30 June 19X5

$$\frac{£(74,000 + 41,000 + 1,600)}{£(60,000 + 24,000 + 15,100 + 15,000)} = 0.37:1$$

Shelton Limited appears to be a profitable company with a healthy balance sheet. The expansion in 19X4/X5, involving new fixed asset acquisitions of £100,000, was financed partly by new medium-term capital (£60,000 bank loan) and partly by the disposal of fixed asset investments. The balance came from funds generated from operations, which amounted to £68,600. Even after paying tax of £10,000 and maintaining the dividend level at £15,000 this was sufficient to finance an increase in working capital of £19,600. The pre-tax rate of return on shareholders' equity was a respectable 23.3%. But there may be short-term liquidity problems: the liquidity ratio is only 0.37:1.

SUGGESTED SOLUTIONS

Workings

1   *Taxation paid in year*

	£	£
Liability at 30 June 19X4		10,000
Add charge for the year:		
On ordinary activities	13,600	
On extraordinary items	1,500	
		15,100
		25,100
Less liability still unpaid at 30 June 19X5		15,100
Tax paid in year		£10,000

2   *Dividends paid in year*

	£
Proposed dividend at 30 June 19X4	15,000
P & L appropriation for year	15,000
	30,000
Less proposed dividend at 30 June 19X5	15,000
Dividend paid in year	£15,000

(b)   (i)

FORECAST STATEMENT OF SOURCE AND APPLICATION OF FUNDS
FOR THE YEAR ENDED 30 JUNE 19X6

	£	£
Source of funds		
Profit before tax *(working 1)*		50,750
Adjustment for item not involving the movement of funds:		
Depreciation of plant		35,000
Total generated from operations		85,750
Application of funds		
Taxation paid (19X4/X5 liability)	15,100	
Dividend paid (19X4/X5 proposed)	15,000	
Loan repayments	60,000	
		(90,100)
Decrease in working capital		£(4,350)
Movements in working capital		
Decrease in stock and work in progress	(9,000)	
Debtors/creditors unchanged	-	
Movement in net liquid funds:		
Increase in bank balance	4,650	
		£(4,350)

(ii)   Estimated pre-tax rate of return on shareholders' equity

$$\frac{£50,750}{£152,500} = 33.3\% \ (working \ 1)$$

(iii)   Liquidity ratio at 30 June 19X6 *(working 2)*

$$\frac{£(41,000 + 6,250)}{£57,000} = 1.83:1$$

The prospects for 19X5/X6 look encouraging. The new plant will be fully operational throughout the year and this is expected to lead to a substantial increase in operating profits. Forecast pre-tax rate of return on shareholders' equity is expected to show a steep rise to 33.5%. Funds generated from operations (£85,750) will be very nearly sufficient to repay the bank loan as well as paying tax of £15,100 and maintaining the dividend level. The small deficiency of £4,350 will be more than offset by the planned £9,000 reduction in stock and work in progress, so that the cash balance will actually rise over the year by £4,650. The current ratio will have weakened only slightly to 1.97:1 by 30 June 19X6.

One point not apparent from the funds statement is that there will be a temporary cash shortage during the quarter from 1 April 19X6 to 30 June 19X6, owing to the need to pay both taxation and dividends during March. This can be illustrated as follows (assuming that funds generated from operations accrue evenly over the year).

	1.7.X5 – 30.9.X5	1.10.X5 – 31.12.X5	1.1.X6 – 31.3.X6	1.4.X6 – 30.6.X6
	£	£	£	£
Opening cash balance	1,600	10,287	18,975	(2,438)
Funds generated from operations	21,437	21,438	21,437	21,438
Reduction in investment in stock	2,250	2,250	2,250	2,250
	25,287	33,975	42,662	21,250
Loan repayments	(15,000)	(15,000)	(15,000)	(15,000)
Taxation paid			(15,100)	
Dividend paid			(15,000)	
Closing cash balance	£10,287	£18,975	£(2,438)	£6,250

Workings

1   *Forecast profit and loss account 19X5/X6*

	£
Operating profits for 19X4/X5	42,000
Less profits for first 6 months of 19X4/X5 (1/3)	14,000
Profits for second 6 months of 19X4/X5	£28,000
Operating profits for 19X5/X6 (2 x £28,000)	56,000
Less interest payable	(5,250)
Profit before tax for 19X5/X6	50,750
Taxation	(18,000)
Profit after tax	32,750
Proposed dividend	(15,000)
Retained profit	£17,750

2   *Forecast balance sheet at 30 June 19X6*

	£	£
Fixed assets		
Plant and machinery £(125,000 – 35,000)	90,000	
Freehold property	25,000	
		115,000
Current assets		
Stock and work in progress	65,000	
Debtors and prepayments	41,000	
Cash and bank (balancing figure)	6,250	
	112,250	
Current liabilities		
Creditors and accruals	24,000	
Taxation	18,000	
Proposed dividend	15,000	
	57,000	
Net current assets		55,250
		£170,250
Capital and reserves		
Ordinary shares		100,000
Reserves £(52,500 + 17,750)		70,250
		£170,250

23. CHADWICK

(a) (i)   STATEMENT OF CASH RECEIPTS AND PAYMENTS
FOR THE YEAR ENDED 31 DECEMBER 19X4

	£	£
Receipts		
From customers		63,500
Loan from friend		2,000
		65,600
Payments		
To suppliers	37,600	
Interest paid on loan	150	
Purchase of plant	8,000	
General expenses	7,300	
Cash drawings	12,000	
		65,050
Net increase in cash balance		£450

(ii)   TRADING AND PROFIT AND LOSS ACCOUNT
                      FOR THE YEAR ENDED 31 DECEMBER 19X4

	£	£
Sales *(working 1)*		64,100
Less cost of sales:		
Opening stock	7,800	
Purchases *(working 2)*	38,050	
	45,850	
Less closing stock	11,000	
		(34,850)
Gross profit		29,250
Expenses:		
Depreciation	6,100	
Interest	150	
General expenses	7,300	
		13,550
Net profit for the year		£15,700

(iii) *Tutorial note.* You may be confused by the term 'sources and applications of working capital'. Essentially however, such a statement is no different from a source and application of funds statement. SSAP10, although it does not provide a definition of 'funds', appears to imply a statement of changes in working capital.

STATEMENT OF SOURCE AND APPLICATION OF WORKING CAPITAL
FOR THE YEAR ENDED 31 DECEMBER 19X4

	£	£
Sales *(working 1)*		64,100
Loan from friend		2,000
		66,100
Cost of sales	34,850	
Cash expenses	7,450	
Drawings	12,000	
		(54,300)
		11,800
Less investment in fixed assets		(8,000)
Net increase in working capital		
£(12,600 *(working 3)* – 8,800)		£3,800

(b)

RECONCILIATION OF PROFIT AND NET CHANGE IN CASH BALANCE

	£	£
Net profit for the year		15,700
Adjustment for item not involving the movement of funds:		
Depreciation		6,100
Funds generated from operations		21,800
Loan from friend		2,000
Total funds generated		£23,800
Funds withdrawn by Chadwick		12,000
Funds invested in fixed assets		8,000
Funds invested in increase in working capital		
Increase in stock	3,200	
Increase in debtors	600	
Increase in creditors	(450)	
		3,350
		23,350
Balance of funds generated (= improvement in cash balance)		450
		£23,800

(c) It can be argued with justification, that 'profit' does not always give a useful or meaningful picture of a company's operations. Readers of a company's financial statements might even be misled by a reported profit figure. For example:

(i) shareholders might believe that if a company makes a profit after tax, of say, £100,000 then this is the amount which it could afford to pay as a dividend. Unless the company has sufficient cash available to stay in business and also to pay a dividend, the shareholders would be wrong;

(ii) employees might believe that if a company makes profits, it can afford to pay higher wages next year. This opinion may not be correct: the ability to pay wages depends on the availability of cash;

(iii) creditors might consider that a profitable company is a going concern. However:

1 if a company builds up large amounts of unsold stocks of goods, their cost would not be chargeable against profits, but cash would have been used up in making them, thus weakening the company's liquid resources;

2 a company might capitalise large development costs, having spent considerable amounts of money on R & D, but only charge small amounts against current profits. As a result, the company might show reasonable profits, but get into severe difficulties with its liquidity position.

(iv) management might suppose that if their company makes a historical cost profit, and reinvests some of these profits, then the company might have a historical cost profit but a current cost accounting loss, ie the operating capability of the firm will be declining;

(v) survival of a business entity depends not so much on profits as on its ability to pay its debts when they fall due. Such payments might include 'profit and loss' items such as material purchases, wages, interest and taxation etc, but also capital payments for new fixed assets and the repayment of loan capital when this falls due (eg on the redemption of debentures).

From these examples, it may be apparent that a company's performance and prospects depend not so much on the 'profits' earned in a period, but more realistically on liquidity - ie cash flows.

The statement of source and application of funds required by SSAP10 does have the merit of showing:

(i)   not an operational performance over a period of time (the profit and loss account);
(ii)   nor a statement of affairs at a single moment in time (the balance sheet) but a dynamic statement of how funds have entered the business and then been used.

The statement although a useful addition to financial reporting, does not show cash flows, although many of the funds flows reported do reflect cash movements.

It has therefore been argued that this type of statement has not removed the need for cash flow accounting. The ability of a company to generate cash in order to survive, grow, repay loans, etc is a crucial issue, which ought to be the subject of a financial report.

The following advantages might be claimed for cash flow accounting:

(a)   survival of a company depends on its ability to generate cash. Cash flow accounting directs attention towards this critical issue;

(b)   cash flow is more comprehensive than 'profit' which is dependent on accounting conventions and concepts;

(c)   creditors (long and short-term) are more interested in an entity's ability to repay them than in its profitability. Whereas 'profits' might indicate that cash is likely to be available, cash flow accounting is more direct with its message;

(d)   cash flow reporting provides a better means of comparing the results of different companies than traditional profit reporting;

(e)   cash flow reporting satisfies the needs of all users better:
    (i)   for management, it provides the sort of information on which decisions should be taken: (in management accounting, 'relevant costs' to a decision are future cash flows); traditional profit accounting does not help with decision-making;
    (ii)   for shareholders and auditors, cash flow accounting can provide a satisfactory basis for stewardship accounting;
    (iii)   as described previously, the information needs of creditors and employees will be better served by cash flow accounting;

(f)   cash flow forecasts are easier to prepare, as well as more useful, than profit forecasts;

(g)   they can be audited more easily than accounts based on the accruals concept;

(h)   the accruals concept is confusing and cash flows are more easily understood;

(i)   cash flow accounting should be both retrospective and also include a forecast for the future. This is of great information value to all users of accounting information;

(j)   forecasts can subsequently be monitored by the publication of variance statements which compare actual cash flows against the forecast.

SUGGESTED SOLUTIONS

Workings

1   *Sales*

	£
Receipts from customers	63,500
Amounts still owing from customers at 31 December 19X4	5,900
	69,400
Less amounts owing from customers at 1 January 19X4	5,300
∴ Sales	£64,100

2   *Purchases*

	£
Payments to suppliers	37,600
Amounts still owed to suppliers at 31 December 19X4	3,950
	41,550
Less amounts owed to suppliers at 1 January 19X4	3,500
∴ Purchases	£38,050

3   *Balance sheet at 31 December 19X4*

	£	£
Fixed assets £(17,900 + 8,000 − 6,100)		19,800
Current assets		
Stock	11,000	
Trade debtors	5,900	
	16,900	
Current liabilities		
Trade creditors	3,950	
Bank overdraft £(800 − (i) 450)	350	
	4,300	
Working capital		12,600
		32,400
Loan		(2,000)
		£30,400
Capital		
At 1 January 19X4		26,700
Net profit for year	15,700	
Less drawings	12,000	
Retained profit for year		3,700
At 31 December 19X4		£30,400

24. MR NIMMO

Tutorial note: if none of the options were taken up, Nimmo would find itself paying interest on its £100,000 deficiency. To put it another way, all three options implicitly guarantee saving that interest. However, that saving is not relevant to any comparison between the options (because it is common to all three).

(a) *Option 1: short-term loan*

Costs: 6 months of interest and arrangement fee

	£
Interest (£100,000 x ½ x 20%)	10,000
Arrangement fee	1,000
	£11,000

Option 2: delaying purchase of plant

Costs: extra operating costs

Operating costs (£3,000 x 6) £18,000

The delayed purchase of £150,000 is more than enough to cover the cash shortage of £100,000. The 'surplus' of £50,000 can be used to repay interest on the bank overdraft, although the £50,000 will reduce by £3,000 each month. Therefore, from the £18,000 operating costs, savings of interest have to be deducted.

Month		*Saving on overdraft interest*
		£
1	£50,000 x 1%	500
2	£47,000 x 1%	470
3	£44,000 x 1%	440
4	£41,000 x 1%	410
5	£38,000 x 1%	380
6	£35,000 x 1%	350
		£2,550

Therefore total cost of option 2 is £18,000 - £2,550 = £15,450

Option 3: take 90 days supplier credit

Costs: cash discounts forgone for each month

Discount forgone £120,000 x 2½% x 6 = £18,000

Taking the 90 days credit provides more than enough to cover the cash shortage of £100,000.

(a) In the first month, £120,000 is gained, less the 2½% cash discount. 2½% x £120,000 = £3,000. So in the first month, £117,000 is gained, representing a surplus of £117,000 - £100,000 = £17,000 over the deficit.

(b) In the second month (because 90 days credit have been taken, not just 60 days), a further £117,000 is gained.

Month		Saving on overdraft interest
		£
1	£17,000 x 1%	170
2	£134,000 x 1%	1,340
3	£131,000 x 1%	1,310
4	£128,000 x 1%	1,280
5	£125,000 x 1%	1,250
6	£122,000 x 1%	1,220
		£6,570

Therefore total cost of option 3 is £18,000 - £6,570 = £11,430

Conclusion

Option 1 (taking out on short-term loan) represents the lowest cost to Nimmo and in the absence of any other factors, is the option to be preferred.

(b) Other considerations which Nimmo should bear in mind when choosing between the options are:

(i)   Are there any tax complications which ought to be taken into account?

(ii) Can the business offer sufficient security for the loan of £100,000?

(iii) What would happen if the cash deficiency went on for longer than 6 months?

(iv) What would be the effect on the workforce if overtime became necessary? What would the unions (if any) say?

(v)   Can the purchase of plant be delayed for more than 6 months? What exactly would be the effect on production?

25. OVEREND

(a) *Cash transactions*

Income	£
Capital	300,000
Sales *(see working 1)*	1,000,000
	£1,300,000

Payments	
Fixed assets	400,000
Purchases *(see working 2)*	880,000
Running expenses	130,000
	£1,410,000

Estimated deficit = £(1,410,000 - 1,300,000) = £110,000

Workings

1. Sales are £1,200,000 ÷ 12 = £100,000 per month. Only 10 months sales will be received in the course of the year (because of the two month credit period). Therefore sales for the year = 10 x £100,000 = £1m.

2. Gross profit margin = 20% sales
    ∴ Purchases during year = 80% x 1,200,000 = £960,000
    ∴ Monthly purchases = £960,000 ÷ 12 = £80,000

    Purchases will actually be made for 13 months (from June 19X7 to June 19X8), to enable trading for the full year. But because of the two month credit period, only 11 months will be physically paid.

    ∴ Purchases (cash) = 11 x £80,000 = £880,000.

(b)

OVEREND LTD
PROFIT AND LOSS ACCOUNT
FOR THE YEAR ENDED 30 JUNE 19X8

	£	£
Sales		1,200,000
Less cost of sales:		
opening stock *(working 1)*	80,000	
purchases	960,000	
	1,040,000	
Less closing stock	80,000	
		960,000
Gross profit		240,000
Less: depreciation *(working 2)*	40,000	
running expenses	130,000	
		170,000
Net profit		£70,000

Workings

1. Opening stock = stock bought (on credit) in June 19X7.

2. Annual depreciation $= \dfrac{£(400,000-40,000)}{9}$

    $= £40,000$

(It is assumed that depreciation is to be made on the straight-line basis.)

OVEREND LTD
BALANCE SHEET
AS AT 30 JUNE 19X8

	Cost £	Depreciation £	NBV £
Fixed assets	400,000	40,000	360,000

Current assets

Stock		80,000	
Debtors *(working 1)*		200,000	
		280,000	

Current liabilities

Cash (deficit)		110,000	
Creditors *(working 2)*		160,000	
		270,000	
Working capital			10,000
Total assets less liabilities			£370,000

Capital and reserves

Share capital (issued and fully paid £1 ordinary shares)	300,000
Retained profit	70,000
	£370,000

Workings
1. Debtors = 2 x monthly sales = £200,000
2. Creditors = 2 x monthly purchases = £160,000

(c) *Assessment of Overend's performance*

Relevant ratios, based on the profit and loss account and balance sheet figures, are:

Return on capital employed $=$ $\dfrac{\text{Profit}}{\text{Capital employed}}$

$= \dfrac{£70,000}{£370,000}$

$= 18.9\%$

Current ratio
$=$ current assets : current liabilities
$=$ 280 : 270
$=$ 1.037 : 1

Quick (liquidity) ratio
$=$ (current assets - stocks) : current liabilities
$=$ 200 : 270
$=$ 0.74 : 1

(d) The return on capital employed figure of 18.9% is not particularly relevant in determining whether the bank should be prepared to finance Overend's deficit:

(i) liquidity ratios (rather than ROCE) are needed to help this kind of decision;
(ii) although 18.9% appears a reasonable figure, there is nothing to compare it with. Other similar companies may have higher ROCE figures.

Nevertheless, the apparently healthy figure of 18.9% tends to confirm that the business is being soundly managed - bearing out the remark in the question that Paul Smith and Phil Davies are experienced businessmen.

'Prudent' current ratios and quick ratios are usually thought to be 2:1 and 1:1 respectively. The current and quick ratios for Overend are not very good compared to these 'ideal' figures (1.037:1 and 0.74:1). Looking at these ratios in isolation, it would not seem to be a good idea to finance the company.

However, it is Overend's first year of trading. The *trading* results have, in fact, been satisfactory (funds generated of £110,000, being profit of £70,000 plus £40,000 depreciation). The liquidity ratios were poor because a considerable initial outlay was made on fixed assets - an outlay which presumably will not take place in future years (or, at least, to not nearly the same extent). Given that trading results are to continue in the same satisfactory vein, annual funds of £110,000 appear sufficient to warrant financing the business.

On the other hand, the quoted figures make no allowances for interest payable, so the picture is not quite as rosy as it might appear. Perhaps the bank may only recover its loan (plus interest) over two - or even three - years.

All in all, it is a close decision. On balance, it appears that the bank will (eventually) be repaid its loan plus interest, and so it should probably undertake to finance Overend's deficit (provided suitable security can be arranged).

(e) The figures in the P&L show a gross profit of £240,000 arising from sales of £1,200,000. In other words, every £100 of sales generates £20 of contribution - which in the case of Overend is the same as net profit, because the only expenses in the P&L account are fixed (not variable).

But an increase in net profit leads to an increase in net assets. The components of net assets are stock, debtors, cash and creditors.

Stock, creditors and debtors are directly related to the sales figure (stock is always $\frac{1}{12}$ of the cost of sales figure, creditors is always $\frac{2}{12}$ of the cost of sales figure, and debtors is always $\frac{2}{12}$ of the sales figure. Remember that cost of sales = 80% of sales). So an increase of £100 in sales will mean a certain increase in stock, creditors and debtors. As we know that the total increase in net assets will be £20, the change in the cash figure will be a balancing figure.

		£
Stock	£100 x $\frac{1}{12}$ x 80%	6.67
Debtors	£100 x $\frac{2}{12}$	16.66
Cash	(balancing figure)	10.00
		33.33
Creditors	£100 x $\frac{2}{12}$ x 80%	(13.33)
Net assets increase		£20.00

So for every £100 of sales, cash is increased by £10.

In fact, an £118,000 increase is required in cash (to meet the £110,000 deficit plus £8,000 advertising expenses).

So additional sales required = £118,000 x 10 = £1,180,000.

(*Note:* those with a mathematical inclination might find the following solution to part (e) easier to follow.

Let sales figure be £X.

	£
Income	
Capital	300,000
Sales	$\frac{10}{12}$X
Payments	
Fixed assets	400,000
Purchases	$\frac{(80\% \times X)}{12} \times 11$
Running expenses	130,000
Advertising expenses	8,000

So, for a zero cash figure:

£300,000 + £$\frac{10}{12}$X = £538,000 + £$\frac{11}{12}$(0.8X)

$\frac{10}{12}$X − $\frac{11}{12}$(0.8X) = £238,000

10X − 8.8X = £2,856,000

X = £2,380,000

ie an increase of sales equal to £2,380,000 − £1,200,000 = £1,180,000 is required)

26. HAMMOND

(a) Sales expected in years 19X7 − 19Y0:

	£
19X7:	1,800,000
19X8:	2,100,000
19X9:	2,400,000
19Y0:	2,700,000

Machines needed in years 19X7 − 19Y0 (sales ÷ £250,000, rounded up if necessary):

19X7:	8
19X8:	9
19X9:	10
19Y0:	11

∴ On the basis of expected sales, two new machines will be needed in 19X7, and one in each year subsequently.

In addition, the 19X2 machines will need replacing in 19X8, the 19X4 machines need replacing in 19Y0, and the 19X5 machine will not need replacing until 19Y1.

Total number of machines needed:

19X7:	2
19X8:	3
19X9:	1
19Y0:	3

(b)

HAMMOND LTD
Summarised profit and loss accounts for years 19X7 - 19Y0

	Working	19X7 £'000	19X8 £'000	19X9 £'000	19Y0 £'000
Sales		1,800	2,100	2,400	2,700
Less:					
Manufacturing costs other than depreciation	1	1,260	1,470	1,680	1,890
Depreciation	2	160	180	200	220
Running expenses		190	200	210	220
Directors' remuneration		81	87	93	99
		1,691	1,937	2,183	2,429
Net profit		109	163	217	271

Workings

1. Manufacturing costs other than depreciation as a percentage of sales in 19X6 =

    $$\frac{£1,050}{£1,500} \times 100\% = 70\%$$

    Manufacturing costs in subsequent years = 70% x sales.

2. *Depreciation*

    Annual depreciation for each machine = $\frac{£120,000}{6}$ x £20,000

    Depreciation in each year = number of machines owned in year x £20,000

19X7:	8 x £20,000	=	£160,000
19X8:	9 x £20,000	=	£180,000
19X9:	10 x £20,000	=	£200,000
19Y0:	11 x £20,000	=	£220,000

HAMMOND LTD
Summarised funds flow statements for years 19X7 - 19Y0

	19X7 £'000	19X8 £'000	19X9 £'000	19Y0 £'000
Profit before tax	109	163	217	271
Adjustment for items not involving the movement of funds:				
Depreciation	160	180	200	220
Total funds generated from operations	269	343	417	491
Application of funds:				
Purchase of fixed assets	240	360	120	360
	29	(17)	297	131
Increase required in working capital	48	48	48	48
Balancing surplus/(deficit)	(19)	(65)	249	83
Cumulative surplus/(deficit)	29	(17)	297	131

(d) The funds flow statement reveals that funds generated from operations for the four years are £269,00, £343,000, £417,000 and £491,000. After the purchase of fixed assets, there is still a surplus of funds in 19X7, 19X9 and 19Y0, but there is a deficit in 19X8.

However, the surplus funds in 19X7 are not sufficient to cover the requirement for working capital: Hammond Ltd will have to increase its bank overdraft (or finance its business in some other way) to the tune of £19,000. Although funds generated from operations are enough to finance purchase of fixed assets, there is certainly no scope for future development using those funds.

In 19X8 the situation is worse. There is already a deficit of funds before the increase in requirements for working capital is met: Hammond Ltd's overdraft will increase to £65,000. Funds generated from operations are not even sufficient to finance the purchase of new machines, let alone any other development.

The situation improves in 19X9: funds generated from operations are sufficient to cover both the purchase of fixed assets and working capital requirements, leaving a surplus of £249,000. At last there is scope for further development using generated funds.

In 19Y0, Hammond Ltd can still look to develop further. Funds generated from operations have easily covered the purchase of fixed assets and working capital requirements, leaving a cash surplus of £131,000.

Finally, it is important to remember that the closing balances for each year do not tell the whole story. Remember that the new machines are bought in January each year: funds earned in that year are not yet available for financing the purchase of machines.

27. COMPTON

Tutorial note: the question provides a table to be filled in – clearly this is the answer format which the examiner requires, and you must adhere to it. But the question is really asking you to adjust the profit and loss account and balance sheet according to the various options: the hard work of this question all lies in the *workings*, not in the final schedule.

Course of action	Net profit for 19X7	Bank balance (or overdraft) at 31/12/X7	Working capital at 31/12/X7	Working capital (current) ratio at 31/12/X7
	£	£	£	
(i)	60,000	(40,000)	160,000	2.6
(ii)	60,000	(10,000)	160,000	2.6
(iii)	37,500	14,500	137,500	3.6
(iv)	60,000	10,000	160,000	2.5
(v)	60,000	(40,000)	160,000	2.6
(vi)	60,000	(80,000)	160,000	2.1

Working 1 Forecast profit and loss accounts for 19X7 under the six options

	(i) £'000	(ii) £'000	(iii) £'000	(iv) £'000	(v) £'000	(vi) £'000
Sales	900	900	900.0	900	900	900
Less: Purchases	720	720	720.0	720	720	760
Stock decrease/(increase) during year	30	30	30.0	30	30	(10)
Cost of goods sold	750	750	750.0	750	750	750
Gross profit	150	150	150.0	150	150	150
Less: depreciation	40	40	40.0	40	40	40
other running expenses	50	50	50.0	50	50	50
cash discount	–	–	3.75	–	–	–
	90	90	93.75	90	90	90
Net profit	60	60	56.25	60	60	60

Working 2   Forecast balance sheets for 19X7 under the six options

	(i) £'000	(ii) £'000	(iii) £'000	(iv) £'000	(v) £'000	(vi) £'000
Fixed assets						
Freehold property less depreciation	300	200	200.0	200	200	200
Plant and machinery less depreciation	125	125	125.0	125	125	125
	425	325	325.0	325	325	325
Current assets						
Stocks	110	110	110.0	110	110	150
Trade debtors	150	150	75.00	150	150	150
Cash at bank	-	-	31.25	10	-	-
	260	260	216.25	270	260	300
Current liabilities						
Trade creditors	60	90	60.0	60	60	60
Bank overdraft	40	10	-	-	40	80
Loan	-	-	-	50	-	-
	100	100	60.0	110	100	140
Net current assets (working capital)	160	160	156.25	160	160	160
	585	485	481.25	485	485	485
Financed by:						
Share capital (£1 ordinary shares)	300	300	300.0	300	500	300
Reserves	285	185	181.25	185	(15)	185
	585	485	481.25	485	485	485

28.   THREE COMPANIES

(a)

		A		B		C	
(i)	Net profit percentage	45/3029	1.5%	67/1556	4.3%	43/206	20.9%
(ii)	Total asset turnover	3029/568	5.3x	1556/1882	0.9x	206/1766	0.1x
(iii)	Return on gross assets	45/568	7.9%	67/1822	3.7%	43/1766	2.4%
(iv)	Liquidity ratio	245/184	1.3	442/301	1.5	1347/778	1.7

(b)   Company C is clearly the finance company. This is shown by the following facts:

   (i)   it has no stocks and negligible fixed assets. This would be expected of a company which is not in the business of buying and selling assets, but is effectively trading in money;

   (ii)   its principal asset is debtors, representing amounts of money out on loan;

   (iii)   it enjoys a high profit percentage on a low revenue figure.

Company A is almost certainly the grocery store chain:

(i)   its level of debtors is very low, especially when compared with its creditors figure, as would be expected from a cash business;
(ii)   it has a high rate of total asset turnover, arising in particular from the rapid turnover of stocks;
(iii)   its net profit percentage is predictably small. This type of business typically enjoys a high turnover, but with low profit margins.

Company B must, by elimination, be the steel manufacturer. Large investment in fixed assets (factory premises, plant and machinery) would be expected of this type of business.

29. GREYWELL AND KENDALL

(a)   Rate of return on total assets:

Greywell $\dfrac{4,000}{30,000}$ = $\underline{13.3\%}$

Kendall $\dfrac{5,000}{25,000}$ = $\underline{20\%}$

(b)   Rate of return on total assets = $\dfrac{\text{return}}{\text{turnover}}$ x $\dfrac{\text{turnover}}{\text{total assets}}$

For Greywell: $\dfrac{4,000}{40,000}$ x $\dfrac{40,000}{30,000}$

                    = 10%   x   1.33
                    = $\underline{13.3\%}$

For Kendall: $\dfrac{5,000}{60,000}$ x $\dfrac{60,000}{25,000}$

                    = 8.3%   x   2.4
                    = $\underline{20\%}$

(c)   Kendall's return on total assets is superior and from the limited information available this is the best indication of overall performance.

The breakdown of the ratio into net profit percentage and assets turnover ratio shows that Greywell has achieved the better net profit percentage, either through working on higher margins or through better control of costs. But Kendall's high rate of asset turnover more than makes up for it, suggesting that Kendall's management is employing its assets more efficiently.

The figures in themselves are not very useful to potential shareholders or creditors. Shareholders would want to know more about stock market ratios, such as price earnings ratio, dividend yield. They will also be interested in gearing levels and the amount of profits paid out as interest.

SUGGESTED SOLUTIONS

Potential loan creditors will want to know about he company's level of income to ensure it is able to pay its interest commitments. They will also be interested in the nature and value of any security available.

30. COTFORD

(a)

	19X8	19X7
Working capital ratio	0.86 : 1	0.79 : 1
Interest cover	3.4 times	3.8 times
Debt/equity ratio	0.56 : 1	0.82 : 1
Total asset turnover	0.63 times	0.85 times
Operating profit percentage	13.0%	12.1%
Return on total assets	8.2%	10.3%
Return on equity	6.3%	10.3%

Notes

1. Working capital ratio = $\dfrac{\text{current assets}}{\text{current liabilities}}$

2. Interest cover = $\dfrac{\text{operating profit}}{\text{interest payable}}$

3. Debt/equity ratio = $\dfrac{\text{current liabilities + long-term borrowing}}{\text{shareholders' funds}}$

4. Total asset turover = $\dfrac{\text{turnover}}{\text{fixed assets + current assets}}$

5. Operating profit percentage = $\dfrac{\text{operating profit}}{\text{turnover}} \times 100\%$

6. Return on total assets = $\dfrac{\text{operating profit}}{\text{fixed assets + current assets}} \times 100\%$

7. Return on equity = $\dfrac{\text{profit after tax}}{\text{shareholders' funds}} \times 100\%$

(b) (i) *Solvency and gearing*

The company is relatively illiquid. The working capital ratio was only 0.79 : 1 in 19X7, and the improvement in 19X8 (to 0.86 : 1) still leaves it looking vulnerable. This is surprising in a business with very good cash flow, as one would expect a hotals and pubs business to be.

The assets of the business are financed to a significant extent by external finance (current liabilities and longer-term borrowing). In 19X7 the ratio of debt to equity was as high as 0.82 : 1. The reduction in 19X6 (to 0.56 : 1) is explained largely by the property revaluation on 30 June 19X8. This reliance on external finance is also indicated by the relatively low interest cover. Operating profits cover interest payments only 3.4 times, and the position has worsened since 19X7 (3.8 times). It would be interesting to know when the longer-term borrowing becomes repayable; it cannot be earlier than twelve months, but if it is only a little longer than that it is hard to see how the repayment will be financed.

(ii) *Asset utilisation*

The company does not appear to be working its assets hard enough. Total assets turned over only to the extent of 85% in 19X7; following the revaluation of properties, the 19X8 position looks even worse (63% turnover, ie total assets turn over only once in 19 months).

The major assets of the company are of course its properties and it seems clear that the public houses and hotels are not generating the level of income that would be expected from them.

(iii) *Profitability*

The operating profit percentage seems reasonable: 12.1% in 19X7, improving to 13% in 19X8. But this disguises two problems:

1. The return is not adequate in absolute terms, because the turnover on which it is based is far less than one would expect from the value of the assets employed (see (ii) above). This is illustrated by the return on total assets, which is only 8.2% in 19X8.

2. A large proportion of the operating profit is absorbed by high interest payments. The return remaining for shareholders is only 6.3% in 19X8. (The fall from 10.3% in 19X7 is mainly a result of the property revaluation.)

Despite all this, the market appears to look favourably on the company's prospects. Earnings per share in 19X8 are 56.7p (1,360/2,400). Since the share price is £6.20, this means that the company's P/E ratio at 10.9 is above average.

31. SOMERTON

Tutorial note. This is one of many questions set by the CIB which require calculation work to begin with, but only as a basis for later criticism or discussion. Part (a) requires calculation of common ratios; part (b) requires an understanding of which ratios are especially interesting to particular user groups; while part (c) calls for practical financial advice.

(a)

		19X3			19X4	
	(i)	807/351 =	2.3:1		758/344 =	2.2:1
	(ii)	350/30 =	11.7x		320/30 =	10.7x
	(iii)	£1.50/44.8p * =	3.3		£1.60/40.6p * =	3.9
	(iv)	350/1,708 =	20.5%		320/1,822 =	17.6%
	(v)	224/1,057 =	21.2%		203/1,178 =	17.2%
	(vi)	300/1,057 =	28.3%		300/1,178 =	25.5%

* Price/earnings ratio = $\dfrac{\text{price per share}}{\text{earnings per share}}$

Earnings per share = (in 19X3) £224,000/500,000 = 44.8p
(in 19X4) £203,000/500,000 = 40.6p

(b) Two ratios of particular interest to shareholders are:

(i) price/earnings ratio; and
(ii) post-tax rate of return on shareholders' equity

Earnings per share is widely used as a measure of a company's performance and is of particular importance in comparing the results over a period of several years. The level of a company's earnings is an important factor in the capital growth of an investor's shareholding; and to the extent that high earnings lead to high dividends, it also influences the value of a shareholding as a source of income. The price earnings ratio is a measure of how solid and well-established a company is perceived to be. A high ratio means that investors are willing to pay a price for the shares which will not be recovered in the form of earnings for many years. In the case of Somerton plc investors are apparently willing to pay £1.60 (19X3 : £1.50) for annual earnings of 40.6p (19X3: 44.8p). The ratio is therefore 3.9 for 19X4, a significant increase on the 19X3 ratio of 3.3.

The rate of return on shareholders' equity discloses to investors how efficiently their funds have been employed in generating profits for themselves. In the case of Somerton plc 19X4 has seen a decline in this ratio from 21.2% to 17.2%. This is mainly because the operating profit for 19X4 has fallen from £350,000 to £320,000, despite a 2.5% increase in turnover.

Two ratios of particular interest to the bank are:

(i) working capital ratio; and
(ii) interest cover.

The working capital ratio indicates the company's ability to meet its short-term creditors from current assets. In Somerton's case the ratio is a healthy 2.3:1 in 19X3 and declines only marginally in 19X4 to 2.2:1. (2:1 is sometimes quoted as an ideal for this ratio, but variations between different industries reduce the usefulness of this generalisation.) The bank can take comfort that the company's short-term liquidity position is good and unlikely to need bolstering by overdraft finance.

The interest cover ratio indicates the company's ability to generate sufficient pre-tax profits to cover interest payments on the 10% debentures. If Somerton were forced to default on interest payments it would be open to the debenture holders to realise their security in a forced sale; this would place the continuing existence of the company in doubt. Despite the 19X4 fall in pre-tax profits, however, the interest payments are covered almost eleven times and no danger appears imminent.

(c) *Project financed by rights issue*

Somerton plc's long-term capital at 1.1.19X5 would be:

	£'000	£'000
Ordinary shares:		
Before rights issue	500	
Rights issue (£500,000/£1.25)	400	
		900
Reserves		
Before rights issue	678	
Share premium on rights issue	100	
		778
Shareholders' funds		1,678
10% debentures		300
		1,978

The company's new debt equity ratio would be:

$$\frac{300}{1,678} = 17.9\%$$

Forecast profit statement for 19X5

	£'000
Operating profit (320 + 200)	520
Less interest payable	30
Profit before tax	490
Less taxation (490 x 30%)	147
Profit after tax	343
Dividends	100
Retained profits for year	243

Interest cover = $\frac{520}{30}$ = 17.3 times

Shareholders' equity at 31.12.19X5 = £1,892,000 (1,649 + 243)

Post-tax rate of return on shareholders' equity = $\frac{343}{1,892}$ = 18.1%

Project financed by loan

Somerton plc's long-term capital at 1.1.19X5 would be:

	£'000	£'000
Shareholders' funds (unchanged)		1,678
Long-term debt:		
10% debentures	300	
Bank loan	500	
		800
		2,478

The company's new debt/equity ratio would be:

$$\frac{800}{1,678} = 47.7\%$$

Forecast profit statement for 19X5

	£'000	£'000
Operating profit		520
Less interest payable:		
On 10% debentures	30	
On bank loan (12% x 500)	60	
		90
Profit before tax		430
Less taxation (430 x 30%)		129
Profit after tax		301
Dividends		50
Retained profits for year		251

Interest cover $= \dfrac{520}{90} = 5.8$ times

Shareholders' equity at 31.12.19X5 = £1,400,000 (1,149 + 251)

Post-tax rate of return on shareholders' equity $= \dfrac{301}{1,400} = 21.5\%$

To finance the project by a bank loan would increase the company's debt/equity ratio to 47.7%. Interest costs would increase to the point where interest cover (on budgeted profits) would be only 5.8 times. This is clearly the riskier alternative, and yet if budgeted figures turn out to be realistic neither the debt/equity ratio nor the interest cover are likely to reach unacceptable levels.

Financing the project by a loan has the advantage of pushing up the post-tax return on shareholders' equity to 21.5% from its 19X4 level of 17.2%. This is because the loan finance is cheap, especially since it is tax-allowable (the after-tax cost of the loan is (12% x 60%) = 7.2%).

The rights issue is the more cautious option. The debt/equity ratio reduces from 25.5% to 17.9% as a result of the new injection of equity, and the interest cover rises to 17.3 times. However, the benefit to shareholders is much smaller: post-tax return on shareholders' equity increases only to 18.1% from the 19X4 level of 17.2%. Unless the company's management is very risk-averse the loan option is likely to be favoured.

32. EASTHOPE AND QUILTER

Tutorial note. Part (a) is straightforward calculation. Part (b) is worth only four marks and presumably therefore requires only a bare statement of the results found in part (c). In part (c) you should concentrate on the areas of most concern to a bank: ability to pay interest, ability to repay the principal and ability to provide security.

(a)

	Easthope		Quilter	
Funds generated from operations	(120 + 50)	£170,000	(130 + 120)	£250,000
Proprietorship ratio	600/860	69.8%	900/1,200	75%
Working capital ratio	455/260	1.75:1	525/300	1.75:1
Net profit: sales	120/2,050	5/9%	130.2/620	5.0%
Return on shareholders' equity	120/600	20%	130.900	14.4%

(b) Areas where Easthope appears to be stronger:

Net profit percentage	(5.9% compared with 5.0%)
Return on equity	(20% compared with 14.4%)

Areas where Quilter appears to be stronger:

Funds generated from operations	(250,000 compared with £170,000)
Proprietorship ratio	(75% compared with 69.8%)

The working capital ratio is the same for both companies.

(c) In terms of their ability to meet interest payments the two companies are evenly matched. Both achieve a similar level of net profit (Easthope £120,000; Quilter £130,000).

In terms of their ability to repay the principal sum advanced Quilter looks a slightly better proposition. Both companies are intending to distribute their entire net profits as dividends and neither proposes any investment in fixed assets. It follows that their respective cash balances are likely to increase by roughly the amount of depreciation charged. This is much higher in Quilter's case than in Easthope's.

In terms of the security they can offer, Quilter again appears to be superior, because a greater proportion of its assets consists of premises. But in this respect the balance sheets may be misleading. It is possible that the two companies' premises are identical, and the difference in book value has been caused by a recent revaluation in Quilter's case. Further information would be needed on this point before a decision was made.

33. PUDSEY

Tutorial note. This is a question requiring knowledge of marginal costing and contribution analysis. As often, the best starting point is to calculate the contribution/sales ratio.

Calculation of contribution/sales (CS) ratio:

	£'000	£'000
Sales		1,600
Less variable costs:		
Cost of goods sold	960	
Variable running costs	160	
		1,120
		480

$$\therefore CS = \frac{480}{1,600} = \underline{30\%}$$

(a) The contribution required to generate a profit of £300,000 is equal to £600,000, since fixed costs of £300,000 must be covered before any profit is earned.

The necessary sales level is therefore 600 x 100/30 = £2,000,000

(*Check:*	£'000	£'000
Sales		2,000
Cost of sales (2,000 x 960/1,600)		1,200
Gross profit		800
Variable running costs		
(2,000 x 160/1,600)	200	
Fixed running costs	300	
		500
Net profit		300

(b)   FORECAST BALANCE SHEET AS AT 31 DECEMBER 19X4

	£'000	£'000
Fixed assets		
Cost		1,000
Depreciation		250
		750
Current assets		
Stock (160 x 2,000/1,600)	200	
Debtors (200 x 2,000/1,600)	250	
Bank (balancing figure)	290	
	740	
Current liabilities		
Trade creditors (80 x 2,000/1,600)	100	
		640
		1,390
Capital and reserves		
Share capital		700
Retained profit (390 + 300)		690
		1,390

(c) The difference between the net profit earned and the change in the bank balance is best shown by a statement of source and application of funds.

STATEMENT OF SOURCE AND APPLICATION OF FUNDS
FOR THE YEAR ENDED 31 DECEMBER 19X4

	£'000	£'000
Source of funds		
Net profit		300
Adjustment for non-cash item (depreciation)		50
Total generated from operations		350
Increase in working capital		
Stock	40	
Debtors	50	
Creditors	(20)	
	70	
Increase in bank balance	280	
		350

34. NEWHAVEN

(a) (i) *Initial investment in June 1988*

	£
Costs of refurbishment	30,000
Purchase of 80 PCs @ £500	40,000
Opportunity cost: cash forgone by not selling premises	120,000
	190,000

(ii) *Breakeven level of sales*

	£
Unit contribution:	
Selling price	600
Less cost	500
	100

	£
Fixed costs:	
Depreciation on refurbishment costs (1/5 x £30,000)*	6,000
Running costs	34,000
	40,000

Breakeven level of sales:

$$\frac{40,000}{100} = 400 \text{ units or } (400 \times £600 =) £240,000$$

* We are not told anything about the depreciation of the premises, and presumably this aspect is to be ignored.

(iii) *Forecast profit*

	£
Contribution (12 x 60 x £100)	72,000
Less fixed costs	40,000
Forecast profit for the year	32,000

(iv) *Margin of safety*

The company expects to sell (12 x 60 =) 720 units per annum.

As calculated above, the breakeven level of sales is 400 units.

The margin of safety is therefore 320 units, or

$$\frac{320}{720} = 44\%$$

(v) *Target level of sales*

	£
Fixed costs to be covered	40,000
Return of 20% to be achieved on initial investment	38,000
Total contribution required	78,000

The target level of sales is therefore:

$$\frac{78,000}{100} = 780 \text{ units}$$

(b) The project is expected to be profitable: if targets are met, it will generate profits of £32,000 per annum. The margin of safety is large: sales volume would need to fall 44% below expectations before the project made a loss.

Even so, it falls short of the financial target normally set by the company. To achieve a 20% return on initial investment sales would need to reach 780 units per annum, more than 8% above forecast.

Factors to be considered before a final decision is made include:

(i)   the reliability of the forecasts;

(ii)   the 'cost' of depreciation on the premises occupied by the project;

(iii) the availability of other projects in which the funds could be invested. If there are no other projects on hand offering the company's target rate of return, this may be the most profitable option available;

(iv) the possibility of undertaking the project on a more profitable basis. For example, is there any room for cutting the £34,000 annual running costs? Is it possible to buy in the computers at a reduced cost, perhaps by negotiating a bulk discount? Is it possible to raise the selling price without reducing demand?

35. ALUMINEX

(a) *Alternative 1*

PROFIT AND LOSS ACCOUNT FOR THE YEAR ENDED 31 DECEMBER 19X3

	Total	First 100,000 units	Next 50,000 units
	£'000	£'000	£'000
Sales at £5 each	750	500	250
Variable costs: at £3 each	525	300	
at £4.50 each			225
Contribution	225	200	25
Less fixed costs:			
Depreciation	20		
Other	122		
	142		
Net profit	83		

(b) *Alternative 2*

PROFIT AND LOSS ACCOUNT FOR THE YEAR ENDED 31 DECEMBER 19X3

	Total	First 100,000 units	Next 50,000 units
	£'000	£'000	£'000
Sales at £5 each	750	500	250
Variable costs at £3 each	450	300	150
Contribution	300	200	100
Less fixed costs:			
Depreciation (20 + 12)	32		
Other	160		
	192		
Net profit	108		

FORECAST BALANCE SHEET AS AT 31 DECEMBER 19X3

	£'000	£'000
Fixed assets:		
Cost (200 + 120)	320	
Depreciation (80 + 32)	112	
		208
Working capital (200 x 150%)		300
		508
Less bank overdraft (balancing figure)		(55)
		453
Share capital		200
Retained profits		
Brought forward	145	
For year	108	
		253
		453

(c) At first sight alternative 2 appears the more attractive, producing a forecast net profit of £108,000 as compared with £83,000 under alternative 1. This conclusion is thrown into doubt by considering the relative risk of the two alternatives.

On alternative 1, the extra sales generate a contribution of £25,000 while costs increase by £2,000, a net increase of £23,000 over the 19X2 profit. This is a very comfortable safety margin. Indeed, since the unit contribution of the extra sales is 50p (£5 - £4.50), only 4,000 units of extra sales need to be made to cover the £2,000 additional costs.

On alternative 2, the unit contribution of the additional sales does not differ from that of the first 100,000 units, ie £2. But fixed costs under this option rise from £140,000 to £192,000 and the extra sales created will need to be at least 26,000 units to cover this increase of £52,000. The margin of safety will be very small if Dowden's estimate of the increased sales is optimistic and his brothers' estimate of 30,000 units more realistic. It is worth noting that at this level of sales the extra profit created is £13,000 (30,000 x 50p - £2,000) under alternative 1 but only £8,000 (30,000 x £2 - £52,000) under alternative 2.

Moreover, alternative 2 involves a heavy initial investment leading to a bank overdraft of £55,000 at 31 December 19X3, assuming that profits of £108,000 are made in the year ended on that date. The overdraft at 1 January 19X3, when the new policy begins, would of course be much larger.

36. MARGINAL

Workings: current budget

The budgeted profit is contribution less fixed overhead, which amounts to	£400,000

	£
Contribution	2,500,000
Variable costs (£18.75 x 80,000)	1,500,000
∴ Sales	£4,000,000
Sales price per unit (÷ 80,000)	£50

(a) *Proposal 1*

	£
Unit sales price (£50 less 10%)	45
Unit variable costs	18.75
Unit contribution	£26.25

	£'000	£'000
Total contribution (100,000 x £26.25)		2,625
Total fixed costs:		
Current budget	2,100	
Extra costs	75	
		2,175
Profit		450

This represents an increase in profit of £50,000 on the current budget, although the contribution/sales ratio falls from 62.5% to 58.3% and with the increase in fixed costs, the breakeven point rises to a turnover of (£2,175,000 ÷ 58.3%) over £3,700,000. The extra sales must be achieved if this proposal is to be profitable.

(b) *Proposal 2*

		£
Unit sales price		55.00
Unit variable cost		18.75
Unit contribution		£36.25

	£,000	£,000
Expected contribution (90,000 x £36.25)		3,262.5
Less fixed costs:		
Current budget	2,100	
Increase in costs (400 + 25 + 20)	445	
		2,545.0
Profit		717.5

This represents a substantial increase in profits over the current budget and even at a sales volume of 80,000 units, the contribution would be £2,900,000 and the profit £355,000 – ie not far short of the current budgeted profit. The large increase in advertising costs is perhaps risky in that the price increase might lead to a fall in sales.

(c) *Proposal 3*

	£'000
Target profit	600
Fixed costs (2,100 + 360 + 25 + 17)	2,502
Target contribution	3,102
Variable costs (88,000 x £18.75)	1,650
Sales revenue	4,752

Sales volume	88,000 units
Sales price per unit	£54

A profit statement is shown in the first 5 lines of the table above.

This is similar to proposal 2, but involves a smaller increase in fixed costs for a smaller profit. Although it is less risky in this respect, it does depend more for success on an increase in sales volume. At a sales level of only 80,000 units, the contribution would be only £2.82 million and the profit £318,000 – substantially less than the current budget.

(d) *Proposal 4*

	£'000	£'000
Sales		4,800
Variable costs (96,000 x £18.75)		1,800
Total contribution		3,000
Fixed costs:		
Production	1,040	
Administration	600	
Marketing (including advertising,		
balancing figure)	640	
		2,280
Profit (15% of £4,800)		720

Since marketing costs are the balancing figure of £640,000 the extra cost of advertising must be £(640,000 - 500,000 - 25,000) = £115,000.

This proposal offers the highest profit at a sales price of only £50. It is questionable, however, whether the increase in advertising expenditure will achieve an increase of 20% in sales volume.

37. PRESBURY

(a) (i) *Breakeven levels*

		Scheme A £	Scheme B £
Contribution:			
Selling price		200	200
Variable costs		150	120
		50	80
Fixed costs:			
Depreciation at 25%		70,000	100,000
Other		130,000	300,000
		200,000	400,000
Breakeven level (in units)		$\frac{200,000}{50}$ = 4,000	$\frac{400,000}{80}$ = 5,000

(ii) *Forecast profit*

	£	£
Contribution		
(7,000 units @ £50; £80)	350,000	560,000
Fixed costs	200,000	400,000
Profit	150,000	160,000

(iii) *Margin of safety*

	Units	Units
Budgeted sales level	7,000	7,000
Breakeven sales level	4,000	5,000
	3,000	2,000
As a percentage of budgeted sales level	43%	29%

(b) Suppose that the required level of sales is N units.

Then the profit (ie contribution less fixed costs) is as follows for each of the two options:

    Scheme A: £50N - £200,000
    Scheme B: £80N - £400,000

For these two amounts to be equal, it follows that:

    £50N - £200,000 = £80N - £400,000

Simplifying the algebra:

    £30N = £200,000
    ∴ N = 6,667 units

(c) Scheme B requires a higher initial investment and higher fixed costs. If budgeted sales are achieved, the profit earned under this scheme is higher than under scheme A (£160,000 compared with £150,000 - see (a)(ii) above). But the risks involved are also greater. To break even under scheme B 5,000 units must be sold; under scheme A the product will break even after only 4,000 units have been sold. Indeed, the profits earned under scheme A exceed those under scheme B for all levels of sales up to 6,667 units; from that point on the higher contribution earned under scheme B leads to superior profits.

Factors to be taken into account by the company before reaching a final decision include:

(i) the reliability of the estimates involved, especially the estimate of sales volume. If there is a significant chance that sales will fail to reach 6,667 units there would be a strong argument for preferring scheme A;

(ii) the availability of finance for the project. It may be much easier to finance the (£280,000 + £60,000 =) £340,000 needed for scheme A than the (£400,000 + £60,000 =) £460,000 that scheme B requires. Even if the higher level of finance is available, it may be hard to obtain at the same cost, ie the increased gearing level might cause investors to demand a higher return.

38. ROPER

Tutorial note. This is a breakeven computation of a popular type (it is very similar to the previous question, Presbury). The schemes are to be compared: one involves a high initial investment compensated for by large profit margins; the other involves minimum outlay but tight margins. The first step should be to calculate the contribution earned under each scheme.

	Plan Y £	Plan Z £
Contribution per £100 of sales:		
Cost of purchases	50	80
Other variable costs	20	5
	70	85
Contribution	30	15
Sales value	£100	£100

(a) (i) Under plan Y, total contribution must be sufficient to cover fixed costs of £290,000 plus the target profit of £100,000. Total contribution must therefore be £390,000. But every £100 of sales earns a contribution of £30. The required level of sales is therefore

$$\frac{£390,000}{£30} \times £100 = £1,300,000.$$

For plan Z, contribution must equal £(50,000 + 100,000) = £150,000. The required level of sales is $\frac{£150,000}{£15} \times £100 = £1,000,000.$

(ii)

	Plan Y £	Plan Z £
Contribution earned from sales of £2,000,000:		
Plan Y £30 x (2,000,000/100)	600,000	
Plan Z £15 x (2,000,000/100)		300,000
Less fixed costs	290,000	50,000
Profit	£310,000	£250,000

(iii) Suppose that the required level of sales is £s.

Then for plan Y, contribution is £30 x s/100 and profit is (£30 x s/100) - £290,000.

For plan Z, contribution is £15 x s/100 and profit is (£15 x s/100) - £50,000.

For profits to be equal, we have:

$$£30,000 \text{ x } s/100 - £290,000 - £16 \text{ x } s/100 - £50,000$$

∴   s/100 (£30 - £15) = £(290,000 - 50,000)

∴   s/100 x £15 = £240,000

∴   s/100 = $\frac{£240,000}{£15}$

∴   s/100 = £16,000

∴   s = £1,600,000

(At this level of sales, profits amount to £190,000 under either plan.)

(b)

FORECAST BALANCE SHEET AT END OF YEAR 1
PLAN Y

	£
Fixed assets	
Working capital	200,000
25p x (1,300,000 - 240,000) + £80,000	345,000
Cash surplus to working capital	105,000
	650,000
15% long-term loan	(450,000)
	£200,000
Capital and reserves	
Share capital	100,000
Profit and loss account	100,000
	£200,000

FORECAST BALANCE SHEET AT END OF YEAR 1
PLAN Z

	£
Working capital	
(10p x 1,000,000)	100,000
Cash surplus to working capital	100,000
	£200,000
Capital and reserves	
Share capital	100,000
Profit and loss account	100,000
	£200,000

Under plan Y the investment required is £545,000 (£200,000 for fixed assets and £345,000 for working capital). This is covered by the share capital of £100,000 and the loan of £450,000, leaving a cash surplus of £5,000. By the end of the year, profit of £100,000 has been earned and the cash surplus has risen to £105,000.

Under plan Z, the initial share capital of £100,000 exactly matches the investment required in working capital. By the end of year 1 the £100,000 profit is represented by the £100,000 cash surplus.

(c) Plan Y involves a higher initial investment and higher fixed costs. If maximum sales are achieved, the profit earned under this plan is much greater than under plan Z (£310,000 compared with £250,000 - see (a) (ii) above). But the risks involved are also greater. To achieve the target profit of £100,000 sales of £1,300,000 must be achieved under plan Y; with plan Z the target will be reached if sales amount to only £1,000,000. Indeed the profits earned under plan Z exceed those earned under plan Y for all levels of sales up to £1,600,000; from that point on the higher contribution earned under plan Y leads to superior profits.

Factors which may influence the decision taken by Roper's management include:

(i) Under plan Y Bowman Ltd will be very highly geared. The gearing ratio at the end of year 1 is 450,000/650,000 - 69%.

(ii) Plan Y requires that suitable premises should be found. This may involve time, trouble and administrative costs.

(iii) Careful estimates need to be made of the level of sales expected. If there is a significant chance that sales will fail to reach £1,600,000 there would be a strong argument for preferring plan Z.

On balance these considerations seem to indicate that plan Z would be the wiser course to adopt.

39. BARENTS

(a) In times of rising prices the year end stock valuation is higher under FIFO than it is under LIFO. This is because under FIFO the stock valuation is based on the assumption that the stock remaining on hand at the year end is the most recently purchased. Under LIFO, the stock on hand is valued at prices prevailing perhaps months previously, leading to a lower valuation when prices are rising. The converse is true when prices are falling.

(i) In 19X0, year end stock has a higher value under LIFO. Prices must have fallen during the year.

(ii) In 19X2, year end stock has a higher value under FIFO. Prices must have risen during the year.

(b) 19X0 was the first year of trading and opening stock therefore does not affect the calculation. The highest profit figure will come from the method which gives the highest valuation for closing stock, namely LIFO.

(c) We know that cost of sales = opening stock + purchases - closing stock. Since the purchases figure is the same under both methods, the lowest cost of sales (and therefore the highest profit) comes from the method which gives the lowest value for opening stock less closing stock.

	LIFO £	FIFO £
Opening stock	36,400	36,000
Less closing stock	(41,800)	(44,000)
	£(5,400)	£(8,000)

The figure for FIFO is lower (minus £8,000 compared with minus £5,400) and therefore the profit under FIFO is higher.

(d) Stock movements for 19X0 and 19X1 do not affect the problem. Only the stock at the end of the three year period is relevant. Since the LIFO valuation at 31 December 19X2 is lower, the LIFO profit for the period will be lower.

(e) As in part (c) the answer to this question depends on the movement in stock over the year.

	FIFO cost £	Lower of FIFO cost and NRV £
Opening stock	36,000	34,000
Less closing stock	(44,000)	(44,000)
	£(8,000)	£(10,000)

The cost of sales is £2,000 higher on the basis of FIFO cost and therefore profit would be £2,000 lower on that basis.

40. PURCHAS

Tutorial note. In this question it is necessary to look at each year in isolation, ie without the benefit of hindsight. Thus the figures for 19X1 are calculated using 19X1 estimates without trying to compare the estimates with actual results in 19X2 and 19X3.

(a) *Calculation of attributable profit:*

	19X1	19X2	19X3 Claim rejected	19X3 Claim rejected
	£'000	£'000	£'000	£'000
Cost incurred	250	2,000	3,100	3,100
Estimated further costs	3,300	1,560	520	1,010
	3,550	3,560	3,630	4,100
Contract price	4,000	4,000	4,000	4,000
Estimated profit/(loss)	450	440	370	(110)

Various methods of calculating attributable profit would be acceptable. Here the formula used is:

$$\text{Attributable profit} = \text{total profit} \times \frac{\text{value of work certified}}{\text{contract price}}$$

(i) 19X1. The contract has hardly begun and it would be imprudent and contrary to SSAP9 to take credit for any profit.

(ii)   19X2. Attributable profit $= £440,000 \times \dfrac{2,500}{4,000}$

$= \underline{£275,000}$

(iii)   19X3. If the insurance claim is accepted:

Attributable profit $= £370,000 \times \dfrac{3,400}{4,000} =$	314,500
Less: taken in 19X2	275,000
Credited in 19X3	£39,500

If the insurance claim is rejected, the whole of the foreseeable loss of £110,000 should be provided for.

(b)   *Balance sheet values.*

SSAP 9 says that the value of long-term contract work in progress should be stated in the balance sheet at cost plus attributable profit less foreseeable losses.

	19X1	19X2	19X3	
			Claim rejected	Claim rejected
	£'000	£'000	£'000	£'000
Cost	250	2,000	3,100	3,100
Attributable profit	-	275	3,155.5	-
	250	2,275	3,414.5	3,100
Less foreseeable loss	-	-	-	(110)
Balance sheet value	£250	£2,275	£3,414.5	£2,990

41. KESTER & CO

(a)   VALUATIONS OF KESTER & CO AT 30 JUNE 19X4

	£'000
(i) *Kester's basis*	
Book value of fixed assets	350
Book value of current assets	355
	705
Less: book value of creditors	105
Book value of net assets to be transferred	600

(NB: the bank overdraft is not to be taken over by the purchaser and therefore does not enter into the calculation).

	£'000
(ii) *Wang's basis*	
Book value as calculated above	600
Add: revaluation of fixed assets	
£(490,000 - 350,000)	140
revaluation of stocks	
£(250,000 - 210,000)	40
Revised valuation	780

(iii) *Pollins's basis*

	19X2 £'000	19X3 £'000	19X4 £'000
Net profit shown by accounts	125	150	145
Less drawings	100	100	100
Adjusted profit	25	50	45

Average adjusted profit = £40,000

Valuation of business: $\dfrac{price}{earnings} = \dfrac{8}{1}$

Price = 8 x £40,000 = £320,000

(iv) *Fraser's basis*

	£'000
Book value as calculated in (i) above	600
Add: revaluation of stock	10
	610
Less: write down of fixed assets	55
Revised valuation	555

(b) Kester's basis has the merit of simplicity but no prospective purchaser would consider it adequate. Accounts are prepared on a going concern basis which is quite inapplicable in the case of a proposed sale. Purchasers will be interested in the future value of the business whereas the accounts show an historical picture.

Wang's method has more to commend it. It attempts to put a value on the individual assets to be taken over by considering the amounts which a purchaser might pay for equivalent assets elsewhere. What is overlooked is that the value of a business as a whole may be greater or less than the sum of its parts.

Pollins is closer in outlook to a prospective purchaser, who will be looking to pay an amount which reflects the value of the business to himself. That value is ultimately dependent on the profitability of the business. The weaknesses in his approach are:

(i) the accounts show profits earned in the past, which may not be an adequate guide to future profitability; and

(ii) the profit figure he suggests as a basis needs to be adjusted as described in (c) below.

Fraser, like Wang, overlooks the difference in the valuations of a business as a whole and of its individual assets. His approach would be suitable if a winding up of the business were being considered, as then the important consideration would be the values of the individual assets separately realised in a quick sale.

(c) Earnings yield valuation:

	19X2 £'000	19X3 £'000	19X4 £'000
Net profit per accounts	125	150	145
Adjustment for stock valuation at 30.6.X2	32		
Revised accounts profits	157	150	145
Add back bank interest*	4	8	10
	161	158	155
Less notional salaries*	60	60	60
Maintainable profits	101	98	95

*The objective is to arrive at the amounts which a purchaser might expect to earn on the assets actually taken over. The bank overdraft is not to be taken over and so there will be no overdraft interest. An adjustment needs to be made also for the amount of salaries which the purchaser might expect to pay to, eg, the directors who will manage the new business.

Average maintainable profits = £98,000 per annum

Earnings yield is (if we ignore tax) the reciprocal of the price earnings ratio, here 1/8 = 12.5%.

This implies a valuation of $\dfrac{£98,000}{12.5\%}$ = £784,000

42. CONNECTICUT

Tutorial note. The earnings yield basis is the most difficult calculation because the valuation depends on estimates of earnings *maintainable in the future*. A number of adjustments are therefore necessary to earnings figures provided for *previous* years.

(a)

	Valuation £'000
Earnings yield basis *(working 1)*	850
Liquidation basis *(working 2)*	808
Dividend yield basis *(working 3)*	667

Workings

1 *Earnings yield basis*

Schedule of maintainable earnings for ordinary shareholders

	19X0 £'000	19X1 £'000	19X2 £'000
Net profit for year	126	210	240
Additional depreciation	(16)	(16)	(16)
Revision of stock valuation			(14)
Exceptional loss added back	56		
Preference dividends	(20)	(20)	(20)
	146	174	190

Average maintainable earnings for ordinary shareholders

$$= 1/3 \ (146 + 174 + 190) = \underline{£170,000}$$

Earnings yield $= \dfrac{\text{earnings for ordinary shareholders}}{\text{value of ordinary shares}}$

∴ Value of ordinary shares $= \dfrac{\text{earnings for ordinary shareholders}}{\text{earnings yield}}$

$$= \dfrac{£170,000}{20\%}$$

$$= \underline{£850,000}$$

2 Liquidation basis

	£'000	£'000
Net worth of ordinary shares as shown in balance sheet		1,550
Less: loss on equipment (800-240)	560	
loss on stock (810-600)	210	
liquidation costs	52	
		822
		728
Add: proposed ordinary dividend (which would not be paid if company was liquidated)		80
Value of ordinary shares		808

3 Dividend yield basis

Ordinary dividend yield $= \dfrac{\text{ordinary dividends}}{\text{value of ordinary shares}}$

∴ Value of ordinary shares $= \dfrac{\text{ordinary dividends}}{\text{ordinary dividend yield}}$

$$= \dfrac{£80,000}{12\%}$$

$$= \underline{£667,000}$$

(b) The liquidation basis is useful as an emergency valuation and in this case it indicates that the company is more than able to pay its creditors even assuming the worst. The earnings yield and dividend yield bases are more useful as attempts to measure the true worth of the ordinary shareholders, but they are hampered in this case by the absence of forecast information. Previous years' results may not be an adequate guide to the future. In the case of the dividend yield basis there is also the problem that the amount of profits actually paid out as dividends may not be a true reflection of the company's profitability. Other factors, such as the availability of attractive investment opportunities or a temporary liquidity problem, may cause even a profitable company to pay low dividends.

All three valuations show a substantial surplus for the ordinary shareholders, though a surplus which is much less than the net worth (£1,550,000) of the ordinary shareholders' interest shown in the balance sheet. It seems likely that the company's assets, particularly the equipment, are overvalued in the balance sheet. Even on a liquidation basis, however, the current ratio is 2.7:1 and the quick ratio is 1.3:1, so it appears that the bank should have no serious worries.

It would still be advisable for the bank to obtain security for its investment in the form of a charge, either a fixed charge over the fixed assets or a floating charge over the total assets of the company.

43. BOLMIN

(a) VALUATION OF TOODEN ON AVERAGE PROFITS METHOD

	Total £	19X1 £	19X2 £
Unadjusted pre-tax profits	26,000	15,000	11,000
Add back:			
Depreciation on equipment	10,000	5,000	5,000
Directors' remuneration	44,000	20,000	24,000
	80,000	40,000	40,000
Deduct:			
Revised depreciation on equipment (10% x £80,000)	(16,000)	(8,000)	(8,000)
Revised directors' remuneration	(22,000)	(10,000)	(12,000)
Adjusted pre-tax profits	£42,000	£22,000	£20,000

Average = £21,000

∴ Valuation = 8 x £21,000 = £168,000

$$\text{Value per share} = \frac{£168,000}{50,000}$$

$$= £3.36$$

(b) (i) The net assets shown in Tooden's 19X2 balance sheet are £186,000. The share value on this basis is therefore:

$$\frac{£186,000}{50,000} = £3.72$$

(ii) The break-up value of Tooden is as follows:

	£
Freehold property	169,000
Equipment	24,000
Stock	17,000
Debtors and bank	69,000
	279,000
Less current liabilities	29,000
	£250,000

The share value on this basis is:

$$\frac{£250,000}{50,000} = \underline{£5.00}$$

(iii) Earnings yield $\quad = \quad \dfrac{\text{earnings}}{\text{market value of shares}}$

$\therefore$ Market value of shares $\quad = \quad \dfrac{\text{earnings}}{\text{earnings yield}}$

$$= \quad \frac{£7,000}{8\%}$$

$$= \quad \underline{£87,500}$$

The share value on this basis is $\dfrac{£87,500}{50,000} = \underline{£1.75}$

(c) The method of valuation suggested by Bolmin's directors appears to be arbitrary. No indication is given either of the reasons for the proposed profit adjustments, or of the reason for choosing eight years as the relevant time span. In addition, the method suffers from the disadvantage that it is based on profits earned in years gone by, which may prove to be an unreliable guide to the future.

It is hard to imagine circumstances in which the second method would be appropriate. Decisions should be based on what is known of the present and what can reasonably be estimated for the future. A historical cost balance sheet is of little use in that respect, especially when, as here, we know that current costs are very different from historical costs.

The break-up basis would of course be the appropriate method if the liquidation of Tooden were contemplated. As a guide to the value of a business purchased as a going concern it is not very useful. In the case of Bolmin and Tooden it is worth noting that the break-up value is greater than the value computed on the directors' suggested method. This means that if the directors' offer is accepted (which is most unlikely) an easy profit could be made simply by liquidating Tooden immediately.

The earnings yield basis is probably the best method in principle, assuming that Bolmin means to take over Tooden as a going concern. This is because it is Tooden's power to generate earnings which will be of most interest to the purchaser. The Chief Accountant's suggestion, however, would need to be examined closely. It is based on unadjusted historical cost earnings rather than on estimates of future earnings adjusted for any changes expected to arise in consequence of the takeover. In addition, its accuracy depends on the closeness of the similarity between Tooden and companies with an earnings yield of 8%.

44. GURNEY

(a) (i) *Tutorial note:* calculating the value of the business on the earnings yield basis means calculating the maintainable profits (after tax - which is to be ignored in this question - and preference dividends, and taking into account any of the adjustments (iii) - (viii) which are relevant) for the last three years. The average of these three profit figures is then divided by the 'typical earnings yield' of 12%, to give the value of the business.

Valuation: earnings yield basis

	19X4 £'000	19X5 £'000	19X6 £'000
Reported profits	715	483	572
Adjustments:			
preference dividends	(40)	(40)	(40)
understatement of opening stock	(140)		
increased in provision for bad/ doubtful debts			(30)
section of business sold off*	(85)		
overcharge of depreciation	35	35	35
	485	478	537

* Excluded from the 19X4 profits because that section of the business no longer exists and so should not be included in any comparison (or averaging calculation) with future years. The £85,000 is not a 'maintainable profit'.

Average profit for the last three years

= (£485,000 + £478,000 + £537,000) ÷ 3
= £1,500,000 ÷ 3
= £500,000
∴ Earnings yield valuation = £500,000 ÷ 0.12 = £4,166,667

(ii) *Tutorial note:* calculating the value of the business on the liquidation basis means using the figures in the most recent balance sheet (adjusted as necessary) to reflect the value of assets less liabilities. Adjustments to take into account are:

1. Plant and equipment, and stocks should be valued at £1,800,000 and £1,406,000 respectively.
2. Debtors should be reduced by the £30,000 bad/doubtful debts.
3. Preference dividends are a liability of the business (£40,000), but the £200,000 proposed ordinary dividend is not.
4. The preference shares themselves are a liability of the business.
5. Liquidation expenses are a liability of the business.

204

Valuation: liquidation basis

	£'000	£'000
Assets		
Plant and equipment		1,800
Stocks		1,406
Debtors		866
Bank		57
		4,129
Liabilities		
Creditors	(509)	
Preference dividends	(40)	
Preference shares	(500)	
Liquidation expenses	(31)	(1,080)
		3,049

(b) Neither the earnings yield nor the liquidation method should be regarded as producing 'absolute' values for the business. They merely provide some figures on which to base a sensible discussion on how a business should be valued.

(i) The earnings yield basis is particularly useful if the business is to continue, because it tries to take account of the expected future earnings of the business. Future profitability is, after all, the subject which most interests a prospective buyer. Adjusting profit figures so that they only reflect 'maintainable' profits is another useful attribute of the earnings yield method. On the other hand, the method suffers from the same problems which beset any attempt to predict the future. For instance, are the historical profit figures a reliable basis on which to predict future profits? For that matter, are the historical figures actually used a fair reflection of the 'maintainable profits' for those years? Finally, the 'typical earnings yield' of 12% used for Gurney is obviously open to question, particularly as it relates to listed companies (and Gurney is an unlisted company).

(ii) The liquidation basis is particularly useful for valuing a business which is not to continue. For that reason, it does not take into account any future values for profit, but only expected 'break-up values. The liquidation method should result in an absolute minimum for the value of the business (ie no lower offers should be considered, because more could be realised simply by selling off the business in bits and pieces). A disadvantage of the method is that a more realistic value of a business ought to be in excess of the liquidation value. Finally, it also suffers from the problem that there is bound to be some uncertainty in the estimated 'break-up' figures.

45. RICHARDS

(a)

		Valuation of one £1 ordinary share
(i)	Book value basis	£1.52
(ii)	Replacement cost basis	£2.48
(iii)	Dividend yield basis	£2.00
(iv)	Price/earnings basis - 19X6 profits	£2.50
(v)	Price/earnings basis - 19X7 profits	£3.40

Workings

(i) Book value of £1 ordinary share

$$= \frac{\text{book value of all assets - long-term and current liabilities}}{8,000,000}$$

$$= \frac{£15,100,000 - £2,900,000}{8,000,000}$$

$$= £1.52$$

(ii) Replacement cost basis valuation of £1 ordinary share

$$= \frac{\text{replacement cost value of all assets - long-term and current liabilities}}{8,000,000}$$

$$= \frac{£22,750,000 - £2,900,000}{8,000,000}$$

$$= £2.48$$

(iii) Dividend yield basis valuation of £1 ordinary share

$$= \frac{\text{dividend per share}}{\text{dividend yield}}$$

$$= \frac{£0.10}{5\%}$$

$$= £2.00$$

(iv) Price/earnings basis valuation of £1 ordinary share (using 19X6 profits)

$$= \text{earnings per share} \times \text{price/earnings ratio}$$

$$= \frac{£2,000,000}{8,000,000} \times 10$$

$$= £2.50$$

(v) Price/earnings basis valuation of £1 ordinary share (using forecast 19X7 profits)

$$= \frac{£2,720,000}{8,000,000} \times 10$$

$$= £3.40$$

(b) (i) Book value of shares is only very approximate. Book values of assets are often unrealistic because of, for example, inflation and the choice of depreciation method to be used by the business. The book value valuation of a share is of no real practical use to shareholders.

(ii) The replacement cost value of shares is an improvement on the book value in that it attempts to use a reasonable estimate of the value of assets. However, the replacement cost method does not take into account the future earnings capacity of a business. The method is useful if the business is not a going concern and is to be sold off, but not otherwise. There is no indication that Richards plc is going to be sold off, and so the replacement cost value of shares is not very important to shareholders. Note that if Richards plc *was* going to come to a halt, then the £2.90 offer from Hadlee plc is very attractive compared to the £2.48 replacement cost valuation.

(iii) The dividend yield basis valuation is useful for small shareholders who are only interested in the dividends they may receive. If the dividend yield basis valuation is likely to remain at £2.00, then the £2.90 offer from Hadlee plc is attractive. But naturally shareholders hope that the directors of Richards plc are right, and that profits (and therefore presumably dividends) will increase as time goes on. In addition, it must be remembered that the 5% dividend yield figure might not be particularly applicable to Richards plc, making the £2.00 valuation somewhat suspect. The dividend yield basis valuation should probably not cause shareholders to sell their shares - but certainly they should keep a close eye on future developments.

(iv) The price/earnings (19X6) basis valuation, at £2.50, does not compare favourably with the £2.90 offer. But the directors of Richards plc maintain that earnings are going to rise in the future and therefore this historical valuation should not persuade shareholders to sell. Assuming that their promises of increased earnings are justified (and a 'leading firm of accountants' seems to think they are), then the directors are probably right: the 19X6 price/earnings valuation does not reflect the value of the business. As usual, it is worth remembering that the price/earnings rates of 10 might not be particularly applicable to Richards plc, thus the valuation, using the figure of 10, may not be realistic.

(v) The price/earnings (19X7) basis valuation is probably the most relevant of the five calculated in part (a) of the question (although, paradoxically, it is the least reliable in that it has no solid evidence to back it up, being based on forecast rather than historic figures). It tries to value the business (and subsequently a share) on the basis of future earnings - in this case, the forecast earnings figures have been approved by a leading firm of accountants, and presumably are a reasonable estimate. This being the case, the £3.40 valuation compares favourably with the £2.90 offer, and the shareholders should firmly reject the take-over bid. There is, of course, the usual proviso that the price/earnings ratio of 10 might not be particularly suitable for Richards plc.

46. HANSARD

Cash flow profile

Year	Capital investment £'000	Cash flows £'000	Discount factor at 15%	NPV £	Discount factor at 11%	NPV £
0	(140)		1	(140,000)	1	(140,000)
1-5		31	3.353	103,943	3.696	114,576
5	50		0.497	24,850	0.594	29,700
				£(11,207)		£4,276

(NB: the first trial was made using a rate of 15%, as the middle of the given range. This led to a negative NPV implying that the actual IRR was below 15%. 11% was therefore taken as a second trial. Any two rates could be chosen, but the resulting approximation to the IRR will be more accurate if values are taken which lead to a small NPV, whether positive or negative.)

The discount factor for years 1-5 is simply the sum of the individual factors for years 1,2,3,4,5.)

Estimate of IRR:

$$IRR = 15\% - \left(\frac{11,207}{11,207+2,276}\right) \times (15-11)\%$$

$$= 12.1\%$$

Since the project's IRR is less than the company's cost of capital, management should be advised not to undertake the project.

47. BURLEY

(a) (i) *Payback method*

	Project A £	Project A £	Project B £	Project B £
Initial investment		80,000		100,000
Paid back:				
End of year 1	40,000		20,000	
End of year 2	60,000		30,000	
		100,000		50,000
Not paid back by end of year 2		£ -		50,000
Paid back at end of year 3				50,000
				£ -

Thus project A is more than paid back by the end of year 2, while project B is paid back at the end of year 3.

(ii) NPV Method

Year	Discount factor at 12%	Project A Cash flow £	Project A NPV £	Project B Cash flow £	Project B NPV £
0	1	(80,000)	(80,000)	(100,000)	(100,000)
1	0.893	40,000	35,720	20,000	17,860
2	0.797	60,000	47,820	30,000	23,910
3	0.712	10,000	7,120	50,000	35,600
4	0.636	5,000	3,180	50,000	31,800
5	0.567	5,000	2,835	50,000	28,350
			£16,675		£37,520

(b) The payback method has the merit of being simple to apply and to understand. By ignoring receipts arising beyond the payback period it shows some (vague) recognition of the fact that receipts are less certain and less valuable the further they are in the future. The NPV method gives more scientific recognition to that fact, by explicitly taking account of the time value of money, and also considers the full effects of a project over the whole of its life. Although project A pays back more quickly, it appears to be a less attractive investment overall.

48. CATALAN

(a) *Payback period*

	£	£
Initial investment		260,000
Paid back:		
in year 1	80,000	
in year 2	90,000	
in year 3	90,000	
		260,000
		-

The payback period of the project is therefore three years.

(b) *Net present value*

The first step is to calculate the company's real cost of capital, using the formula:

$$(1 + rr)(1 + rpi) = (1 + mr)$$

(Remember: rr is the real cost of capital
rpi is the rate of inflation
mr is the money cost of capital)

Here: $(1 + rr)(1 + 0.08) = (1 + 0.19)$

$\therefore$ $1 + rr = \dfrac{1.19}{1.08}$

$= 1.10$

$\therefore$ Real cost of capital = 0.10 or 10%

The estimated annual cash inflows are given to us in real terms, ie in May 19X8 prices. They should therefore be discounted at the real cost of capital, 10%. However, the amounts realised at the end of year 5 in respect of plant and working capital are given to us (presumably) in year 5 prices. There are two methods of coping with this.

(i)   We could translate the £12,000 and £60,000 to May 19X8 prices by discounting them at the rate of inflation, 8%. We would then discount the May 19X8 prices at the real cost of capital.

(ii)   Alternatively, we could simply discount the year 5 prices at the money cost of capital.

Both methods give the same result, and method (ii) is simpler (one stage instead of two). However, the question specifically states that the real cost of capital must be used, so method (i) is adopted in this solution. We must first translate the £62,000 into May 19X8 prices:

£62,000 x 0.680 = £42,160

The cash flows are therefore as follows:

Year	Cash flow	Discount factor at 10%	Present value
	£		£
0	(260,000)	1	(260,000)
1	80,000	0.909	72,720
2	90,000	0.826	74,340
3	90,000	0.751	67,590
4	50,000	0.683	34,150
5	*72,160	0.620	44,739
			33,539

* £(30,000 + 42,160) = £72,160

(c)   *Advantages of each method*

(i)   *Payback method*

It is simple to use and easy to understand
It emphasises the importance of returns in the early years of a project's life.
It deals with cash flows expected in the near future which may therefore be more reliably predicted.

(ii)   *Discounting*

It takes account of the time value of money
It takes account of cash flows throughout the life of the project, and not just during the early stages.

49. VETCH

Tutorial note. The weighted average cost of capital (WACC) can be calculated by computing the return required by each category of investor separately and then aggregating them and dividing by the total finance provided. This method is used in the solution to part (a).

(a)

	Amount provided £'000	Return required %	£'000
Equity investors	300	20	60
Bank	200	12	24
	500		84

The total return required on the £500,000 provided is £84,000. The WACC is therefore 84/500 x 100% = 16.8%.

To the nearest whole per cent WACC = 17%

(b) Net present values at 17%.

Year	Discount factor	Project A Cash flow £'000	NPV £'000	Project B Cash flow £'000	NPV £'000
0	1	(500)	(500)	(500)	(500)
1	0.855	200	171	400	342
2	0.731	300	219	200	146
3	0.624	200	125	200	125
4	0.534	400	214	200	107
			229		220

(c) Both projects show substantial positive NPVs at 17% discount rate; both are therefore well worth undertaking. The NPV of project A is very slightly higher than that of project B; against that, project B has a quicker payback period (1½ years, as compared with two years for project A). No clear-cut recommendation is possible between the two projects without considering other material factors such as the degree of risk inherent in each. If the given cash flows are taken as certain the slight superiority of A's NPV would give it the edge over B.

50. BARRON

Tutorial note. There are three options to be considered:

(i) immediate sale of the warehouse;
(ii) letting the warehouse for five years and selling it at the end of that period;
(iii) using the warehouse for five years to purchase and sell widgets. Again, the warehouse would be sold at the end of the five years.

The present value of cash receipts from each option needs to be calculated and the results compared. The book value of the warehouse is irrelevant. So too is the cost of the feasibility study, since the money is already spent. It cannot affect a decision based on the best course to take for the future.

(a) *Option (i)*
This has a present value of £275,000.

Option (ii)
Five amounts of £12,000 are received. The first is received immediately (because the rent is payable in advance); the others are received at the ends of years 1,2,3 and 4. The present value of this option is:

	Cash flow £	Discount factor	Present value £
Year 0	12,000	1	12,000
1	12,000	0.877	10,524
2	12,000	0.769	9,228
3	12,000	0.675	8,100
4	12,000	0.592	7,104
5	500,000	0.519	259,500
			£306,456

Option (iii)

	Cash flow	Discount factor	Present value
Year 0	(30,000)	1	(30,000)
1	25,000	0.877	21,925
2	25,000	0.769	19,225
3	25,000	0.675	16,875
4	25,000	0.592	14,800
5	525,000	0.519	272,475
			£315,300

(b) The option with the highest net present value is option (iii), to use the warehouse for purchasing and selling widgets. This option is some £9,000 more profitable than letting the warehouse for five years; letting the warehouse is in turn some £31,000 more profitable than immediate disposal.

However, these figures do not disclose the amount of risk involved in each option. If immediate disposal is chosen, there is virtually no risk; £275,000 is received immediately. At the other extreme, the cash flows arising from option (iii) must be regarded as very uncertain, even though a feasibility study has been carried out. It could easily happen that demand for widgets or the gross profit achievable on sales turns out to be less than expected.

Taking risk into account, option (ii) may be regarded as the wisest choice. Its expected present value is only £9,000 less than that of option (iii) and the cash flows are more certain. Provided that a five-year rental contract is signed immediately, the income should be safe against all eventualities other than the failure of the lessee firm.

51. DORMAN

(a)

Year	Discount	Cash inflow/ (outflow) £	NPV £
0	1	(100,000)	(100,000)
1 – 5	*3.605	40,000	144,200
			£44,200

*The discount factor for years 1–5 is simply the sum of the separate factors for years 1–5.

The project has a substantial positive NPV and, on the basis of these estimates, should be undertaken.

(b) If the project is to be accepted the NPV of the £40,000 annual cash inflows should at least equal the NPV, £100,000, of the original cash investment. The minimum acceptable discount factor is therefore

$$\frac{100,000}{40,000} = 2.5$$

The sum of the discount factors for years 1–3 is 2.402. The project should therefore last a little over three years if it is to be acceptable.

(c) Using the same reasoning as in (b) above, but assuming a discount factor of 3.605 (ie a project life of 5 years) the minimum acceptable average net cash annual inflow is:

$$\frac{100,000}{3.605} = £27,740$$

52. BARBICAN

PROFIT AND LOSS ACCOUNT FOR THE YEAR ENDED 31 MARCH 19X8

	£'000
Operating profit before tax	450.0
Taxation (W1)	102.5
Profit after tax	347.5
Dividends (73 + 15% x 1,000)	223.0
Retained profit for the year	124.5
Profits brought forward	260.0
Profits carried forward	384.5

BALANCE SHEET AT 31 MARCH 19X8

	£'000	£'000
Fixed assets		
Cost	1,250	
Depreciation	820	
Net		430
Current assets		
Stock, debtors and cash	1,558	
Creditors: amounts falling due within one year		
Trade creditors and accruals	372	
Proposed dividend	150	
ACT on proposed dividend	50	
Corporation tax (W2)	15	
	587	
		971
		1,401
Provisions for liabilities and charges		
Deferred tax (W3)		(16.5)
		1,384.5
Capital and reserves		
Called up share capital		1,000
Profit and loss account		384.5
		1,384.5

Workings

1. *Taxation charge for the year*

	£'000
Corporation tax: profits of £400,000 @ 25%	100.0
Deferred tax: timing differences of £50,000 @ 25%	12.5
Tax charge in respect of 19X8	112.5
Less overprovision in previous year	10.0
	102.5

2. *Corporation tax liability*

	£'000
Total corporation tax charge for year	100
Less ACT paid in year	85
Mainstream liability	15

3. *Deferred tax*

	£'000
Balance brought forward	54.0
Charge for the year (W1)	12.5
	66.5
Less ACT on proposed dividend	50.0
	16.5

SUGGESTED SOLUTIONS

53. MAWDSLEY

Tutorial note. The examiner often requests that answers should be presented in a particular format. This not only simplifies the task of marking but also provides a useful guide for students who are uncertain how to structure their answer. Obviously in this case your answer should begin with the figures required by the examiner, in the format prescribed. Cross references to workings should then indicate how your figures are derived.

There is one ambiguity in the question. Part (b) refers to the mainstream corporation tax charge for the year debited to the profit and loss account. But the tax charge in the P & L account includes the *total* corporation tax liability computed for the year, not just the mainstream liability. Since the mainstream liability must be calculated in part (f) it is assumed here that part (b) refers to the total corporation tax charge for the year.

	19X6 £	19X7 £
Taxable profit *(working 1)*	100,000	80,000
Mainstream corporation tax charge *(working 2)*	25,000	20,000
Transfer to (from) the deferred tax account *(working 3)*	2,500	(2,500)
Advance corporation tax payable *(working 4)*	7,000	5,000
Balance on the deferred tax account *(working 5)*	2,500	-
Mainstream corporation tax liability *(working 6)*	25,000	13,000

Workings

1.

	19X6 £	19X7 £
Taxable profit for the year		
Taxable profit	140,000	110,000
Less capital allowances:		
WDA @ 25%	(40,000)	
WDA @ 25% x (160 - 40)		(30,000)
Taxable profit after capital allowances	£100,000	£80,000

2. *Corporation tax charge for the year*

Charge - 25% of taxable profits	£25,000	£20,000

3. *Transfer to (from) deferred tax account*

Capital allowances for the year *(working 1)*	40,000	30,000
Depreciation charge for the year	30,000	40,000
Originating (reversing) timing difference	£10,000	£(10,000)
Deferred tax debit (credit) @ 25%	£2,500	£(2,500)

4. *ACT payable*
   ACT is payable on the proposed dividends:

25/75 x £21,000	£7,000	
25/75 x £15,000		£5,000

5. *Balance on deferred tax account*
    19X6 charge (- balance at end of 19X6) £2,500
    In 19X7 this is reduced by the £2,500
    deferred tax credit in that year £ -

6. *MCT liability*
    In 19X6 no ACT is actually paid. The
    mainstream liability is therefore the same
    as the charge for the year £25,000

    In 19X7, ACT of £7,000 *(working 4)* is paid on
    the 19X6 dividend. This reduces the total
    19X7 liability of £20,000 *(working 2)* to £13,000) £13,000

54. EASY

PROFIT AND LOSS ACCOUNT FOR THE YEAR ENDED 31 DECEMBER 19X8
(EXTRACTS)

	£'000
Income from fixed asset investments:	
Debenture interest receivable (21 x 100/75)	28
Tax on profit on ordinary activities *(working 1)*	113
Dividends paid and proposed (21 + 10.5)	31.5

BALANCE SHEET AS AT 31 DECEMBER 19X8 (EXTRACTS)

	£'000
Taxation payable *(working 2)*	101
Proposed dividend	10.5
Deferred taxation *(working 3)*	23.5

Workings

1 Tax on profit on ordinary activities

	£'000
Estimated corporation tax for 19X8	112
Deferred taxation	5
	117
Less tax overprovided in 19X7	4
	113

216

2   Taxation payable

	£'000	£'000
Estimated corporation tax for 19X8		112
Less ACT paid in year*:		
On 19X7 final dividend	5	
On 19X8 interim dividend (25/75 x £21,000)	7	
	12	
Tax already suffered by deduction at source - 25/75 x £7,500	2.5	
		(14.5)
Mainstream corporation tax liability		97.5
Add ACT on proposed 19X8 dividend (25/75 x £10,500)		3.5
		101

3   Deferred taxation

	£'000
Provision for timing differences at 1.1.X8	22
Add transfer from profit and loss account	5
Provision for timing differences at 31.12.X8	27
Less ACT on proposed final dividend **	(3.5)
	23.5

* Only ACT actually *paid* during 19X8 can be deducted from the 19X8 tax liability. This means that the ACT relating to the 19X7 final dividend is included, whereas that relating to the 19X8 final dividend is excluded, as it will not be paid until 19X9.

** The £5,000 ACT which was brought forward at 1.1.X8 has now been 'recovered', in that it has been used to reduce the taxation liability in the 19X8 balance sheet (see *working 2*). It therefore disappears from the deferred taxation account and is replaced by the corresponding amount relating to the 19X8 proposed dividend.

55. ANGLO

Tutorial note. Bangle is a subsidiary company. It was acquired on 31 December 19X3 and therefore all its profits are pre-acquisition. Carmen is an associated company since Anglo holds 25% of its equity and takes an active part in running the company. It was acquired on 1 January 19X3 and its profits earned up to that date are pre-acquisition. The profit earned in 19X3 is post-acquisition. The group structure is:

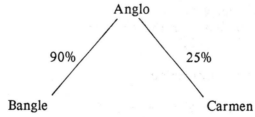

(a)

CONSOLIDATED BALANCE SHEET
AS AT 31 DECEMBER 19X3

	£'000	£'000
Fixed assets		
Tangible fixed assets		
Freehold property (200 + 300)		500
Plant and equipment (756+107)		863
		1,363
Investment in associated company *(working 4)*		819
		2,182
Current assets (521+351)	872	
Current liabilities (374+106+138)	618	
Net current assets		254
Total assets less current liabilities		2,436
Minority interest *(working 3)*		(62)
		2,374
Capital and reserves		
Share capital (Anglo only)		1,000
Capital reserve arising on consolidation *(working 2)*		118
Consolidated profit and loss reserve *(working 1)*		1,256
		2,374

(b) The consolidated balance sheet enables the bank to assess the financial strength and stability of the group as a whole. However, the bank's contractual relationship is with Anglo Ltd only, not with Bangle and Carmen, and unless there are cross guarantees within the group it may be that the holding company balance sheet is of more use to Anglo's bank than the consolidated balance sheet. This is because it is only against Anglo's assets that the bank may make a direct claim for repayment of any monies advanced.

Workings

1   *Consolidated profit and loss reserve*

		£'000	£'000
Anglo:	at 1 January 19X3	950	
	profit for year	247	
			1,197
Bangle:	at 1 January 19X3	210	
	profit for year	90	
	revaluation of freehold property		
	(300 – 180)*	120	
		420	
	less: pre-acquisition	420	–
Carmen:	group share of undistributed		
	post-acquisition profits		
	(25% x 236)		59
			1,256

*This revaluation is not reflected in Bangle's accounts but it should be made as a consolidation adjustment so as to establish the 'fair value' of Bangle's assets at the date of acquisition. See the calculation of goodwill in *working 3* below.

2   *Goodwill on acquisition*

	Bangle	*Carmen*
	£'000	£'000
Share capital	200	2,000
Reserves at date of acquisition (see *working 1*)	420	128
Net worth of company	620	2,128
Proportion acquired by Anglo	90%	25%
∴ Net worth of assets acquired	558	532
Cost of acquisition	440	760
(Discount)/premium on acquisition	(118)	228

3   *Minority interest in Bangle*

	£'000
Minority share capital	20
Minority interest in retained profits	
10% x 420 (see *working 1*)	42
	62

4   *Investment in associated company*

	£'000	£'000
Group share of goodwill in the books		
of Carmen (25% x 104)		26
Premium on acquisition *(working 2)*		228
		254
Group share of Carmen's net assets other than goodwill:		
Net assets per accounts (2,893–529)	2,364	
Less goodwill	104	
	2,260	
Group share (25%)		565
		819

This is the analysis required by SSAP 1.

56. PARK AND GATE

Tutorial note. As usual, the problem figures in a consolidated balance sheet are those for goodwill arising on consolidation, minority interest and consolidated reserves. Bear in mind that since the publication of SSAP 22 *Accounting for goodwill* the normal method of accounting for goodwill is to cancel it against reserves. If, as in this case, no accounting treatment is specified, this is the policy which should be adopted.

Workings

1 *Goodwill arising on consolidation*	£
Share capital of Gate Limited at 31 December 19X3	80,000
Retained profits at 31 December 19X3	37,500
Net assets of Gate Limited at 31 December 19X3	£117,500
Share of net assets acquired by group	
(48,000/80,000 = 60%)	70,500
Cost of shares acquired	72,000
Goodwill arising on consolidation	£1,500

2	*Minority interest in Gate Limited*		£
	Minority interest in:		
	Share capital		32,000
	Retained profits £(37,500 + 28,500) x 40%		26,400
			£58,400

3	*Consolidated reserves*	£	£
	Park Ltd: as at 31 December 19X3	45,100	
	retained profit for 19X4	17,600	
			62,700
	Gate Ltd: post-acquisition profits	28,500	
	group share (60%)		17,100
			79,800
	Less goodwill *(working 1)*		1,500
			£78,300

(a)
CONSOLIDATED BALANCE SHEET
AS AT 31 DECEMBER 19X4

	£	£
Fixed assets		
Freehold property	99,000	
Other	217,300	
		316,300
Current assets	130,100	
Creditors: amounts falling due within one year	(79,700)	
Net current assets		50,400
Total assets less current liabilities		366,700
Creditors: amounts falling due after more than one year		
Unsecured loan repayable 19X9	30,000	
Minority interest *(working 3)*	58,400	
		(88,400)
		£278,300
Capital and reserves		
Ordinary shares of £1 each		200,000
Reserves		78,300
		£278,300

(b) The consolidated balance sheet of Park Limited hardly looks strong enough to support a loan of £400,000, unless the freehold property of Gate Limited has a market value above its book value. Park Limited has net assets of £262,700; the net assets of Gate Limited are £146,000 at net book value.

It is important to remember that a group is not a separate legal entity and any loan must be made to one or other of the individual companies. One solution would be for the bank to make a loan to Gate Limited, but to insist on a written guarantee of support from Park Limited. Any loan made should be secured by a floating charge over the assets and enterprise of the business.

57. MARTENS

Tutorial note. Martens owns 75% of the equity of Tasman, which is therefore a subsidiary company. Martens also owns 22% of the equity of Wood and has board representation in that company. Wood is therefore accounted for as an associated company.

		£'000	£'000
Consolidated reserves			
Martens:	per draft	438	
	sub-standard materials charged to Wood	4	
			442
Tasman:	per draft	64	
	less pre-acquisition	(16)	
	post-acquisition	48	
	group share (75%)		36
Wood:	per draft	64	
	sub-standard materials	(4)	
		60	
	less pre-acquisition	10	
	post-acquisition	50	
	group share (22%)		11
			489

Goodwill on acquisition

	Tasman £'000	Wood £'000
Share capital	200	10
Reserves at date of acquisition	16	10
Net worth at acquisition	216	110
Proportion acquired by Martens	75%	22%
∴ Net worth of assets acquired	162	24.2
Cost of acquisition	200	50.0
∴ Premium on acquisition	38	25.8

Minority interest in Tasman

	£'000
Minority share capital	50
Minority interest in reserves (25% x 64)	16
	66

Investment in associated company

	£'000
Group share of net assets of Wood (22% x (100 + 64 – 4))	35.2
Premium on acquisition	25.8
Amount owed by associated company (42 + 4)	46.0
	107.0

(a)

CONSOLIDATED BALANCE SHEET
AS AT 30 JUNE 19X3

	£'000	£'000
Fixed assets		
Intangible assets		
Goodwill on consolidation		38
Tangible assets		
Property	464	
Plant and machinery	438	
		902
Investment in associated company		107
		1,047
Current assets		
Stocks and work in progress	184	
Debtors and prepayments	217	
Cash at bank and in hand (including £6,000 in transit)	35	
	436	
Creditors: amounts falling due within one year		
Bank overdraft	25	
Other creditors	103	
	128	
Net current assets		308
Total assets less current liabilities		1,355
Minority interest		(66)
		1,289
Capital and reserves		
Called up share capital		800
Reserves		489
		1,289

(b) If Martens held only 19% of the shares of Wood there would be a presumption that associated company status did not exist. If that presumption were true Martens would account for Wood simply as an investment and would take credit for Wood's profits only to the extent that they were distributed as dividends.

In this case, however the presumption would probably be rebutted on the grounds that Martens is still in a position to influence the financial policies of Wood, despite having a shareholding below 20%. The ability to exercise such influence is the principal criterion for establishing associated company status.

58. HAKLUYT

(a)

CONSOLIDATED BALANCE SHEET
AS AT 30 SEPTEMBER 19X1

	£'000	£'000
Tangible fixed assets (2,833 + 364)		3,197
Current assets		
Stock (396 + 103)	499	
Debtors (1,500 + 185)	1,685	
Bank (60 + 12 + 5 in transit)	77	
	2,261	
Current liabilities		
Trade creditors (198 + 78)	276	
Net current assets		1,985
Total assets less current liabilities		5,182
Minority interest (working 2)		(159)
		5,023
Capital and reserves		
Called up share capital		4,000
Profit and loss account *(working 3)*		1,023
		5,023

Workings

		£'000
1	*Goodwill arising on consolidation*	
	Share capital of Cook Limited	400
	Reserves at date of acquisition	36
	Net assets of Cook Ltd at date of acquisition	436
	Share of net assets acquired by group (75%)	327
	Purchase consideration	350
	∴ Goodwill	23

		£'000
2	*Minority interest at 30.9.X2*	
	Share capital of Cook Limited	400
	Reserves at 30.9.X2	236
		636
	Share owned by minority (25%)	159

		£'000	£'000
3	*Consolidated profit and loss reserve at 30.9.X2*		
	Retained earnings of Hakluyt plc		896
	Retained earnings of Cook Ltd:		
	Shown in draft accounts	236	
	Less pre-acquisition reserves	36	
	Post acquisition reserves	200	
	Group share (75%)		150
			1,046
	Less goodwill *(working 1)* written off in accordance with SSAP 22		23
			1,023

(b) *(Note.* The approach to this part of the question should be to compute the relevant ratios as they are now and then to calculate the effect of altering Cook's ratios so as to bring them into line with those of Hakluyt.)

		Hakluyt		*Cook*
Gross profit percentage	4,840/7,220	67.0%	460/880	52.3%
No of days stock	396/2,380x365	60.7	103/420x365	89.5
No of days sales in debtors	1,500/7,220x365	75.8	185/880x365	76.7
No of days purchases in creditors	198/2,380x365	30.4	78/420x365	67.8

If Cook's gross profit percentage rose to 67.0% on sales of £880,000 the company's cost of sales would be 33% of £880,000, ie £290,400.

The company's revised working capital position, assuming the same ratios as Hakluyt plc for stock, debtors and creditors, would then be as follows:

	£'000
Stock (60.7/365 x £290,400)	48.3
Debtors (75.8/365 x £880,000)	182.8
	231.1
Less creditors(30.4/365 x £290,400)	24.2
Net investment in working capital	206.9

This compares with the company's current investment in working capital of:

	£'000
Stock	103
Debtors	185
	288
Less creditors	78
	210

This implies that the reduction in working capital, and the consequent increase in funds available, would amount to only £3,100 under the accountant's scheme even if the scheme were practicable. In fact, it is very doubtful whether Cook Limited could suddenly increase its gross margin by nearly 15%. Even if it could, the scheme involves running down stock levels by one third (90 days to 61 days) which may not be feasible for Cook Limited.

It is worth noting that if the accountant's suggestion were modified, so that creditors remained at the existing level of 67.8 days purchases, there would be a further £29,700 funds available ((67.8 - 30.4)/365 x £290,400).

59. A AND B

Working

A LIMITED - CONSOLIDATION SCHEDULE

	Group £	Group £	A Limited £	A Limited £	B Limited £	B Limited £
Turnover		3,000,000		1,000,000		2,000,000
Cost of sales	2,100,000		600,000			(1,500,000)
Inter-company profit	6,000		6,000			
		(2,106,000)		(606,000)		
		894,000		394,000		500,000
Expenditure:						
General administration	489,000		98,000		391,000	
Depreciation	49,000		29,000		20,000	
Audit	2,300		1,200		1,100	
		(540,300)		(128,200)		(412,100)
		353,700		265,800		87,900
Debenture interest		(3,000)		2,000		(5,000)
Profit on ordinary activities		350,700		267,800		82,900
Corporation tax		(141,880)		(108,720)		(33,160)
		208,820		159,080		49,740
Minority interest (25% of £49,740)		(12,435)				(12,435)
		196,385				37,305
Inter-company dividends		-		22,500		(22,500)
Group profit for the year		196,385		181,580		14,805
Dividend proposed		(190,000)		(190,000)		
Retained profits/ losses for the year		6,385		(8,420)		14,805
Profits brought forward (post acquisition)		82,000		82,000		-
		88,385		63,580		14,805
Transfer to capital reserves		(41,250)		(30,000)		(11,250)
		£47,135		£43,580		£3,555

The transfer to the group reserves includes 75% of the (post-acquisition) retained profits for the year of B Limited, ie 75% of £15,000 = £11,250.

A LIMITED
CONSOLIDATED PROFIT AND LOSS ACCOUNT
FOR THE YEAR ENDED 31 DECEMBER 19X0

	£
Turnover	3,000,000
Cost of sales	(2,106,000)
	894,000
Expenditure	(540,300)
	353,700
Interest payable	(3,000)
Profit on ordinary activities	350,700
Tax on ordinary activities	(141,880)
	208,820
Minority interest	(12,435)
Profit for the year attributable to the group	£19,638
Profit for the year	196,385
Proposed dividends	(190,000)
Retained profit for the year (note)	£6,385

Note

	Group	*Holding Company*	*Subsidiary Company*
	£	£	£
Movements on revenue reserves			
Profits b/f	82,000	82,000	–
Retained profits/losses for the year	6,385	(8,420)	14,805
	88,385	73,580	14,805
Transfer to capital reserves	(41,250)	(30,000)	(11,250)
Unappropriated profits c/f	£47,135	£43,580	£3,555

60. APPLE BANANA AND CHERRY

Tutorial note. This is quite a complex question on preparing a consolidated balance sheet. You should keep in mind two main points:

(i) Because there is a sub-subsidiary, two consolidations are needed. First consolidate the balance sheets of Banana and Cherry, then combine this first consolidation with the balance sheet of Apple.

(ii) It is necessary to calculate goodwill *after* revaluing Banana's fixed assets. The revaluation is a pre-acquisition profit.

(a) *Consolidation of Banana and Cherry*

	£'000
Fixed assets (960 + 700)	1,660
Net current assets	780
Total assets less current liabilities	2,440
12% long-term loans	(750)
	1,690
Capital and reserves	
Share capital	1,000
Reserves *(working 1)*	690
	1,690

Workings

1. *Reserves*

	£'000	£'000
At 1 January 19X5:		
Per draft accounts*		300
Revaluation of Banana's assets		450
Less goodwill eliminated (W2)		150
		600
Profit for year:		
Per draft accounts (120 + 60)	180	
Less increase in depreciation charge	90	
		90
At 31 December 19X5		690

*Cherry's reserves at 1 January 19X5 are of course pre-acquisition profits and are not included in consolidated reserves.

2. *Goodwill*

	£'000
Share capital and reserves acquired	700
Cost of investment	850
Goodwill to be eliminated	150

The balance sheet prepared above can now be consolidated with that of Apple.

CONSOLIDATED BALANCE SHEET
AS AT 31 DECEMBER 19X5

	£'000	£'000
Fixed assets (800 + 1,660)		2,460
Net current assets (270 + 780)		1,050
Total assets less current liabilities		3,510
12% Long-term loans (650 + 750)	1,400	
Minority interest (40% x 1,690)	676	
		(2,076)
		1,434
Capital and reserves		
Share capital		1,200
Reserves *(working 3)*		234
		1,434

3. *Reserves*

	£'000
At 1 January 19X5*	563
Profit for year (157 + 60% x 90)	211
	774
Less goodwill eliminated *(working 4)*	540
At 31 December 19X5	234

*The reserves at 1 January 19X5 of the Banana-Cherry sub-group are of course pre-acquisition profits and are not included in consolidated reserves

4. *Goodwill*

	£'000
Share capital of Banana	1,000
Reserves at 1 January 19X5 *(working 1)*	600
	1,600
Net assets acquired by Apple (60% x 1,600)	960
Cost of investment	1,500
Goodwill to be eliminated	540

(b) *Debt/equity ratios*

Apple:	650.1,920	=	33.8%
Banana:	500/1,420	=	35.2%
Cherry:	250/760	=	32.9%
Group:	1,400/1,434	=	97.6%

(c) The individual members of the group have very similar debt/equity ratios, ranging from a low of 32.9% (Cherry) to a high of 35.2% (Banana). The ratio for the group as a whole is very different: 97.6%.

The difference is a matter of arithmetic. While the debt of the group as a whole is simply the sum of the debt of the individual companies, the group's equity is not the sum of the individual companies' equity. This is because much of the group companies' equity consists of pre-acquisition profits which do not appear in consolidated reserves in the group balance sheet. A potential lender would be well advised to inspect the individual balance sheet of the company he intends to lend to, rather than the group balance sheet, because it is the individual company rather than the group which will be legally liable for interest payments and capital repayments.

61. DINOS AND NIVIS

Tutorial note. It is important to work out the movements on Nivis Ltd's fixed assets.

	£'000
Book value at 1 January 19X7	930
Depreciation for year	87
	843
∴ Additions during year	77
Book value at 31 December 19X7	920

Under the acquisition method, these assets will be shown in the consolidated balance sheet at their fair value. Using the merger method, no adjustment to book values is needed.

	£'000
Fair value of fixed assets at 1 January 19X7	1,200
Add cost of new assets acquired in year	77
	1,277
Less fair value of depreciation charge for year	(116)
Fair value of fixed assets at 31 December 19X7	1,161

The profit for the year must be reduced, under the acquisition method, to take account of the higher depreciation charge arising from the use of fair values. The profit reduction will amount to £(116,000 – 87,000) = £29,000, so that the profit for the year will be £(143,000 + 285,000 – 29,000) = £399,000.

Suggested solution

(a) CONSOLIDATED BALANCE SHEET
 AS AT 31 DECEMBER 19X7

(Acquisition method)

	£'000	£'000
Fixed assets (2,465 + 1,161)		3,626
Net current assets		1,483
		5,109
Share capital (3,000 + 400)		3,400
Share premium account (400,000 @ £2.50)		1,000
Reserves at 1 January 19X7 (W)	310	
Profit for 19X7	399	
Reserves at 31 December 19X7		709
		5,109

Working: goodwill

	£'000
Fair value of Nivis Ltd's net assets at 1.1.19X7:	
Share capital	600
Reserves	300
Revaluation surplus (1,200 – 930)	270
	1,170
Purchase consideration (400 x £3.50)	1,400
∴ Goodwill	230

The goodwill is to be written off against reserves. Group reserves at 1 January 19X7 are therefore:

		£000
Nivis Ltd: all pre-acquisition		-
Dinos Ltd: per draft		540
less goodwill written off		230
		310

(b) CONSOLIDATED BALANCE SHEET
AS AT 31 DECEMBER 19X7

(Merger method)

	£000	£000
Fixed assets (2,465 + 920)		3,385
Net current assets		1,483
		4,868
Share capital (3,000 + 400)		3,400
Revenue reserves at 1 January 19X7 (540 + 300)	840	
Profit for the year (143 + 285)	428	
Revenue reserves at 31 December 19X7	1,268	
Reserve arising on consolidation (600 - 400)	200	
		1,468
		4,868

(c) SSAP 23 states that consolidated accounts may be prepared on merger accounting principles if *all* of the following conditions are met:

(i)   The business combination results from an offer to the holders of all equity shares and the holders of all voting shares which are not already held by the offeror.

(ii) The offeror has secured, as a result of the offer, a holding of:

1.   at least 90% of all equity shares (taking each class of equity separately); and
2.   shares carrying at least 90% of the votes of the offeree.

In other words, if any significant minority interest remains after the combination is complete, it cannot be treated as a merger.

(iii) Immediately prior to the offer, the offeror does *not* hold:

1.   20% or more of all equity shares of the offeree (taking each class of equity separately); or
2.   shares carrying 20% or more of the votes of the offeree.

(iv) At least 90% of the fair value of the total consideration given for the equity share capital (including that given for shares already held) is in the form of equity capital; at least 90% of the fair value of the total consideration given for voting non-equity share capital (including that given for shares already held) is in the form of equity and/or voting non-equity share capital. In other words, the payment for the shares acquired must consist mainly of shares in the acquiring company: if any significant part of the payment is made in cash, the combination cannot be treated as a merger.

If any or all of these conditions are not met, the business combination is an acquisition and the principles of acquisition accounting, as stated in SSAP 14, must be applied. Even if all the conditions are met SSAP 23 only says that merger accounting principles *may* be used. The investing company may still choose to use acquisition accounting.

The principles underlying merger accounting are only valid in cases where the two combining companies are left in the same position afterwards as they were before. If significant resources have left the group (which would be the case if payment for the shares acquired was made in cash) there is a change in the financial position. In such circumstances it would be essential to use acquisition accounting.

62. ACCOUNTING POLICIES

(a) The use of LIFO will produce the lower profit figure. The reason is that closing stock under FIFO is assumed to consist of the most recent purchases which, when prices are rising, cost more than older purchases. Under LIFO, the closing stock valuation will be based on prices prevailing perhaps months before the balance sheet date and will therefore be more conservative.

Another way of looking at it is to consider the cost of sales, which will be higher under LIFO. The reason is that each time a sale is made the cost of that sale is taken as the cost of the most recent stock item purchased. Under FIFO the item sold is assumed to be the oldest item in stock, perhaps purchased months ago at a much lower cost. Since LIFO cost of sales is higher, it follows that LIFO profit is lower.

(b) In this case a marginal costing system will produce a lower figure of reported profit. This is because under such a system all fixed costs are written off as incurred. In a total cost system a proportion of the fixed costs incurred in the period is capitalised and carried forward in the stock valuation.

(c) The answer and the reason for it are the same as for (b) above.

(d) If there is any difference at all under the two methods it will be the first method (separate valuation for each stock item) that will lead to the more conservative figure for reported profit. The reason is that in looking at a group of similar items it is possible that a loss on one is masked by an unrealised profit on another.

For example, suppose a company has three similar items of stock, each costing £10, which normally have a net realisable value of £14 each. One of the items is damaged and will realise only £8. If the cost/NRV comparison is done individually a valuation of £28 (£10 + £10 + £8) is arrived at. If it is done for the group as a whole, we have a total cost of £30 compared with a total NRV of £36 and the valuation is consequently £20, £2 higher than before. The loss of £2 on the damaged item has been masked by the anticipated profits on the other two items.

(e) The reducing balance method will produce higher depreciation charges, and therefore lower profits, in the early years of an asset's life. This is because a higher depreciation rate is needed under this method to write off the cost of the asset in the same time as under the straight line method. For example, if an asset costing £13,000 and with a residual value of £1,000 is estimated to have a four year life, the depreciation charges in the profit and loss account would be as follows:

	Reducing balance at 47.3%	Straight line at 25%
	£	£
Year 1: cost	13,000	13,000
depreciation	6,149	3,000
NBV	6,851	10,000
Year 2: depreciation	3,241	3,000
NBV	3,610	7,000
Year 3: depreciation	1,708	3,000
NBV	1,902	4,000
Year 4: depreciation	900	3,000
residual value	£1,002	£1,000

(f) Under a current cost system the asset will be revalued upwards each year, but this will have no effect on reported profit, since the revaluation surplus will go straight to current cost reserve. What *will* affect profit is the depreciation charge, which will be higher under the current cost system. This system will therefore produce the lower figure for reported profit.

63. HATFIELD

A   Note: it is assumed that 'total cost' in the question means 'cost computed in accordance with SSAP 9' ie with the inclusion of an appropriate amount of production overheads. Marginal cost is not permitted under SSAP9 and is therefore ignored here. The comparison of cost and net realisable value must be done separately for the different groups of stock items. A single overall comparison would be incorrect.

	Cost	Net realisable value (NRV)	Lower of cost and NRV
	£	£	£
Group A	25,000	36,000	25,000
Group B	12,000	4,000	4,000
Group C	71,000	94,000	71,000
Group D	51,000	67,000	51,000
Balance sheet total			£151,000

B   SSAP9 permits the inclusion of an amount of attributable profit in the valuation of long-term contract work in progress. Here the attributable profit might be calculated as 60% of the total estimated profit, ie £18,000.

The balance sheet figure for work in progress would therefore be:

	£
Cost	51,000
Attributable profit	18,000
	£69,000

Tutorial note. The question has been printed as it was originally set in 1984. Under the rules introduced by SSAP 9 (revised) much more information would be needed to establish the appropriate disclosure.

C   (i)

		£
Cost of land and buildings		380,000
Accumulated depreciation at 1.7.X3		
(10 yrs x 4% x £300,000)		120,000
Net book value at 1.7.X3		260,000
Revaluation at 1.7.X3		800,000
∴ Profit on revaluation		£540,000

Depreciation charge for year ended 30.6.X4

$$= \frac{£(60,000-100,000)}{20}$$

$$= \underline{£25,000}$$

Balance sheet valuation at 30.6.X4:	£
Valuation of land and buildings	800,000
Less: depreciation	25,000
	£775,000

(ii)   This is a change of accounting policy which will be shown in the accounts as a prior year adjustment. The machine had evidently been depreciated for three years as at 30 June 19X3. If the reducing balance method had been used from the outset the accumulated depreciation at 30 June 19X3 would have been as follows:

	Cost/NBV	Depreciation charge
	£	£
Year ended 30 June 19X1:		
Cost	100,000	
Depreciation at 30%	30,000	30,000
Net book value	70,000	
Year ended 30 June 19X2:		
Depreciation at 30%	21,000	21,000
Net book value	49,000	
Year ended 30 June 19X3:		
Depreciation at 30%	14,700	14,700
Net book value	34,300	
Accumulated depreciation		65,700
Year ended 30 June 19X4:		
Depreciation at 30%	10,290	10,290
Net book value	£24,010	£75,990

The prior year adjustment would consist of a reduction in opening reserves of £35,700, being the revised accumulated depreciation of £65,700, less the depreciation accumulated on the previous basis, £30,000.

D   Research expenditure should always be written off as incurred. Development expenditure may be carried forward as an asset provided the strict criteria of SSAP 13 are met. The criteria relate principally to the eventual viability of the project and would appear not to be satisfied in this case since there is doubt in the minds of a majority of directors. The development expenditure therefore should also be written off to profit and loss account.

E   The profit and loss taxation charge will comprise:

	£
UK corporation tax at 30% on the profits for the year	90,000
Transfer to deferred taxation account (£25,000 x 30%)	7,500
	£97,500

The balance sheet will include a liability of £90,000 in respect of corporation tax and a provision for deferred taxation amounting to £87,500 (£80,000 + £7,500).

Summary

Extracts from profit and loss account:

	£	£
Profit on long-term contracts (included in gross profit)		18,000
Revaluation surplus (possibly shown as extraordinary item)		540,000
Depreciation charge: buildings	25,000	
machinery	10,290	
		35,290
Research and development expenditure		6,500
Tax charge		97,500
Prior year adjustment (debit)		£35,700

Extracts from balance sheet

	Cost/ valuation £	Dep'n £	Net £
Tangible fixed assets			
Land and buildings	800,000	25,000	775,000
Machinery	100,000	75,990	24,010
	£900,000	£100,990	£799,010
Current assets			
Stocks and work in progress		220,000	
Creditors: amounts falling due within one year			
Taxation		90,000	
Provisions for liabilities and charges			
Taxation including deferred taxation		87,250	

64. GUYON

(a) The assets of Rayner will for the most part simply be absorbed into those of Guyon. The goodwill requires separate consideration.

SSAP 22 and the Companies Act 1985 permit two accounting treatments in respect of purchased goodwill. It may either be eliminated immediately against reserves, or it may be capitalised as an intangible asset and amortised over its expected useful economic life.

(b) Guyon has acquired 40% of Tours Ltd's equity and is represented on its board of directors. Tours is therefore an associated company of Guyon and should be accounted for in accordance with the requirements of SSAP 1 and the Companies Act 1985.

In its individual profit and loss account, Guyon will take no credit for the earnings of Tours because no dividends have been paid. In the consolidated profit and loss account (if Guyon prepares consolidated accounts) credit will be taken for 40% of the £36,000 profits, or £14,400.

In its individual balance sheet, Guyon will show the investment in its associated company at cost of £110,000. In the consolidated balance sheet (if any) the carrying value of the investment should be analysed as follows:

(i)   Guyon's share of net assets other than goodwill; plus
(ii) Guyon's share of goodwill (if any); plus
(iii) any premium paid on acquisition.

The total of these amounts can also be derived from a different formula, namely:

	£
Cost of shares acquired	110,000
Group share of post-acquisition retained profits	14,400
	124,400

However, it must be remembered that the amounts under (ii) and (iii) above represent purchased goodwill, which must either be written off immediately or at least amortised. In either case, the effect will be that the carrying value of the asset in the consolidated balance sheet will be less than the £124,400 calculated above.

(c) SSAP 9 requires that stock should be valued at the lower of total cost and net realisable value. The figures relating to prime cost are therefore irrelevant and may be ignored.

The comparison between total cost and net realisable value should be carried out (as required by SSAP 9 and the Companies Act 1985) item by item. This leads to the following valuation:

Type	£
V	61,000
W	5,000
X	23,200
Y	15,600
X	41,200
	146,000

(d) The proposed dividend (1,000,000 x 5p = £50,000) should be shown as a current liability in the balance sheet.

The associated ACT (25/75 x £50,000 = £16,667) should also be shown as a current liability. However, it is a liability which will eventually be recoverable against future payments of corporation tax. It should therefore also be disclosed as a debit balance in the balance sheet. This can be achieved by deducting the amount from the provision for deferred taxation, if there is one, or alternatively by including the amount under current assets. In the latter case, a note should disclose that it will be recoverable after more than twelve months.

(e) The disposal of a freehold property is likely to fall within the definition of an extraordinary item. The amount of the capital gain will be subject to corporation tax at 35%. For the sake of simplicity, assume that the capital gain is equal to £(300,000 – 140,000) = £160,000. (In practice, it would not be as simple as that: for example, there would be allowable costs associated with the disposal.) Attributable taxation would then be £56,000. The gross gain of £160,000, the taxation of £56,000 and the net gain of £104,000 would all be disclosed in the profit and loss account below the figure of 'profit on ordinary activities after taxation'.

The taxation of £56,000 would be included with any other corporation tax liability under 'Creditors: amounts falling due within one year'.

65. PORTLAND

(a) Extraordinary items are defined in SSAP 6 as 'material items which derive from events or transactions that fall outside the ordinary activities of the company and which are therefore expected not to recur frequently or regularly'.

The explanatory note to SSAP 6 quotes the profits or losses arising from the following as possible extraordinary items:

(i) the discontinuance of a business segment, either through termination or disposal;

(ii) the sale of an investment not acquired with the intention of resale;

(iii) the expropriation of assets.

Exceptional items are defined in SSAP 6 as 'material items which derive from events or transactions that fall within the ordinary activities of the company, and which need to be disclosed separately by virtue of their size or incidence if the financial statements are to give a true and fair view'.

Again, the explanatory note quotes examples of items which might fall to be treated as exceptional:

(i) abnormal charges for bad debts and write-offs of stocks and work in progress;

(ii) abnormal provisions for losses on long-term contracts; and

(iii) redundancy costs relating to continuing business segments.

(b)   PROFIT AND LOSS ACCOUNT
FOR THE YEAR ENDED 30 JUNE 19X3

Note		£	£
	Turnover		17,500
	Cost of sales (see working)		10,585
	Gross profit		6,915
1	Administration expenses	3,660	
	Distribution costs	1,200	
			4,860
	Profit on ordinary activities before taxation		2,055
	Tax on ordinary activities		805
	Profit on ordinary activities after taxation		1,250
2	Extraordinary loss		590
	Profit for the financial year		660
	Dividends		100
	Retained profit for the financial year		560
	Retained profits brought forward:		
	As previously reported	7,200	
3	Prior year adjustment	425	
			7,625
	Retained profits carried forward		£8,185

Notes:

1   Administration expenses include an exceptional bad debt of £750,000 arising from the liquidation of the company's major customer.

2   The extraordinary loss is the loss arising on closure of the company's factory in Scotland, net of attributable taxation of £170,000.

3   The prior year adjustment arises from a change in the company's accounting policy for valuing stock from a marginal cost to a total cost basis.

Working: cost of sales	£'000
Per question	19,800
Add increase in value of opening stock	425
	11,225
Less increase in value of closing stock	640
	10,585

66. SELHURST

Tutorial note. Although the question was set (in the April 1985 paper) in two parts, the answer to part (a) in fact emerges as part of the answer to part (b). The suggested solution below is presented as a single statement.

The main difficulty of the question lay in the three items covered by SSAP 6 on extraordinary items and prior year adjustments. The factory closure, being material, non-recurring and outside the company's normal activities is an extraordinary item; the bad debt is part of the company's normal activities but exceptional on account of its size, and therefore separately disclosed as an exceptional item; and the decision to depreciate the freehold buildings is a change of accounting policy falling within the SSAP 6 definition of a prior year adjustment.

PROFIT AND LOSS ACCOUNT
FOR THE YEAR ENDED 31 DECEMBER 19X4

	Note	£	£
Turnover			6,174,000
Cost of sales			4,850,000
Gross profit			1,324,000
Distribution costs		135,600	
Administrative expenses *(see working)*		644,100	
			(779,700)
Operating profit (answer to part (a))	1		544,300
Income from fixed asset investments			10,000
			554,300
Interest payable	3		(22,300)
Profit on ordinary activities			532,000
Tax on profit on ordinary activities	4		(217,000)
Profit on ordinary activities after taxation			315,000
Extraordinary loss, net of tax	5		(126,500)
Profit for the financial year			£188,500

STATEMENT OF RETAINED PROFITS

	Note	£	£
Balance at 1 January 19X4:			
As previously reported		736,400	
Prior year adjustment	6	(72,000)	
			664,400
Profit for the financial year		188,500	
Less: dividends		(64,000)	
transfer to preference share redemption reserve		(30,000)	
Retained profit for the financial year			94,500
Balance at 31 December 19X4			£758,900

NOTES TO THE PROFIT AND LOSS ACCOUNT

1   *Operating profit*
Operating profit is stated after charging:

	£
Exceptional bad debt	108,000
Directors' emoluments (note 2)	68,000
Auditors' remuneration	33,900
Depreciation (9,300 + 27,200 + 8,000)	44,500

2   *Directors' emoluments*

	£
As directors (£5,000 + 3 x £3,000)	14,000
For other services	54,000
	£68,000

	£
Chairman's emoluments	£5,000
Emoluments of highest paid director	
£(20,000 + 3,000)	£23,000

Two other directors received emoluments as follows
£15,001 - £20,000	1
£20,001 - £25,000	1

3   *Interest payable*
On bank overdraft   £22,300

4   *Tax on profit on ordinary activities*

	£
UK corporation tax at ?% on the profit	
for the year	180,000
Tax associated with dividends received (25/75 x £9,000)	3,000
Deferred taxation	34,000
	£217,000

5   *Extraordinary loss*
The extraordinary loss represents the costs (net of attributable taxation) associated with closure of the company's South Wales factory.

6   *Prior year adjustment*
This relates to a change of accounting policy. The directors have decided to depreciate the freehold office buildings acquired at the beginning of 19W5. The prior year adjustment represents depreciation for the nine years 1 January 19W5 to 31 December 19X3.

Working

Administrative expenses

	£
Balance per question	528,100
Exceptional item - bad debt (75% x £144,000)	108,000
Depreciation on office buildings £(250,000 - 10,000)/30	8,000
	£644,100

67. SHEPPARTON

(a) BALANCE SHEET AS AT 30 SEPTEMBER 19X8

	Note	Cost £	Dep'n £	Net £
Fixed assets				
Freehold property		305,000	10,100	294,900
Plant and machinery		100,000	20,000	80,000
		405,000	30,100	374,900
Current assets				
Stocks			153,400	
Debtors	1		86,600	
Investments	2		6,200	
Cash at bank			1,300	
			247,500	
Creditors: amounts falling due witin one year				
Bank loan			20,000	
Trade creditors			32,100	
Other creditors including				
taxation and social security	3		53,800	
			105,900	
Net current assets				141,600
Total assets less current liabilities				516,500
Creditors: amounts falling due after more than one year				
Debenture loan	4		150,000	
Bank loan	5		60,000	
				(210,000)
				306,500
Capital and reserves				
Called up share capital				
200,000 ordinary shares of £1 each				200,000
Reserves				
Share premium account			80,000	
Profit and loss account			26,500	
				106,500
				306,500

NOTES TO THE BALANCE SHEET

1. *Debtors*

	£
Trade creditors	78,500
Prepaid expenses	3,100
ACT recoverable (£15,000 x 25/75)	5,000
	86,600

The £5,000 ACT will be recoverable after a period of more than twelve months.

2. *Investments*

This comprises an investment in the shares of an unlisted company.

3. *Other creditors including taxation and social security*

	£
Corporation tax	7,700
National Insurance	4,800
Proposed dividend	15,000
ACT on proposed dividend	5,000
Interest payable	21,300
	53,800

4. *Debenture loan*

This is a 12% debenture repayble in ?

5. *Bank loan*

This is repayable by instalments, all of which fall due in less than five years.

(b) *The principal limitations of published accounts*

(i) Published accounts are almost always, since the withdrawal of SSAP 16, based on historical costs. The values of assets are not current and the balance sheet therefore does not provide a realistic valuation of the company. Depreciation charges do not represent the true value of the asset used. Holding gains are included in profit. The effect of inflation on capital maintenance is not shown. Comparisons over time are unrealistic. Many of these difficulties were reduced by the system of current cost accounting advocated by SSAP 16, but the system as a whole was eventually discarded as unsatisfactory.

(ii) Many external users of accounts (such as creditors or potential investors) are less interested in the historical picture provided by accounts than in the company's future prospects. Historical results are often an inadequate basis for estimating future profitability, and as yet there is no requirement for companies to publish forecast financial information.

(iii) The variety of possible accounting treatments makes it difficult to compare companies with different accounting policies. Accounting standards are meant to limit the areas of difference, but in practice they are often fairly permissive documents. For example, SSAP 22 allows companies to write off purchased goodwill immediately or to amortise it gradually over an undefined period. Companies with several 'blocks' of purchased goodwill may even adopt different policies in respect of each block.

(iv) Various forms of off balance sheet finance (factoring debts, discounting bills receivable, leasing and more elaborate schemes) enable companies to disguise the true extent of their liabilities while remaining within the law.

68. MALHAM

BALANCE SHEET
AS AT 31 MARCH 19X4

Notes		£'000	£'000
	Fixed assets		
	Intangible assets		
1	Goodwill		48
2	Tangible assets		
	Freehold properties	1,050	
	Fixtures and fittings	141	
			1,191
			1,239
	Current assets		
	Stocks	436	
3	Debtors	404	
	Cash at bank and in hand	99	
		939	
	Creditors: amounts falling due within one year		
4	Bank loan	20	
	Trade creditors (206-15)	191	
	Proposed dividend	64	
		275	
	Net current assets		664
	Total assets less current liabilities		1,903
	Creditors: amounts falling due after more than one year		
4	Bank loan	120	
	Accruals and deferred income	15	
			(135)
			1,768
	Capital and reserves		
5	Called up share capital		800
6	Revaluation reserve		270
6	Profit and loss account *(see working)*		698
			1,768

NOTES TO THE BALANCE SHEET

1	*Fixed assets: intangible assets*	
		£'000
	Goodwill at cost	60
	Less: amortisation	12
		48

The directors estimate the useful economic life of the goodwill to be five years and are amortising it over that period in equal instalments.

2 *Fixed assets: tangible assets*

	Total	Freehold properties	Fixtures & fittings
	£'000	£'000	£'000
Cost/valuation			
At 1 April 19X3	930	780	150
Additions in year	67	-	67
Revaluation surplus	270	270	-
At 31 March 19X4	1,267	1,050	217
Depreciation			
At 1 April 19X3	54	-	54
Charge for year	22	-	22
	76	-	76
Net book value			
At 31 March 19X4	1,191	1,050	141

The freehold properties were valued at 31 March 19X4 by Messrs Collins & Co, chartered surveyors.

3 *Debtors*

	£'000
Trade debtors	391
Prepayments	13
	404

4 *Bank loan*

	£'000
Repayable within one year	20
Repayable after one year but within five years	80
Repayable after more than five years	40
	140

The loan carries interest at a fixed rate of 12% per annum and is repayable by annual instalments of £20,000.

5 *Called up share capital*
800,000 ordinary shares of £1 each, fully paid   £800,000

6 *Reserves*

	Revaluation reserve	Profit and loss account
	£'000	£'000
Balance at 1 April 19X3	-	573
Retained profit for year	-	125
Surplus on revaluation of freehold properties	270	-
Balance at 31 March 19X4	270	698

Working

	£'000	£'000
Calculation of retained profits at 31.3.19X4		
Brought forward at 1 April 19X3		573
Profit for the year:		
Per question	229	
Write down of stock (group X) to net realisable value	(28)	
Amortisation of goodwill (1/5 x £60)	(12)	
Proposed dividend (800,000 x 8p)	(64)	
		125
		698

(Note. No adjustment is required for depreciation, since the £22,000 has already been accounted for. This is clear from the fact that the balance of accumulated depreciation is as at 31 March 19X4, ie it includes the charge for the year. Nor is any adjustment needed in respect of the loan interest, which was paid on the last day of the year and will already have been entered in the books).

69. MILFORD

(a)

PROFIT AND LOSS ACCOUNT
FOR THE YEAR ENDED 31 DECEMBER 19X3

	£	£
Turnover		862,150
Cost of sales *(working 1)*		512,700
Gross profit		349,450
Distribution costs	25,000	
Administration expenses *(working 2)*	208,800	
		233,800
Operating profit		115,650
Interest payable		12,000
Profit on ordinary activities before taxation		103,650
Tax on profit on ordinary activities		77,000
Profit on ordinary activities after taxation		26,650
Retained profits as at 1 January 19X2:		
As previously reported	96,800	
Prior year adjustment	23,300	
As restated		120,100
Retained profits as at 31 December 19X2		£146,750

Workings

1	*Cost of sales*	£
	As shown in draft accounts	484,500
	Revision of method of stock valuation	23,300
	Invoice omitted	4,900
		£512,700

2   *Administration expenses*

	£
As shown in draft accounts	185,700
Research costs written off	15,000
Amortisation of goodwill (1/5 x £33,000)	6,600
Additional depreciation	1,500
	£208,800

(Tutorial note: SSAP 13 and Companies Act 1985 allow *development* expenditure to be capitalised in certain circumstances. *Research* expenditure must always be written off as incurred).

BALANCE SHEET
AS AT 31 DECEMBER 19X2

	£	£
Fixed assets		
Intangible assets		
Development costs	9,100	
Goodwill £(33,000 - 6,600)	26,400	
		35,500
Tangible assets		
Land and buildings £(120,000 - 3,500)	116,500	
Plant and machinery	126,600	
		243,100
		278,600
Current assets		
Stocks	139,400	
Debtors	91,200	
Cash at bank and in hand	14,000	
	244,600	
Creditors: amounts falling due within one year		
Trade creditors £(57,100 + 4,900)	62,000	
Current corporation tax	77,000	
	139,000	
Net current assets		105,600
Total assets less current liabilities		384,200
Creditors: amounts falling due after more than one year		
12% debenture		100,000
		£284,200
Capital and reserves		
Called up share capital		100,000
Share premium account		4,450
Revaluation reserve *		33,000
Profit and loss account		146,750
		£284,200

*£2,000 depreciation was charged in the draft accounts for 19X2 and at the end of that year the land and buildings appeared in the accounts at £85,000. Clearly their book value at 1 January 19X2, the date of the revaluation, must have been £87,000. The amount of the revaluation was therefore £120,000 - £87,000 = £33,000.

(b) Profits available for distribution are the accumulated realised profits of a company less its accumulated realised losses. (In the case of public companies, such as Milford plc, this amount must be reduced by any excess of *unrealised* losses over *unrealised* profits. However, Milford plc does not have any unrealised losses and this restriction therefore has no effect.) The revaluation surplus is not a realised profit and therefore does not enter the calculation. Realised losses normally include depreciation, but any part of a depreciation charge which relates to a revaluation is excluded from this general rule.

Milford plc's profits available for distribution are therefore as follows:

	£
Accumulated profits at 31 December 19X2	146,750
Add back depreciation relating to revaluation	1,500
	£148,250

70. BOLT

Tutorial note. Goodwill is the difference between the value of a business as a going concern, and the aggregate value of its tangible assets less liabilities. 'Value' in this context means fair value or market value - book values are irrelevant.

(a) *Calculation of goodwill*

	£
Aggregate fair value of tangible assets*	
Fixed assets	21,600
Stocks	14,700
Debtors £(9,600 - 500)	9,100
	45,400
Price offered by Briston Ltd	60,000
Difference (= Briston's valuation of goodwill)	£14,600

*No account need be taken of liabilities, because Briston Ltd is not intending to take over Bolt's liabilities.

(b) It is usual for the value of a business as a whole to differ from the aggregate values of its individual assets less liabilities. The difference is described as goodwill. Usually the value of the business as a whole will exceed the value of its net assets; this may be because the business has a superior management team, good labour relations, a strategic location or some similar intangible asset not reflected in its balance sheet. However, the reverse is also possible and in that case the business is said to have negative goodwill.

Although it is possible to list factors such as those in the preceding paragraph, which may contribute to creating goodwill, it is not possible in practice to value them. Any estimate of the value of the intangible asset goodwill must therefore be very subjective. For this reason it is not good accounting practice to induce goodwill in the balance sheet of a business, although it is an asset inherent in most businesses.

An exception to this general rule occurs when the value of goodwill is evidenced in a purchase transaction, ie when one business buys another as a going concern. In this case the value of goodwill is measured as the difference between the price paid for the net assets of the business acquired and the fair value of those net assets taken separately. It is then appropriate to refer to *purchased* goodwill; until that point, although the goodwill evidently exists in the acquired business (*inherent* goodwill) no monetary amount for it should appear in the balance sheet.

SSAP 22 does not permit any value for inherent goodwill to be included in a company's balance sheet. But when a company acquires a business as a going concern, and purchased goodwill arises, it is permissible to show the goodwill in the accounts of the acquiring company. SSAP 22 permits two accounting treatments of purchased goodwill:

(i) Purchased goodwill may be eliminated from the accounts immediately by writing it off against reserves. Under this method, purchased goodwill is given the same status as inherent goodwill.

(ii) Purchased goodwill may be recorded as an asset in the balance sheet of the acquiring company. If this policy is chosen the intangible asset must be gradually amortised over its estimated useful life.

SSAP 22 states that method (a) (immediate elimination against reserves) will normally be more appropriate, but leaves the choice to the judgement of management. The Companies Act 1985 treats both methods as equally acceptable. Both are agreed that goodwill should never be treated as an asset unless it is purchased goodwill: inherent goodwill must never appear in a company's accounts (and will rarely be found even in those of a sole trader or partnership).

(c) The main advantage of writing off goodwill on acquisition is that it rids the balance sheet of an asset generally regarded as dubious. Since the continued existence of goodwill can never be relied on and since it is not an asset upon which creditors can rely, immediate write-offs is clearly the most prudent policy. This treatment reflects the view that goodwill is essentially a premium paid on acquisition, a once only expense rather than an asset.

A second reason for writing off goodwill straight away is that there is a lack of consistency in showing purchased goodwill as an asset in the balance sheet, whereas inherent goodwill is not shown at all. Furthermore, the balance sheet of one company which grows by acquiring other operating units (and which therefore might record purchased goodwill) would not be properly comparable with the balance sheet of another company which grows by internal expansion only, (and which therefore has no purchased goodwill).

The approach in method (ii) (carrying goodwill as an intangible asset to be amortised over its useful economic life) may be justified by the accruals concept. When one business buys another the purchased goodwill is a cost which is incurred in anticipation of future earnings (arguably, in anticipation of future superprofits). The cost of goodwill should therefore be written off against the profits of those future years.

71. HERAPATH AND BLACKWALL

Tutorial note. This is a fairly straightforward question. According to the examiner's report the main difficulty was caused by the requirement to show the changes made to Blackwall's reported profit. Three adjustments are necessary: one for depreciation, one for the closing stock values in 19X4 and 19X5 and one for the opening stock value in 19X5.

(a)

BLACKWALL LIMITED
SUMMARISED BALANCE SHEET
AS AT 31 DECEMBER

	19X4 £'000	19X5 £'000
Plant at cost	300	300
Accumulated depreciation	30	60
	270	240
Stocks	150	210
Net liquid assets	45	05
	465	555
Share capital	375	375
Profit (see below)		
19X4	90	90
19X5	-	90
	465	555

	19X4 £'000	19X5 £'000
Profit per draft	10	42
Adjustment for depreciation:		
19X4 (90 - 30)	60	
19X5 (63 - 30)		33
Adjustment for closing stock:		
19X4 (150 - 130)	20	
19X5 (210 - 175)		35
Adjustment for opening stock:		
19X5 (130 - 150)		(20)
Revised profit	90	90

(b) Return on shareholders' equity = $\dfrac{\text{Profit}}{\text{Share capital + reserves}}$

Herapath Ltd

19X4	Return	=	$\dfrac{60}{310}$	=	19.4%
19X5	Return	=	$\dfrac{60}{370}$	=	16.2%

Blackwall Ltd (unadjusted figures)

19X4   Return $= \dfrac{10}{385} = 2.6\%$

19X5   Return $= \dfrac{60}{427} = 9.8\%$

Blackwall Ltd (adjusted figures)

19X4   Return $= \dfrac{90}{465} = 19.4\%$

19X5   Return $= \dfrac{90}{555} = 16.2\%$

After adjusting Blackwall's policies on depreciation and stock valuation, the percentage return earned for shareholders is identical with that of Herapath.

(c)   The accounting policies adopted by companies can have a material effect on their reported results and asset values. This is illustrated by the computations above relating to Blackwall Ltd. When using Blackwall's unadjusted accounts it appears that the company's return on shareholders' equity is very much poorer than that of Herapath; when the figures are adjusted to correspond with Herapath's accounting policies it emerges that the return on equity is identical for both companies. The apparently poorer performance of Blackwall does not arise from any operational inefficiency, but is purely a result of its more conservative accounting policies on depreciation and stock valuation.

if the accounts of different companies are used to compare their performance and financial position it is important to eliminate any differences caused merely by accounting policies. If all companies used the same accounting policies such comparisons would be made much easier. Statements of standard accounting practice attempt to limit the possible variations but they are not so prescriptive as to impose identical accounting policies on all companies. For example, both Blackwall's and Herapath's policies on depreciation are permitted by SSAP 12.

72. GURNEY

Tutorial note. The main point to grasp here is that distributable profits include any profits accumulated in previous years and not already distributed. The dividend for a given year may exceed the profits earned in that year if there are sufficient brought forward profits to cover it.

(a)   The planned dividends for the coming years are set out below. In each case the dividend per share, given in the question, is multiplied by 400,000 (the number of shares in issue).

Year	Planned dividends
	£'000
19X4	60
19X5	64
19X6	68
19X7	72
19X8	76
19X9	80

(b)

	19X4	19X5	19X6	19X7	19X8	19X9
	£'000	£'000	£'000	£'000	£'000	£'000
Distributable profits:						
Balance b/f	–	50	6	33	–	124
Profits for year	110	20	95	320	200	(20)
	110	70	101	63	200	104
Less dividend	60	*64	68	**63	76	* 80
Balance c/f	50	6	33	–	124	24

* In these two cases, profits for the year are insufficient to cover the planned dividend. But there is no obligation to restrict the dividend, because distributable profits include any accumulated realised profits brought forward from previous periods.

** In this case, even profits brought forward are insufficient to meet the planned dividend. The dividend payment must therefore be restricted to the total of distributable profits available, ie £63,000.

(c) The profits available for capitalisation at the end of 19X9 are £24,000. The company will make a bonus issue of 3 shares for every 50 shares already sold.

73. NEWTON

	£'000	£'000
(a) Balance of profit for year to 31/3/X7		471
Less:		
Debenture interest	72	
Transfer to debenture redemption reserve	20	
Depreciation	225	
Stock write-off	17	
R&D expenditure	84	
Goodwill	72	
		490
		(19)
Retained profit at 1/4/X6		108
Retained profit for year to 31/3/X7		89

SUGGESTED SOLUTIONS

(b)
NEWTON LTD
BALANCE SHEET
AS AT 31 MARCH 19X7

	Note	£'000 Cost	£'000 Dep'n	£'000
Fixed assets				
Tangible assets				
Plant and machinery	1	1,800	1,125	675
Investments				
Shares in group company	2			430
				1,105
Current assets				
Stocks	3		567	
Debtors			719	
Cash			35	
			1,321	
Creditors: amounts falling due within one year				
Bank loan	4	40		
Creditors		375		
Accruals		72		
			487	
Net current assets				834
Total assets less current liabilities				1,939
Creditors: amounts falling due after more than one year				
Debentures	5		600	
Bank loan			160	
				760
				1,179
Capital and reserves				
Called up share capital	6			800
Share premium account	7			150
Debenture redemption reserve	7			140
Profit and loss account	7			89
				1,179

Notes (NB workings marked with * are given to illustrate the answer to the question only, and would not normally appear in published accounts)

1. *Plant and machinery*	£'000	£'000
Cost at 1/4/X6		1,800
Additions		-
Cost as at 31/3/X7		1,800
Accumulated depreciation at 1/4/X6	900	
Charge for year to 31/3/X7*	225	
Accumulated depreciation at 31/3/X7		1,125
Net book value		675
		£'000
* NBV at start of 19X7 =		900
Remaining life = 4 years		
∴ New annual depreciation = £900,000 ÷ 4 =		225

251

2. Norfolk Ltd is a subsidiary company. Norfolk Ltd has a total issued share capital of 250,000 ordinary shares of £1 each. Newton Ltd holds 200,000 of those shares.

3. Stocks are valued at the lower of their cost and net realisable value.*

*	Group	Lower of cost and NRV
		£'000
	X	90
	Y	326
	Z	151
		567

The extracted balance of £584,000 is based on the total of the cost figures - ie it is incorrect by £17,000, entirely accounted for by the fact that group X should be valued at £90,000 and not £107,000. The difference of £17,000 is written off in the profit and loss account.

4. *Bank loan*
The bank loan of £200,000 is repayable in five annual instalments of £40,000. The first such instalment is classified as a 'creditor: amounts falling due in one year' figure. The remaining instalments, totalling £160,000, are classified as 'creditors: amounts falling due after more than one year'.

5. *Debentures*
12% debentures repayable 2010.

6. *Share capital*

Authorised share capital, ordinary shares of £1 each	£X
Called up share capital, ordinary shares of £1 each fully paid	£800,000

7. *Reserves*

	Share premium account	Debenture redemption reserve	Retained profit
	£'000	£'000	£'000
Balances at 1/4/X6	150	120	108
Movements during year to 31/3/X7:			
Transfer to reserve		20	
Retained profit for year			(19)
Balances at 31/3/X7	150	140	89

(c) (i) *Goodwill*, according to SSAP 22, can either be written off immediately against reserves, or be amortised over its estimated economic life. In this answer, it has been written off immediately. But it would be equally correct to maintain goodwill of £54,000 in the balance sheet, writing off £18,000 (ie £72,000 ÷ 4) through the profit and loss account.

(ii) *Research* expenditure, according to SSAP 13, should be written off immediately against profits. The SSAP allows *development* expenditure to be carried forward if (among other conditions) there is a reasonable expectation that the cost will be met by related future revenue. This is not the case for Newton Ltd, because 'the majority of the directors have substantial reservations concerning the prospects of the new product'. Therefore, both the research and the development expenditure, totalling £84,000, should be written off immediately against profits.

74. KYLSANT

	(a) £'000	(b) £'000	(c) £'000	(d) £'000	(e) £'000
Ordinary shares	200	800	400	280	150
Preference shares	100	100	100	-	100
Share premium account	60	-	460	60	60
Revaluation reserve	320	-	-	-	-
Capital redemption reserve	-	-	-	20	50
Retained profits	685	145	685	685	610
	1,365	1,045	1,645	1,045	970
Fixed and net current assets	1,365	1,045	1,645	1,045	970

Notes
1. In scheme (b), 600,000 ordinary shares are to be issued. The issue is financed firstly from share premium account and, when that is exhausted, the balance (£540,000) is financed from retained profits.

2. In scheme (c), 200,000 ordinary shares are to be issued at £3 each. Assets rise by £600,000 (the cash received); ordinary share capital rises by £200,000 (the nominal value of the new shares); and share premium account rises by £400,000.

3. In scheme (d), the preference shares are redeemed and are partly replaced by a new issue of 80,000 ordinary shares. The shares not so replaced (£20,000) must be replaced instead by a non-distributable capital redemption reserve (CRR).

4. In scheme (e), assets fall by the amount of cash paid to redeem the shares (50,000 x £1.50 = £75,000). The premium on redemption (£25,000) is charged to distributable profits and a £50,000 transfer to CRR from distributable profits must also be made.

75. GOWER

(a) (i) SSAP 9 says that both FIFO and average cost are acceptable methods for valuing stocks. In order to provide the *lowest* possible profit figure for 19X6, the lowest of the two valuations should be used (because closing stock reduces the cost of sales, which in turn reduces gross profit. Therefore the lower closing stock valuation leads to a higher cost of sales, which in turn gives a lower profit figure).

(ii) SSAP 12 says that both the straight line and the reducing balance methods of calculating depreciation are acceptable. In order to provide the *lowest* possible profit figure for 19X6, the highest depreciation figure should be used (because depreciation is a deduction in the profit and loss account).

Straight line method
Annual depreciation $= £\dfrac{1,000,000 - 240,000}{4}$

$= £190,000$

Reducing balance method
19X6 depreciation $= 30\% \times £1,000,000$
$= £300,000$

Therefore the reducing balance figure of £300,000 should be used.

(iii) SSAP 13 says that *research* expenditure should be written off in the year in which it is incurred, but *development* expenditure may be written off in the year in which it is incurred or in certain defined circumstances deferred and matched against future income. In order to provide the lowest possible profit figure for 19X6, Gower Ltd should write off both the research and the development expenditure immediately (a total of £54,000).

(b)

GOWER LTD
PROFIT AND LOSS ACCOUNT
FOR THE YEAR ENDED 31 DECEMBER 19X6

	£'000	£'000
Sales		1,650
Less manufacturing costs*		900
Gross profit		750
Less: depreciation	300	
research and development expenditure	54	
admin, selling and distribution expenses	216	570
Net profit		180

* Manufacturing costs of £1,100,000 less closing stock valued at £200,000.

GOWER LTD
BALANCE SHEET
AS AT 31 DECEMBER 19X6

	Cost £'000	Dep'n £'000	£'000
Fixed assets			
Plant and machinery	1,000	300	700
Current assets			
Stocks		200	
Debtors		350	
Cash at bank		36	
		586	
Creditors: amounts falling due within one year			
Creditors		106	
Net current assets			480
			1,180
Capital and reserves			
Called up share capital (ordinary shares of £1 each)			1,000
Retained profit			180
			1,180

(c)

GOWER LTD
PROFIT AND LOSS ACCOUNT
FOR THE YEAR ENDED 31 DECEMBER 19X6

	£'000	£'000
Sales		1,650
Less manufacturing costs*		880
Gross profit		770
Less: depreciation	190	
research expenditure	14	
admin, selling and distribution expenses	216	420
Net profit		350

* Manufacturing costs of £1,100,000 less closing stock valued at £220,000.

GOWER LTD
BALANCE SHEET
AS AT 31 DECEMBER 19X6

	Cost £'000	Dep'n £'000	£'000
Fixed assets			
Intangible assets			
Development costs			40
Tangible assets			
Plant and machinery	1,000	190	810
			850
Current assets			
Stocks		220	
Debtors		350	
Cash at bank		36	
		606	
Creditors: amounts falling due within one year			
Creditors		106	
Net current assets			500
			1,350
Capital and reserves			
Called up share capital (ordinary shares of £1 each)			1,000
Retained profits			350
			1,350

(d)   (i)   Although SSAP 9 allows both FIFO and average cost as a basis for valuing (closing) stock, it also suggests that a business should use whichever method is most appropriate. It is not possible to say which is most appropriate for Gower Ltd, as there is insufficient information given in the question. But in real life, one method would be chosen on some rational basis.

If the lower value (average cost basis of £200,000) is used for closing stock, giving lower 19X6 profits, then the profit figure for 19X7 will be correspondingly higher. Alternatively, if the higher closing stock value is used, giving higher 19X6 profits, then the profit figure for 19X7 will be correspondingly lower.

Whichever method Gower Ltd chooses for stock valuation, it should not change that method in future years (SSAP 2).

(ii)   Again, although both straight line and reducing balance methods of depreciation are allowed by SSAP 12, a business will usually choose one method on a rational basis. If an asset wears out equally over time, then the straight line method is probably the most appropriate. But if an asset wears out more quickly in early years than in later years, the reducing balance method is probably the most appropriate.

If the straight line method is chosen, depreciation will be equal each year (£190,000), and will reduce profit by that amount annually. If the reducing balance method is chosen, depreciation will be high in early years (reducing profit considerably) but lower in later years (having less effect on profit figures).

Whichever method Gower Ltd chooses to use for calculating depreciation, it should stick to that method in future years (SSAP 2).

(iii)   Development expenditure can be deferred and matched against future income – provided that the future income arises directly from whatever product has been developed. This is an application of the matching concept which is noted both in SSAP 2 and CA 1985. The development expenditure, if deferred, should be amortised over the period in which income from the project is received.

If the development expenditure is not deferred, it will reduce the 19X6 profits by the full £40,000. If it is deferred, it will not affect 19X6 profits at all, but instead will reduce 19X7 profits. Presumably, some proportion of the £40,000 will be written off in 19X7, then some more in 19X8, and so on according to some rational amortisation basis. The question does not give sufficient information to determine exactly how the expenditure could be deferred (possibly it could be written off in full in 19X7).

76. DEXTER

(a) If the £1,000,000 is raised by making a rights issue of 400,000 (ie 1,000,000 x 2/5) £1 shares at £2.50 each, it will be recorded in the books as:

	£
Extra share capital issued (all at £1)	400,000
Share premium account	600,000
	1,000,000

DEXTER LTD
Forecast profit and loss accounts
for the years 19X7-19X9

	19X7	19X8	19X9
	£'000	£'000	£'000
Net profit before tax	520	240	600
Less corporation tax (30%)	156	72	180
	364	168	420
Less dividends	364	168	420
Retained profit for the year	-	-	-
Retained profit b/f	70	70	70
Retained profit c/f	70	70	70

DEXTER LTD
Forecast balance sheet as at 31 December 19X9

	£'000
Fixed assets and net current assets	2,070
Financed by:	
Share capital (£1 shares)	1,400
Share premium account	600
Retained profits	70
	2,070

(b) If the £1,000,000 is raised by issuing a 12% debenture, Dexter Ltd will incur interest of 12% x 1,000,000 = £120,000 each year.

DEXTER LTD
Forecast profit and loss accounts
for the years ended 19X7-19X9

	19X7	19X8	19X9
	£'000	£'000	£'000
Net profit	520	240	600
Less debenture interest	120	120	120
Net profit before tax	400	120	480
Corporation tax (30%)	120	36	144
	280	84	336
Less dividends	280	84	336
Retained profit for the year	-	-	-
Retained profit b/f	70	70	70
Retained profit c/f	70	70	70

DEXTER LTD
Forecast balance sheet as at 31 December 19X9

	£'000
Fixed assets and net current assets	2,070
Creditors: amount falling due after more than one year	
Debenture loan	1,000
	1,070
Financed by:	
Share capital (£1 shares)	1,000
Retained profit	70
	1,070

(c) (i) If the £1m is raised by a rights issue, Dexter Ltd has no debt capital and so the debt:equity ratio is meaningless. Gearing is zero.

$$\text{Return on shareholder's equity} = \frac{\text{Profit after interest and tax}}{\text{Ordinary share capital + reserves}}$$

19X6	*19X7*	*19X8*	*19X9*
$\dfrac{£140,000}{£1,070,000}$	$\dfrac{£364,000}{£2,070,000}$	$\dfrac{£168,000}{£2,070,000}$	$\dfrac{£420,000}{£2,070,000}$
= 13.1%	= 17.6%	= 8.1%	= 20.3%

(ii) If the £1m is raised by issuing a debenture:

Debt:equity ratio =

19X6:	meaningless (no debenture in 19X6)		
19X7:	£1m : £2.07m	=	1 : 2.07
19X8:	£1m : £2.07m	=	1 : 2.07
19X9:	£1m : £2.07m	=	1 : 2.07

Return on shareholder's equity =

19X6:	$\dfrac{£140,000}{£1,070,000}$	=	13.1%
19X7:	$\dfrac{£280,000}{£1,070,000}$	=	26.1%
19X8:	$\dfrac{£84,000}{£1,070,000}$	=	7.8%
19X9:	$\dfrac{£336,000}{£1,070,000}$	=	31.4%

(d) (i) *Shareholders of Dexter Ltd*

The advantages of a rights issue to shareholders are:

1. Their investment is more secure than it would be if the company became geared. There may be years when the additional profits generated by debenture funds are insufficient to cover the interest payable. This is illustrated by the return on shareholders' equity in 19X8 which is lower if the debenture issue is used than if the rights issue is used.
2. They are entitled to *all* of the additional profits which may be expected to accrue from the new funds invested.

The advantages of a debenture issue to shareholders are:

1. The new funds should in theory earn profits greater than the interest charges accruing to the debenture holders. The excess is effectively a free gift to the shareholders. This is illustrated by the much higher return on shareholders' equity earned in 19X7 and 19X9 if the debenture issue is used.
2. They do not have to raise any cash themselves.

(ii) *Management*

The advantages of a rights issue to management are:

1. It does not use up any borrowing power which may be conferred on the directors by the Articles of Association. This leaves them with greater scope for borrowing in the future.
2. It avoids any charge which would normally be attached to the company assets if a debenture was issued.

The main advantage of a debenture issue to management is that debenture interest is an allowable deduction for tax purposes; dividends paid to shareholders are not.

77. GARNER

(a) (i) SSAP 6 defines *exceptional* items as:

'material items which derive from events or transactions that fall within the ordinary activities of the company, and which need to be disclosed separately by virtue of their size or incidence if the financial statements are to give a true and fair view'.

(ii) *Extraordinary items* are defined in SSAP 6 as:

'material items which derive from events or transactions that fall outside the ordinary activities of the company and which are therefore expected not to recur frequently or regularly. They do not include exceptional items nor do they include prior year items merely because they relate to a prior year'.

(b)
GARNER LTD
PROFIT AND LOSS ACCOUNT AND STATEMENT
OF RETAINED EARNINGS FOR YEAR ENDED 30 JUNE 19X7

	£'000	£'000
Turnover		37,200
Cost of sales *(working 1)*		25,120
Gross profit		12,080
Distribution costs		(3,600)
Administration expenses		(6,200)
Net profit		2,280
Extraordinary loss *(note 1)*		(7,300)
Loss for the financial year		(5,020)
Retained profit brought forward		
As previously reported	12,600	
Prior year adjustment *(note 2)*	(2,140)	
As re-stated		10,460
Retained profit carried forward		5,440

Workings

1. Cost of sales is increased by the write-off of closing stock of £520,000. This item would not normally be shown separately on the face of the account or in the notes – it is certainly not exceptional or extraordinary.

Notes

1. Loss on closure of manufacturing division £7,300,000.
2. Prior year adjustment of (£2,140,000) has been made to retained profit b/f, necessitated by a fundamental bookkeeping error.

78. LANGOSTA

(a) The first step is to calculate the retained profit for 19X6. We can then work back up the profit and loss account to arrive at the figure of profit before tax.

	£'000
Profit and loss account at 31.12.19X6	182
Profit and loss account at 31.12.19X5	76
∴ Retained profit for the year	106

PROFIT AND LOSS ACCOUNT
FOR THE YEAR ENDED 31 DECEMBER 19X6

	£'000	£'000
Profit before taxation (balancing figure)		346
Taxation *		91
Profit after taxation		255
Dividends *	36	
Transfer to capital redemption reserve	70	
Transfer to debenture redemption reserve	20	
Transfer to plant replacement reserve	23	
		149
Retained profit (as above)		106

* It is assumed that no payments of tax or dividends have been made during the year, other than those relating to 19X5 and appearing as liabilities in the 19X5 balance sheet.

(b) STATEMENT OF SOURCE AND APPLICATION OF FUNDS
FOR THE YEAR ENDED 31 DECEMBER 19X6

	£000	£000
Source of funds		
Profit before tax		346
Adjustment for item not involving the movement of funds:		
Depreciation		26
Total generated from operations		372
Other sources of funds		
Issue of shares (100 + 80)		180
		552
Application of funds		
Purchase of plant and machinery	110	
Redemption of preference shares	250	
Payment of tax	65	
Payment of dividends	55	
		480
		72
Movement in working capital		
Increase in stocks	8	
Increase in debtors	25	
Increase in creditors	(5)	
Movement in net liquid funds:		
Increase in bank balance (37 + 7)	44	
		72

(c) The share premium account has arisen from the issue of ordinary shares during the year. The shares were issued at a premium of 80p, or £80,000 in total.

The capital redemption reserve (CRR) has been created to compensate for the reduction in fixed capital caused by the redemption of preference shares. Although the fall in fixed capital (£250,000) has been partly made good by the proceeds (£180,000) of a new share issue, there is still a balance of £70,000 to make good by reclassifying distributable reserves (the profit and loss account) as a non-distributable CRR.

(d) Distributable profits are the excess of accumulated *realised* profits over accumulated *realised* losses.

The property revaluation reserve is not distributable because it is an unrealised profit. It would only become realised if the land and buildings were actually sold for their revalued amount.

The capital redemption reserve is also undistributable. The reserve has been created, as explained in (c) above, to maintain the level of the company's fixed capital. Companies legislation requires that this should be done in circumstances such as a share redemption when the creditors' buffer would otherwise be reduced. Clearly it would defeat the purpose of the legislation if the reserve were allowed to be distributed.

The debenture redemption reserve is distributable. It represents funds earmarked by the directors to replace the loan capital due to be repaid shortly. But there is no legal obligation to earmark funds for this purpose and the directors are at liberty to distribute the reserve.

79. HOLFORD

SUMMARISED CURRENT COST PROFIT AND LOSS ACCOUNT
FOR THE YEAR ENDED 31 DECEMBER 19X2

	£'000	£'000
Historical cost operating profit		29,000
Current cost operating adjustments:		
Cost of sales *(working 1)*	6,840	
Additional depreciation *(working 2)*	13,000	
		(19,840)
Current cost operating profit		9,160
Gearing adjustment *(working 3)*	6,613	
Interest payable	(5,000)	
		1,613
Current cost profit on ordinary activities		
before taxation		10,733
Taxation		10,000
Current cost profit attributable to shareholders		773
Less dividends		7,000
Retained current cost loss for the year		(6,227)

Workings

1   *Cost of sales adjustment*

Since Holford plc holds an average of three months' stock the average cost of stock held at 31 December is that which prevailed 1½ months previously, ie in mid-November.

To arrive at the current cost of goods sold we must restate the historical cost of opening and closing stocks to average values for the year. The difference between current cost of goods sold and historical cost of goods sold is the cost of sales adjustment.

The calculation is as follows:

	£'000
Opening stock at average cost (35,000 x 135/120)	39,375
Purchases	200,000
	239,375
Less closing stock at average cost (50,000 x 135/142)	47,535
Current cost of goods sold	191,840
Less historical cost of goods sold	185,000
Cost of sales adjustment	6,840

2   *Additional depreciation adjustment*

This adjustment is the difference between historical cost depreciation and depreciation based on the replacement cost of the fixed asset. Here we will use the average current cost valuation of £330,000.

	£'000
Current cost depreciation (£330,000x1/10)	33,000
Historical cost depreciation	20,000
Additional depreciation adjustment	13,000

3   *Gearing adjustment*

This is calculated by multiplying the total current cost adjustment by the gearing proportion, which is the proportion of net borrowing to net operating assets, here one third.

	£'000
Current cost adjustments:	
COSA (debit)	6,840
ADA (debit)	13,000
	19,840

∴ Gearing adjustment = £19,840,000 x 1/3
                     = £6,613,000 (credit)

80. BELL

Tutorial note. Remember that the cost of sales adjustment is the difference between historical cost of sales and current cost of sales; while the depreciation adjustment is the difference between depreciation on the historical cost basis and depreciation on the current cost basis.

(a)

CURRENT COST PROFIT AND LOSS ACCOUNT
FOR THE YEAR ENDED 31 DECEMBER 19X4

	£'000	£'000
Historical cost operating profit		160
Current cost adjustments:		
COSA	16	
ADA	51	
		67
Current cost operating profit		93

Workings

1   COSA

	£'000	£'000
Opening stock at average cost		
300 x 124/120	310	
Less opening stock at historical cost	300	
		10
Closing stock at historical cost	360	
Less closing stock at average cost		
360 x 124/126	354	
		6
		16

2   ADA

	£'000
Depreciation based on current cost	
£150,000 x 134/100	201
Depreciation based on historical cost	150
	51

263

(b) Historical cost accounts have a number of disadvantages at times when prices are rising.
   (i)   fixed asset values become out-of-date and unrealistic;
   (ii)   holding gains on stocks are included in profit;
   (iii) the true effect of inflation on capital maintenance is not shown;
   (iv)   comparisons over time are unrealistic.

Despite this the decision to adopt a current cost basis of accounting is not an obvious one.
   (i)   The professional accountancy bodies have been unable to agree amongst themselves as to the form such accounts should take.
   (ii)   The degree of subjectivity in preparing current cost figures is greater than under the historical cost basis.
   (iii) Current cost accounting is conceptually difficult and users of accounts may not understand what the figures mean.
   (iv)   There is additional time and expense involved in preparing the calculations and analyses required for a set of current cost accounts.

81. NORWICH

(a)
CURRENT COST OPERATING PROFIT FOR 19X6

	£m	£m
Historical cost operating profit		15
Current cost adjustments:		
Depreciation adjustment	3	
Cost of sales adjustment	5	
		(8)
Current cost operating profit		7

SUMMARISED CURRENT COST BALANCE SHEET
AS AT 31 DECEMBER 19X6

	£m	£m
Fixed assets		85
Current assets		
Stocks	21	
Debtors	30	
Bank	2	
	53	
Current liabilities	30	
		23
		108
Long-term liability		(20)
		88
Capital and reserves		88

(b) (i) *Interest cover*

HC accounts: 15 ÷ 3 - 5 times
CC accounts: 7 ÷ 3 = 2.3 times

(ii) *Return on shareholders' equity*

HC accounts: 12 ÷ 62 = 19.4%
CC accounts: 4 ÷ 88 = 4.5%

(iii) *Debt/equity ratio*

HC accounts: 20 ÷ 62 = 32.3%
CC accounts: 20 ÷ 88 = 22.7%

(c) (i) *Interest cover*

Companies must maintain their capital base if they wish to stay in business. The significance of the interest cover calculation is that it indicates the extent to which profits after tax are being eaten into by payments to finance external capital. The figures calculated above indicate that only one-fifth of historical cost profit is being absorbed in this way, while four-fifths are being retained to finance future growth. On the face of it, this might seem satisfactory; however, the current cost interest cover is only 2.3 times, indicating that, after allowing for the impact of rising prices, interest payments absorb nearly half of profits after tax.

(ii) *Return on shareholders' equity*

This is the ratio of profits earned for *shareholders* (ie profits after interest) to shareholders' equity. Once again, the position disclosed by the historical cost accounts is more favourable than appears from the current cost ratio. The historical cost profit is higher than the current cost profit because no allowance is made for the adverse impact of rising prices; and at the same time the denominator in the historical cost fraction is lower because shareholders' capital is stated at historical values rather than their higher current values.

The significance of the ratio is that it enables shareholders to assess the rate of return on their investment and to compare it with alternative investments that might be available to them.

(iii) *Debt/equity ratio*

The significance of this ratio is as a measure of the extent to which the company's net assets are financed by external borrowing and shareholders' funds respectively.

In times of rising prices it can be beneficial to finance assets from loan capital. While the assets appreciate in value over time (and the gain accrues to shareholders), the liability is fixed in monetary amount. The effect of this is that current cost accounts tend to give a more favourable picture of the debt/equity ratio than historical cost accounts. In the ratios calculated above, the amount of debt is £20m in both balance sheets. This represents nearly one-third of the historical cost value of shareholders' funds, but only one-fifth of the equity calculated on a current cost basis.